1 & 2 KINGS

THE PEOPLE'S BIBLE COMMENTARY

STEPHEN B. DAWES

A BIBLE COMMENTARY FOR EVERY DAY

Introducing the
People's Bible Commentary
Series

Congratulations! You are embarking on a voyage of discovery—or rediscovery. You may feel you know the Bible very well; you may never have turned its pages before. You may be looking for a fresh way of approaching daily Bible study; you may be searching for useful insights to share in a study group or from a pulpit.

The People's Bible Commentary (PBC) series is designed for all those who want to study the scriptures in a way that will warm the heart as well as instructing the mind. To help you, the series distils the best of scholarly insights into the straightforward language and devotional emphasis of Bible reading notes. Explanation of background material, and discussion of the original Greek and Hebrew, will always aim to be brief.

- If you have never really studied the Bible before, the series offers a serious yet accessible way in.

- If you help to lead a church study group, or are otherwise involved in regular preaching and teaching, you can find invaluable 'snapshots' of a Bible passage through the PBC approach.

- If you are a church worker or minister, burned out on the Bible, this series could help you recover the wonder of scripture.

Using a People's Bible Commentary

The series is designed for use alongside any version of the Bible. You may have your own favourite translation, but you might like to consider trying a different one in order to gain fresh perspectives on familiar passages.

Many Bible translations come in a range of editions, including study and reference editions that have concordances, various kinds of special index, maps and marginal notes. These can all prove helpful in studying the relevant passage. The Notes section at the back of each PBC volume provides space for you to write personal reflections, points to follow up, questions and comments.

Each People's Bible Commentary can be used on a daily basis, instead of Bible reading notes. Alternatively, it can be read straight through, or used as a resource book for insight into particular verses of the biblical book.

If you have enjoyed using this commentary and would like to progress further in Bible study, you will find details of other volumes in the series listed at the back, together with information about a special offer from BRF.

While it is important to deepen understanding of a given passage, this series always aims to engage both heart and mind in the study of the Bible. The scriptures point to our Lord himself and our task is to use them to build our relationship with him. When we read, let us do so prayerfully, slowly, reverently, expecting him to speak to our hearts.

CONTENTS

PBC 1 & 2 KINGS: INTRODUCTION

An old, old story

This collection of ancient tales, adding up to a story of failure and disappointment, was a message for the present and the future of the people of God. Whenever and wherever they were first told, they appear where they do in the Hebrew Bible as part of a longer tragedy. The books of Joshua, Judges, Samuel and Kings tell the story of the people of Israel from a bright beginning on the wrong side of the Jordan River into and then out of the promised land, and away to exile in Babylon in 587BC. This tragic story is followed by four explanations (Isaiah, Jeremiah, Ezekiel and the Twelve Minor Prophets) which repeat the same message: the people of Israel are the people of God and the tragedy is that their misfortune is of their own making. The theme of the story and the message of the explanation are the same: they have brought the catastrophe of the exile upon themselves by their disobedience and wrongdoing.

This message becomes clearer and clearer as we read through 1 and 2 Kings. In 722BC the Assyrians destroyed the northern kingdom, Israel, and deported its people. 2 Kings 17:7–8 explains that tragedy like this:

> *This occurred because the people of Israel had sinned against the Lord their*
> *God, who had brought them up out of the land of Egypt from under the*
> *hand of Pharaoh king of Egypt. They had worshipped other gods and walked*
> *in the customs of the nations whom the Lord drove out before the people of*
> *Israel, and in the customs that the kings of Israel had introduced.*

2 Kings 24:20 accounts for the catastrophe of 587BC in the same way and in the simplest and starkest of terms: 'Jerusalem and Judah so angered the Lord that he expelled them from his presence.'

But what sort of story is this? Is it history, or fiction, or bits of both or neither? It is traditional among Christians to call the books from Joshua to Nehemiah the 'Historical Books' and, as the story probably began originally with Deuteronomy, to call the one who wove it together the 'Deuteronomic Historian'. 'History' is, however, a misleading word unless we remember that all history, ancient and modern, is not straight reporting but has a message to convey.

1 and 2 Kings is a book with a message—about 'the meaning of life, the universe and everything', about God, about faith in God and about faithfulness to God then and now. It is first and foremost a book of theology, of talk about God, which uses a range of types of writing, including 'history' and 'creative storytelling', to make its point and proclaim its message. It is as if its anonymous writer, numerous editors and those who included it in our Bibles are saying to us, 'If you have eyes to see, then see!' That is how I invite you to read 1 and 2 Kings with me.

The text

In this commentary we will read Kings—and I will call it that or the 'book of Kings' even though it is in two parts—as we have it in our modern Bibles. The particular version I will use is the New Revised Standard Version (NRSV), though I will refer occasionally to other modern versions, especially the Revised English Bible (REB), the New International Version (NIV), the New Jerusalem Bible (NJB), the Good News Bible (GNB) and the New Jewish Publication Society translation called 'Tanach' (NJPS).

Kings covers the period from the death of King David in the tenth century BC to the middle of the exile in Babylon in the sixth. There are several parallel accounts of this period in the Old Testament, the biggest of which is 1 Chronicles 28 to 2 Chronicles 36. Parts of Kings are actually found in the books of Isaiah and Jeremiah, and these and other prophets operated during the period in question. I shall not often refer to the parallel accounts in these other books and I certainly will not get involved in discussing the frequent differences between Kings and Chronicles in an attempt to explain those differences or decide which is 'correct'. In this commentary we shall be reading Kings in its final form—simply because that is the book as we have it.

Kings—and the Deuteronomic History of which it is the last part—is and always has been anonymous. Sometimes, therefore, I will simply refer to the author as 'our writer' or 'writers' but often I will call him (for the writer almost certainly was a man) or them, the 'Deuteronomic Historian(s)' or the 'Deuteronomists'.

Scholars agree that almost all those responsible for the book reaching its final form, whether as original author or authors or as editors and revisers, share the same outlook and theology and belong to the same party or group in ancient Israel. They call them the 'Deuteronomists' because their outlook and theology are found in the book of Deuteronomy. Exactly who they were is not so easy to say. Most scholars identify them as a group who emerged in the northern kingdom (Israel) in the eighth century BC, who were passionate in their belief in the Lord as the one God for Israel who was calling his people into a covenant with himself. When that kingdom was destroyed in 722BC, they moved south to Judah, where their way of looking at things eventually prevailed and their viewpoint became the accepted orthodoxy. Their theology can be summed up in a sentence: The God who has made himself known to Israel as the Lord ('Yahweh'), calling Israel into being as his particular people and blessing them with the gift of their own land, demands exclusive loyalty and obedience from his chosen people.

A distinctive feature of their approach, particularly noticeable in Judges, is a fourfold cycle of events: the people of Israel disobey God and cease to walk in his ways; they suffer for their disobedience, often through foreign attack or invasion; they turn back to God, who hears and answers their cry for help; they live happily and successfully for a while until they disobey again; and the cycle continues. All of this is expressed in a distinctive vocabulary which features not only in Deuteronomy itself but throughout the books of the Deuteronomic History and in the books of a number of the prophets too, especially Jeremiah. If they began their work in the eighth century, it certainly continued until after the return from exile in the sixth.

Story and plot

The Deuteronomists tell a good story. There is detail and there are dates, but rarely does the story slow down enough for readers to get bogged down in the detail or to have to worry about the dates. It begins with the intrigues which lead to Solomon's accession to the throne in Jerusalem on the death of David, and then highlights the glories of his building schemes—the Temple and the palace. But there is no adulation of monarchy here. Time and again the story—here by a hint, there directly—points an accusing finger at the king. We follow the division of the kingdom on his death, with a tendency to dwell longer on Israel and the faults of its succeeding dynasties than Judah and its continuing Davidic line. We watch the end of that kingdom, of a nation and its kings who never listened to God's prophets or heeded his guidance; and then see the same mistakes repeated, with the same result, a century and a half later in Judah. We notice the constant appearances of prophets who insist on the Deuteronomic line that righteousness is rewarded and sin is punished. We see the way that king after king fails to behave as they should and how the nation, often just as bad, is caught up in the consequences. The end is the destruction of Solomon's glories and the exile of his people, but it's an end with a twist in it.

Kings (as well as Joshua, Judges and Samuel) are primarily books about God, a fact clearly indicated in the title of all these books in the Hebrew Bible, where they are called the 'Former Prophets'. This title does not simply mean that they happen to feature some of the 'former prophets' like Samuel, Nathan, Elijah and Elisha, but that they are books which speak of the will and purpose of God—they convey what God was believed to be saying and doing, and talk about what it means to be God's people. To put it another way, I shall read Kings as a theology book, an anthology of stories told, incidents recounted and conversations shared, not because this is what happened and we are interested in what happened (though it might be and we may be) but so that we and all God's people of yesterday, today and tomorrow might understand what the will and purpose of God is. For me, these books are books about God, his will and his ways—books which give lessons for the people of God in every age and in every place, lessons from the past for the present and the future.

Although Kings is not a history textbook, there are times when I will put dates on particular events or to the reigns of kings. There is, however, a small problem here. Because of the difficulty of working out a chronology of events from the data given in the Old Testament itself, there are two different sets of dates currently in use. For most of the time they do not differ much and they never differ hugely, but anyone who reads Kings in the NJB (New Jerusalem Bible) will notice at several points that I am using the other scheme.

What about the 'nasty bits'?

There are plenty of 'nasty bits' in the story of God and ancient Israel in Kings, and they do not make the book an easy or comfortable read. They focus the general problem of God, the Bible and violence so sharply that some readers reject the story completely as an expression of attitudes and values which we have now outgrown. Others seem to see no problem with God and his people perpetrating acts of violence then or now, but that frightening observation is another story! It would be easy to dismiss Kings as a collection of barbaric tales from an ancient and barbarous age, but we ought to take the 'nasty bits' in Kings a bit more seriously than that, not least because a moment's thought might make us pause to reflect how anyone in our century could dare to accuse another age or place of barbarism.

Be that as it may, Kings is, of course, a book from its own age which expresses attitudes and values different from ours. That age, for example, was not a 'democratic' one in which government was accountable to the people and where bad governments could be removed and replaced via the ballot box. Thus, what alternative was there to the coup—even a coup as bloody as Jehu's—if things became unbearable? Neither, in that age, was the worship and service of the Lord, the God of Israel, or any other god, the kind of religion that could be divorced from public life and practised as a private hobby for those who liked that sort of thing. Life-and-death issues were involved in religion—Queen Jezebel's faith permitted her to use her royal power to get rid of the peasant Naboth for her own profit, but Elijah's faith drove him to oppose her—and that at least ought to help us to see why the story is told with all the passion that it is.

Suggestions for further reading

Iain W. Provan, *1 and 2 Kings*, New International Biblical Commentary, Hendrickson/Paternoster, 1995.

G.H. Jones, *1 and 2 Kings* (2 volumes), the New Century Bible Commentary, Eerdmans, 1984.

A PRAYER

Eternal and generous God, whose gift of the Bible we cherish because it speaks of your great love for us and of your power and will to save us; grant that our study of it may not be spoiled by the callousness and carelessness of our hearts, but that by it we may be moved to penitence, renewed in hope, strengthened for service and, above all, filled with a true knowledge of you.

The RULERS *of* JUDAH & ISRAEL

The united monarchy

Saul
David
Solomon

The divided kingdoms

Judah		Israel	
Rehoboam	931–916	Jeroboam	932–911
Abijam	916–914		
Asa	914–874	Nadab	911–910
		Baasha	910–887
		Elah	887–886
		Zimri	886
		Omri	886–875
Jehoshaphat	874–850	Ahab	875–854
		Ahaziah	854–853
Jehoram	850–843	Joram	853–842
Ahaziah	843–842		
Athaliah	842–837	Jehu	842–815
Jehoash	836–797	Jehoahaz	815–799
Amaziah	797–769	Joash	799–784
Uzziah (Ahaziah)	769–741	Jeroboam II	784–753
		Zechariah	753–752
		Shallum	752–751
		Menahem	751–742
		Pekahiah	742–741
Jotham	741–734	Pekah	741–730
Ahaz (Jehoahaz)	734–715	Hoshea	730–722
Hezekiah	715–697		
Manasseh	697–642		
Amon	641–640		
Josiah	639–609		
Jehoahaz II	609		
Jehoiakim	609–598		
Jehoiachin	598		
Zedekiah	598–587		

A KING'S OLD AGE

A great king

The great King David is old and frail. The fact that he is 'old and advanced in years' testifies that he has been richly blessed by God, and that phrase invites us to see him on a par with Abraham and Joshua (Genesis 24:1; Joshua 13:1). King David has built the united kingdom of Israel out of struggling and competing tribal groups, given his new nation peace and prosperity and even made a place for it, though a small one, on the international scene. The threat from the Philistines which had dogged the fate of Israel's first king, Saul, from the beginning of his reign to its tragic end, is a thing of the past, destroyed by David (see 1 Samuel 13:2–23; 31:1–13 and 2 Samuel 5:17–25; 8:1). Instead it is Israel which stands tall among the petty kingdoms between the Mediterranean Sea and the great Arabian Desert, albeit because the world powers of Egypt in the south and the Mesopotamian states in the north are too preoccupied with other things to worry too much about it. He rules as God's anointed king in Jerusalem, his own city, the 'City of David', whose capture from the Jebusites had finally rid the promised land of its previous occu-pants and, in the process, shown David's personal skills as a com-mander and military tactician (2 Samuel 5:6–10). Only briefly under Solomon will Israel's borders be bigger, and after that they will never reach this extent again, stretching from a hundred miles north of Damascus to the borders of Egypt and from the Mediterranean itself to nearly as far beyond the River Jordan in the east. Israel has arrived at genuine nationhood, and it is David who has brought it there. But in his old age, personal problems loom largest: he can't get warm (v. 1). Worse is to follow: he has lost control of his own family.

A flawed man

His days of greatness are now behind him; but so too, it appears, are the turbulent times. The account of David's reign in 1 Samuel 16 to 2 Kings 2:11 is a strangely frank one. It makes no attempt to disguise —indeed at times it seems to emphasize—that alongside the real greatness of his political and military successes there is a flawed humanity. David is a victor. He is also a survivor. He has reached old age despite a long military career, and despite personal trauma, family crises and armed coups. But the stories give him little credit for surviving these things because they are quick to point out that it was usually his own folly, wrongdoing or shortcomings which had caused them in the first place. For example, the legacy of abducting and raping Bathsheba (for that is what his crime amounts to) and arranging for her husband to be killed (2 Samuel 11:2–27) is not simply that David grieves when the baby son conceived in that act dies. It is that Bathsheba and her second son, Solomon, are for ever involved in palace intrigues and that Solomon sows seeds which eventually reap the break-up of all that David had achieved. Or again, David might have subdued the Philistines but he couldn't control his own sons (2 Samuel 19:9). Absalom had even forced him to flee from Jerusalem and live in internal exile (2 Samuel 15:14—20:3). But all that too is now past. The man who found what he wanted, and took it when he found it, now has to have a woman found for him, and can do nothing with her even when he is given every opportunity. David's nubile hot-water bottle, though very attractive, is simply that and his nurse; nothing more (v. 4).

But what next?

These opening verses set a scene which is both rather pathetic and not lacking in irony. They introduce us to an aged king, his loyal and caring servants and the beautiful Abishag from the village of Shunem in the plain of Esdraelon. It all looks remarkably innocent, until we remember that old age means the approach of death and that the death of a king raises the question of succession to the throne. There may be, as yet, no mention of God, but there is the beginning of a plot.

FOR MEDITATION

David was a great king and a flawed man.
His achievements show God's high purposes for humanity.
His human fallibility is a picture of our own.
He is a model of all of us—though not a model for us!

TROUBLE AS BEFORE

The calm of the book's opening scene is shattered by verse 5. Adonijah stages a palace coup. Israel is a new nation; its dynastic principles and rules of succession have not yet been established. Adonijah, David's fourth and oldest surviving son (2 Samuel 3:4), sees his father's infirmity and stakes his claim.

A new Absalom?

The full horror of this threat is unfolded in six short phrases. Adonijah 'exalts himself'. He makes his claim—'I will be king'. By now, readers who have been reading the story from the beginning and have just turned over from the story of David's reign in 2 Samuel will be hearing warning bells, and their fears grow when Adonijah backs his claim by a show of power, mustering an unspecified number of chariots and horsemen and fifty 'outrunners'. Here we are reminded of the beginning of Absalom's attempt to become king (2 Samuel 15:1), but Adonijah's coup is backed by military technology not seen in Israel before—cavalry as well as chariots and infantry. Verse 6 can be read in different ways, one which puts blame on Adonijah by saying that his father had never given him any reason to rebel like this, and the other which puts blame on David by saying either that he had never bothered to exercise any proper parental control over his son or that he made no attempt to stop what was happening now. More memories of Absalom are stirred by the fifth phrase, that Adonijah was 'handsome' (see 2 Samuel 14:25), and then the ominous name itself is mentioned in the sixth phrase. Adonijah is Absalom's younger brother. We now know what to expect.

Taking sides

Adonijah is joined by two of David's most loyal leading statesmen. Joab was David's nephew and commander-in-chief (2 Samuel 8:16). He had a long string of victories for David to his credit, and a lifetime of ruthless and dedicated service to David behind him. He was the one who had arranged Uriah's death (2 Samuel 11:14–16), brought about the initial reconciliation between David and Absalom (2 Samuel 14), killed Absalom when he finally rebelled against his father (2 Samuel 18:14) and then tackled David when he was distraught with grief over Absalom's death (2 Samuel 19:5–7). He was cunning and brutal (see 2 Samuel 20:8–10) but, until now, prepared to do what David ordered even when he believed it to be wrong (2 Samuel 24:1–9). Abiathar, who shared the chief priestly responsibility with Zadok (2 Samuel 8:17), had been with David since David's earliest outlaw days. He had joined him when Saul had killed his family (1 Samuel 22:20–21) and remained loyal to him throughout. We are not told of their motives for joining Adonijah.

The list of non-joiners is longer. First named is Zadok, the other chief priest; then Benaiah, the captain of David's bodyguard (2 Samuel 8:18); the prophet Nathan who had advised David over his hopes to build a temple (2 Samuel 7:1–17) and then dramatically rebuked him over his treatment of Uriah (2 Samuel 12:1–15); and Shimei and Rei about whom nothing is known. David's bodyguard also refuses to side with Adonijah. The split seems to be the 'old guard' versus the 'young bloods'.

The coup

Adonijah offers a lavish sacrifice to mark the launch of his campaign, just as Absalom had done (2 Samuel 15:12). Its location, En-rogel, was a spring in the Kidron valley just outside Jerusalem, and it too has links with Absalom's revolt for it was the place where David's spies waited for news (2 Samuel 17:17). None of the non-joiners are invited and neither is 'his brother Solomon'. With mention of that name and that relationship, the shape of the coming struggle begins to be seen—and not only that, but the shape of the whole of the book of Kings which will tell about kingdoms and loyalties divided and point up the terrible cost. As yet, King David knows nothing of what is going on.

FOR PRAYER

Pray for the leaders of the nations and all who hold political power, that they may seek not to rule but to serve.

The PROPHET & *the* QUEEN

Here we meet two key players in the drama, Nathan the prophet and
Bathsheba the queen.

Hatching a plot

Nathan, the official prophet at Court, was no 'yes man'. In the past
he had been forthright in confronting the king (2 Samuel 12:1–15)
but now he plots behind his back (vv. 11–14). This story, like so
much Old Testament storytelling, tells us nothing about motives.
Does Nathan see himself following in the footsteps of Samuel as
prophet and king-maker? Or is he, knowing what is afoot, taking
steps to make sure that God's will is done? The last time Nathan
appeared in the story was when Solomon was born, and he had been
sent to say that the baby was also to be called 'Jedidiah', 'Beloved of
the Lord' (2 Samuel 12:25). Has the time come for Nathan to show
what that name really means? Whatever the case may be, Nathan
doesn't confront the king but plots with the queen.

He begins by asking a far-from-innocent question. Has Bathsheba
not heard (of course she has!) … that her rival's son (why else call
Adonijah 'the son of Haggith'? She knows full well who his mother
is) … has become king; and obviously David doesn't know about it
(else he would have told her, wouldn't he?). Then he suggests a plan
of action which involves reminding David of the solemn oath he had
sworn in which he had promised his throne to her son, Solomon. No
such oath has been heard in the story so far. Is Nathan, for whatever
reason, resorting to tricking an old man for a blessing, like Jacob had
done (see Genesis 27:1–45)?

Executing it

Having agreed tactics, Bathsheba goes in to the king (vv. 15–21). She
had been summoned to him on their first meeting but now the initiative is hers. She needs no permission to be admitted to his royal
presence, though she does follow the proper protocol (v. 16). The
story reminds us that the king is old and dependent (v. 15). His question shows that some things never change: what does she want?
Bathsheba keeps to the script and leads the king by the nose. She

reminds him that he swore an oath, and then builds on it, point upon point. At the end he is in an impossible position. Does he want to be seen to be failing in his duty by not making a declaration about his successor? Can he die in peace, knowing what will happen to her and her son? She is under no illusion about what happens to potential rivals for thrones, and David too has seen how brutal his sons can be to each other (2 Samuel 13:29). Did not Nathan say as much (2 Samuel 12:10)?

There are two very different ways of looking at death in the Old Testament. One is where death comes at its proper time, peacefully in old age, at the end of a full life. Here, relatives, though naturally grieving, can rejoice over a life 'faithfully lived and peacefully died', as with Abraham in Genesis 25:8. The other view sees death as vicious, terrifying and evil; destroying, hurting and defacing what is beautiful, good and healthy, as in Psalm 18:4–5. David is soon to 'sleep with his ancestors' (v. 21). Although that phrase might simply mean being put in the family tomb, it may be picking up the images of being 'gathered to his people' as Abraham was. With that good death before him, can David condemn his wife and child to the other?

Then, right on cue, enter Nathan (vv. 22–27), with due ceremony and proper introduction. He too has remembered the script and carefully prepared his tactics. He begins by asking the king if he has said that Adonijah shall succeed him, because that is what Adonijah and his supporters are claiming. They have proclaimed him king by acclamation already. Is that wise, Nathan hints, without the blessing of prophet and priest? Of course, if the king has approved this, then that is fine, and if he has simply forgotten to tell some of those who ought to have been told about it...

We are now in no doubt about the dangers facing the kingdom. The king is dying. Opposing forces are gathering. Who will succeed —the Adonijah we have met or the Solomon we have yet to meet?

FOR REFLECTION

*How can we discern the will of God in the political choices
we have to make?*

'LONG LIVE KING SOLOMON!'

Three scenes follow in quick succession.

The king and Bathsheba

Nathan disappears from the king's presence, as Bathsheba had on his arrival. She is summoned back and stands before him, making no obeisance this time. He acts on what she has said. He swears a new solemn oath that he will do what he swore before and do it immediately. Bathsheba's bow and stylized response, 'May my lord King David live for ever' (v. 31), surely invite a wry smile.

King David swears a new oath (which is much more than 'making a promise' as in GNB) and he does so on the very name of the living God 'who has saved his life from every adversity' (v. 29). David has not led a trouble-free life. His family life alone has been a catalogue of anguish. Yet, through it all, he acknowledges the help of God which has strengthened and sustained him.

The king and the leading officials

The king then summons Solomon's key supporters—Zadok, one of the two chief priests, Nathan the court prophet and Benaiah the captain of the guard (see 1:8). He commands them to take the royal guard and make Solomon king. He gives precise instructions about how to do it.

Solomon must ride on the royal mule. Horses were not yet common in Palestine and mules appear in David's time as royal mounts (2 Samuel 13:29; 18:9). He must go to the spring at Gihon, which is in the same valley as En-rogel and just out of sight of the place where Adonijah is celebrating. This was Jerusalem's main source of water, and possibly therefore the city's main public space. The priest and prophet must anoint him there with holy oil, as the prophet Samuel had anointed the first king, Saul (1 Samuel 10:1), and the people had anointed the second, David (2 Samuel 2:4). The trumpet must be blown (as it had been to announce that Absalom had become king in 2 Samuel 15:10) and he must be acclaimed as king (see 1:25). Then he must lead them back into the city and take his seat on his father's throne.

David's decision is that Solomon is to be the 'ruler over Israel and over Judah'. Note that phraseology. The two tribal groups, Israel and Judah, had been united under David's personal kingship. First, he had been made king of Judah at Hebron (2 Samuel 2:4) and then, seven years later, he became king of Israel (2 Samuel 5:3–5). Now, by his own royal fiat, his son is to be ruler of both states. Not only is this coronation rushed, it lacks any of the community assent which had given both thrones to David.

Benaiah, who is neither priest nor prophet but the longtime leader of David's personal troops, shouts 'Amen!' ('It shall be done!') and prays for the new king's success.

The officials and Solomon

Verses 38–40 add detail as the commands are carried out. The royal guard are named as the 'Cherethites and Pelethites,' which may be a corruption of 'Cretans and Philistines'—foreign troops whose personal loyalty to David had been proved during Absalom's revolt against his father some years before (2 Samuel 15:18). Zadok takes oil from the 'tent' (v. 39). At this time Jerusalem had no temple and the two nations had no national sanctuary other than the tent (or 'tabernacle') in which the sacred Ark, containing various holy relics, was kept. David had previously ensured that this holy box, from the old days of wandering in the desert, was lodged in Jerusalem (2 Samuel 6:12–19). Nathan is not involved in the anointing. Note verse 39: the people make the acclamation in response to the official declaration. This is a very public event, in marked contrast to Adonijah's private party. Verse 40 may simply mean that they were celebrating very noisily, but the phrase about the earth 'quaking' suggests that these were truly momentous, earth-shattering events in which God was present and at work (see how the same word is used at Numbers 16:31).

FOR PRAYER

Pray for those who minister to those in power,
and for honesty and integrity in places of plot and intrigue.

1 KINGS 1:41-53

The DEED IS DONE

Six scenes have quickly passed since we last saw Adonijah and his supporters. The plot hatched by Nathan has worked. The old king has acted decisively not only to name his successor but also to enthrone him. Solomon's name has been frequently mentioned but so far he has neither spoken nor acted.

Bad news

The details of Solomon's accession are repeated for the third time in Jonathan's report of it (vv. 43-45), which leads to the bald and pointed statement of fact in verse 46, 'Solomon now sits on the royal throne.' This speech marks the end of the dynastic struggles which began as early as 2 Samuel 15, and sets the scene for the next ten chapters of 1 Kings. Solomon is king—fact. This is not good news to Adonijah and company, but the way in which Jonathan's report begins by stating the fact, continues by describing how it has come about and ends with restating it indicates that it is a fact to be accepted. His comment that the 'king's servants' have given it their backing (v. 47), by which he clearly means Benaiah as well as the royal guard, strongly suggests that opposition to this *fait accompli* is futile. Notice how Benaiah's blessing has grown in the telling.

Jonathan concludes his report with two comments about David. First, that he 'bowed in worship on the bed' (v. 47). This might be the Deuteronomic Historians' way of telling us that he was too frail to do it properly on the floor; more likely it is their invitation to readers who know the longer story to make the link with Jacob ('Israel') in Genesis 47:31. Solomon is the chosen one who will carry out the old man's last wishes, just as Joseph did for his father. Then King David went on to 'bless the Lord' (v. 48).

'Blessed be the Lord, the God of Israel, who...' is a standard formula which occurs frequently in the Old Testament. The Hebrew verb is often translated as 'praise', as in NIV and GNB here, or 'thank'. But to 'bless the Lord' is more than to thank him or praise him. It is to acknowledge, affirm and acclaim that he alone is God and that he has acted to demonstrate his divine power. That is exactly its powerful meaning here. David acclaims that the Lord, the God of

Israel, is indeed God, and that it is he who has brought about this great event. Psalm 89 is a whole psalm which 'blesses the Lord' on the same theme as this verse.

Adonijah pleads for mercy

Verses 49–53 set out the reaction to the news. Adonijah's supporters disappear. Adonijah, fearing Solomon, seeks sanctuary at the altar in or, more likely, just outside the holy tent. The 'horns of the altar' were projections at each corner on which the blood of the sacrifices was smeared (Exodus 29:12; 30:10). The fear, on which Bathsheba had played in her appeal to David in 1:21, was a real one. Because of her success, it is Adonijah who is now afraid. All this is reported to Solomon.

In verse 52 Solomon speaks for the first time. His words seem wise, fair and reassuring. They do, however, contain a warning to Adonijah and leave Solomon with room to manoeuvre and an answer to any later critics should he need to rid himself of his step-brother. Adonijah is to be a 'worthy man' ('an honourable man'—REB), as he himself had recognized Jonathan to be. Solomon's first action as king is to have Adonijah brought to him, sanctuary or no (v. 53). Adonijah is to retire from public life. A deal has been struck. Adonijah pledges good behaviour in return for the king's clemency.

The kingdom is intact and there has been no bloodshed. Solomon is king. David sees this as the will of God. Adonijah and his supporters have little choice but to accept the reality, however reluctantly.

A PRAYER

Blessed are you, O Lord, the God of our ancestor Israel,
for ever and ever. Yours, O Lord, are the greatness, the power,
the glory, the victory, and the majesty; for all that is in the heavens
and on the earth is yours; yours is the kingdom, O Lord,
and you are exalted as head above all.

1 Chronicles 29:10–11

6

LAST WILL & TESTAMENT

David prepares to die. He leaves his successor both good advice (vv. 1–4) and bad instructions (vv. 5–9).

Good advice

David's charge to Solomon focuses on obedience to the 'Torah of Moses' (v. 3). Most modern versions use the traditional translation of this phrase, 'the law of Moses', but NJPS has 'the Teaching of Moses'. 'Law' is a much misunderstood word in Christianity, which immediately associates it with 'legalism' and sees it as something bad, to be contrasted with 'the gospel' which is good. In the Old Testament, 'Torah' is seen in an entirely positive way. It is God's great gift to Israel, his life-giving guidance, instruction and teaching. It is no exaggeration to say that the word 'gospel' itself would be a good equivalent for 'Torah', for 'Torah' is God's 'good news' for his people. This is clearly seen in Exodus 20:1–2, where, having rescued his people from Egypt, God gives them his good advice about how they can live their new and liberated life, free from bondage and terror of any kind, in the land he is giving them. The teaching goes into detail at times, for there are very practical and specific things to do or to avoid if such freedom is to be protected (Deuteronomy 4:40; 11:8–15), but 'Torah' is not burden and demand. It is gift and blessing, as can be seen in Psalm 119.

In three expressions in verses 3–4 we see the writer's Deuteronomic point of view. 'Walking in God's ways' is a favourite expression in Deuteronomy itself (see, for example, 8:6; 10:12; 11:22). 'All their heart and all their soul' takes us straight to the central text of this outlook in Deuteronomy 6:4–5, called the *Shema* after its opening word in Hebrew. The Deuteronomic foursome of statutes, commandments, ordinances and testimonies (this last one is more helpfully called 'decrees' in NJB, 'requirements' in NIV and 'solemn precepts' in REB) does not refer to four different kinds of regulations or obligations but is a standard expression for everything which God has made clear Israel is to do.

David reminds Solomon about all this. He will enjoy the blessings his father has received, and avoid the curses, if he heeds the good guidance of Torah. God keeps his promises, as Solomon will discover if he takes God's advice seriously. For the promise referred to, see 2 Samuel 7:11–16 and also Psalm 89. It is, however, not to be presumed upon. Kings, Solomon is reminded, are not free to use their power as they please (see also Deuteronomy 17:14–20).

Bad instructions

Verses 5–9 reveal the flaws of the old king all too clearly. He leaves to Solomon the job of tying up loose ends by disposing of Joab and Shimei. Is it because Joab had supported Adonijah that David now decides that old wrongs must be punished? (For the incidents mentioned, see 2 Samuel 3:26–27 and 20:9–10.) The treatment of Shimei (one of Solomon's key supporters, 1 Kings 1:8) seems especially underhand. The original oath was that he should not die (see 2 Samuel 19:23 for the oath and 16:5–14 and 19:18–23 for the background) and not that *David* would not kill him. That, however, is how David speaks of it now, and putting it that way makes it possible for Solomon to kill him (v. 8). Neither Joab nor Shimei are to live to the end of their natural lives. Their punishment is that their 'grey heads will not go down to Sheol in peace'. Sheol, the place where all the dead gradually fade into nothingness, is to receive these two before their due time. That is their punishment for their misdeeds. Solomon, David recognizes, is 'wise' enough to do both killings discreetly (vv. 6, 9). It is disconcerting that the first two mentions of Solomon's proverbial wisdom in Kings should be in connection with such deeds. That the sons of Barzillai are to continue to receive royal maintenance for their family's help to David in his hour of need (see 2 Samuel 17:27–29 and 19:31–39) does little to counterbalance the sad impression of a great king left by these last instructions.

There may, however, be political rather than personal reasons operating here. Does Joab represent the old guard from Judah, and Shimei the nationalists of Israel, both of which represent threats to a united kingdom around Solomon's table?

FOR REFLECTION

The longest psalm of all, Psalm 119, is a song of praise for the Torah. Read verses 33–40 for a good example of a worshipper's 'delight in God's law'. Sadly, the dying king falls short.

7

TWO DEATHS

The death of King David

David dies peacefully at the age of seventy (see 2 Samuel 5:4–5). He is buried in his own city (v. 10). Jerusalem is 'the city of David' because he captured it from the Jebusites (2 Samuel 5:6–9). It is his personal possession, which he has developed and improved. It belongs to him, not to Israel or Judah, the twin states over which he has ruled.

Solomon sits on his father's throne. That he is David's son has been mentioned often in the story, but here the comment is pointed that his throne is his father's throne. The comment in verse 12 (and compare v. 24) that his rule is 'firmly established' is, in one sense, premature. Such a comment can only safely be made when his rivals and their supporters have been eliminated (2:46). On the other hand, 'established' is a key word in the promise to David in 2 Samuel 7:11–16, and one point of this postscript to David's reign is that that promise has proved true. Solomon is being deliberately described as what David was—God's chosen and appointed king.

The death of Prince Adonijah

The calm of verse 12 is shattered by verse 13. Adonijah reappears. He comes to the queen mother with a request. He is again called 'Adonijah son of Haggith'. Bathsheba is pointedly referred to as 'Solomon's mother'. There may be some playing on words here, for Haggith means 'festivals' and Bathsheba means 'daughter of the oath', and we have already seen both a feasting Adonijah and the role of oaths in securing the throne for Solomon. Does this introduction to the scene suggest that Adonijah is doomed to fail? In these two verses five people are named—the father David, his two sons and the two mothers. We are reminded that the tragic story of David and his dysfunctional family is not yet over.

There is some inevitable fencing with words. Bathsheba asks about his intentions: does he come 'peaceably' ('as a friend', REB)? After saying 'yes' and making the point that he accepts that it is the Lord's will that the crown, which everyone expected to be his, is now Solomon's, he makes his request for her to ask King Solomon to give him the beautiful Abishag as his wife (v. 17). Again, we are not let into his motives. Does he love her? The frightening story of Amnon and Tamar at least shows us that such love was a possibility (2 Samuel 13:1–15). On the other hand, there is the story of Absalom sleeping with ten concubines out of David's harem after he had exiled David from his city (2 Samuel 16:21–22), and that was clearly a public and political act.

Bathsheba goes to speak to the king, and is received with respect and due ceremony; Solomon bows to her (v. 19) and sets her throne on the right-hand side of his, the place of honour. We are not told anything about her motives either. She is hardly a political innocent. She cannot wish to further Adonijah's claim. Is it that here is an opportunity not to be missed? By making Adonijah's request, she can give Solomon the chance to be rid of him. She uses Adonijah's line of approach almost word for word, adding only that she has a 'small' request and adding the words 'your brother' before the mention of Adonijah's name (v. 21). She may be asking Solomon to help his brother or she may be reminding him that his brother remains a threat to his throne.

Solomon is not slow to seize his chance. He sees the request as an attempt to gain power (v. 22) and a breach of the trust he had placed in Adonijah in the deal they had made (1:52). This is no little request: it is a plot. Adonijah is indeed his brother, his elder brother, and all the more of a threat because of it. And who else wants to join in with a request? Solomon then swears the most powerful oath voiced so far in the book. In it he repeats three times the point that Adonijah had made once, that it was the Lord who had given him the throne (v. 24). The oath is that Adonijah must die. Verse 25 starkly recounts how he does.

A PRAYER

Almighty Father, who dost give
The gift of life to all who live,
Look down on all earth's sin and strife,
And lift us to a nobler life.
Thy world is weary of its pain,
Of selfish greed and fruitless gain,
Of tarnished honour, falsely strong,
And all its ancient deeds of wrong.

J.H.B. Masterman (1867–1933)

BLOOD & BANISHMENT

The fate of Abiathar

Adonijah's request has put his supporters in jeopardy; but Abiathar gets off lightly. He is banished to his family home in Anathoth (v. 26), three miles north of Jerusalem, with a death sentence hanging over him. He is spared death on account of his loyalty to David in two crises in David's life, the first in the early days when David was outlawed by King Saul (1 Samuel 22:20–23; 23:6–14), and the second when David fled from Jerusalem after Absalom had taken control of the city (2 Samuel 15:24–37).

This banishment is an illustration of the basic Deuteronomic principle that righteousness is rewarded and sin is punished. At one level, Abiathar's internal exile is his punishment for the sin of supporting Adonijah, while the fact that he is not killed is his reward for his goodness in supporting David. In the longer term, his fate is the final stage of the punishment on Eli's house which a prophet had announced when Samuel was a mere boy in the temple at Shiloh, for Abiathar is Eli's great-great-grandson (1 Samuel 2:27–36). With Abiathar deprived of his place as one of the two chief priests, Zadok is given sole authority (v. 35). His descendents will later be seen as the true priestly succession.

The 'fulfilment' of the 'word of the Lord', as in verse 27, is an important phrase in the vocabulary of the Deuteronomic Historians. The Davidic dynasty owes its existence to the 'word of the Lord' spoken through the prophet Nathan (2 Samuel 7:4), just as the ending of Eli's priestly line is the result of God's word spoken through a prophet whose name is not mentioned (v. 27).

The fate of Joab

Joab hears the news and flees to the holy tent and its altar for sanctuary, as Adonijah had done (1 Kings 1:50–53). Benaiah hesitates to carry out his orders, but does so after Solomon explains why Joab must die. He must now receive the reward for his killings of Abner, to whom David had given safe passage (2 Samuel 3), and Amasa, whom he had greeted with the right hand of peace just before disembowelling him with the sword in his left (2 Samuel 20:4–10). Benaiah carries out his orders and the king gives him Joab's job (vv. 34–35). The one who had lived by the sword has died by it. Their 'blood comes back' on Joab's head (vv. 32–33), another example of the Deuteronomic principle at work. Solomon's justification for violating the sanctuary of the altar is that Joab deserved his fate. He has brought this action on himself. David's prayer in 2 Samuel 3:39 has been answered. Note too the idea that both wrongdoing and well-doing have wide and long-term effects in which the 'descendants' of those who do them are caught up (v. 33).

The fate of Shimei

The fate of Shimei is unjust. There are no grounds to suggest that this Shimei is a different one from the one who had supported Solomon against Adonijah (1 Kings 1:8). In addition to being a supporter of Solomon, he had received David's pardon for cursing him (2 Samuel 16:5–14; 19:16–23). Now, because of David's malice, he is placed under curfew. He must build a house in Jerusalem, away from his family home, and he must not leave Jerusalem on pain of death. Note here too the 'blood on your own head' idea in verses 37 and 44. Shimei brings his death upon himself, first in consequence of his sin in cursing David, and second as a consequence of breaking his oath. The story rather suggests that Solomon is only waiting for a pretext, and a very insignificant and innocent incident supplies it. Solomon has neatly contrived Shimei's death in such a way that no blame or 'blood guilt' attaches to the king. David's confidence in his son's wisdom to find a way to deal with Shimei has been fully justified— but it does Solomon no credit.

The kingdom is established

Solomon is king. His only rival is dead. The two great offices of state, commander-in-chief and chief priest, are held by his nominees. He is secure.

FOR REFLECTION

The story is not an edifying one. There have been oaths sworn, broken and reinterpreted to suit David's and Solomon's purposes. Deaths which were politically advisable have been justified on religious pretexts. There is blood on those royal hands.

A Prayer *for* Wisdom

Doing what kings do

Solomon continues to do what kings do by making a marriage alliance with the nearest world power. There are mixed messages here. On the one hand, Solomon is now a player on the world stage and his kingdom on the world map. Even Egypt is prepared to recognize the people who used to slave in its brickyards as a sovereign nation. On the other, the mention of that name is ominous. In the long story of Israel's past, Egypt has been the source of most of Israel's troubles, and in that story they have been warned both about kings who get too close to the old oppressor (Deuteronomy 17:16) and against marrying foreigners (Deuteronomy 7:3).

Roles are now reversed. The last pharaoh's daughter we met took the infant Moses into her family (Exodus 2:5–10). Now the king brings one, whose name we do not know, into 'the city of David' (v. 1). The 'city of David' was the old Jebusite walled city which David had captured on a southern spur of the main ridge (2 Samuel 5:6–9). When Solomon has finished building, his walled city will extend northwards up the hill, with the palace and the temple occupying its summit area.

The 'high places' were local, open-air places of worship. REB calls them 'shrines', for not all of them were on the tops of hills. In the 'however' of verse 2, the writer sounds another warning note. The writer is working on the principle of Deuteronomy 12:1–14, that it is only in Jerusalem and only in the temple that God is to be worshipped. That will be the only acceptable 'house for the name of the Lord', a favourite Deuteronomic phrase. The fate of the kingdom will turn out to be bound up with the tensions between the temple that Solomon will build and the local shrines and sanctuaries which it will only slowly replace.

The dream

Verse 3 is not entirely complimentary about Solomon. He loves the Lord, but we shall see later that he also loves his foreign wives (1 Kings 11:1–2). He 'walks' in God's ways as his father had done, but at the same time he actively supports the local shrines in ways which David had not. It is at Gibeon, the principal local shrine where he habitually and lavishly worships, that he has his famous dream (vv. 5–14). In it we see Solomon at his best. He refuses to ask for power or glory but offers his great responsibilities to God and prays for wisdom (vv. 7–9). He dreams that his prayer is heard, his wish granted and more besides (vv. 10–14). In the next chapter we will learn more about Solomon's 'wisdom'.

The last sentence in the dream, in verse 14, begins with 'If…'. Solomon is not given a blank cheque. There are conditions to be fulfilled if he is to receive these blessings. He is to behave—and God has defined what good behaviour is. In the dream he is told to model himself on his father, but the mention of 'statutes and commandments' takes us back to Moses. For him, good government meant keeping certain rules and observing certain conditions, as we have seen (Deuteronomy 17:14–20, a passage which is in the background throughout 1 and 2 Kings). Solomon is inheriting his throne from his father, and well might he be grateful to God for it and for the promises to his father in 2 Samuel 7:15–16; but he must not presume upon them.

There are two pen portraits in verse 6. See 1 Kings 8:23–24 and the comments in Study 20, where the portrait of God is filled out. The portrait of David is warm and affirming. It notes his 'faithfulness'—God could always rely on him; his 'righteousness'—he always did what he should have done; and his 'uprightness of heart'—he did it all with integrity and honesty.

A sacrifice and a feast

In gratitude Solomon returns to Jerusalem and offers sacrifices before the 'Ark of the Covenant'.

A PRAYER

Almighty God, to whom our needs are known before we ask, help us to ask only what accords with your will; and those good things which we dare not or in our blindness cannot ask, grant us, for the sake of your Son, Jesus Christ our Lord. Amen.

The GIFT of WISDOM

Solomon's reign is described in 1 Kings 3—11, and two features of it are emphasized. The first is that Solomon built the temple. The second is Solomon's wisdom. Having prayed for the gift of wisdom and received it, in this passage we see how it is put to the test (vv. 16–27). The story is tense and dramatic. Who is telling the truth? An infant life lies in the balance. Solomon's reputation is established.

Solomon's wisdom has become proverbial. Whether that reputation is justified we will discuss at the end of his reign with reference to 1 Kings 11:41–43. To be able to do that, we must look at what is meant by 'wisdom'.

Wisdom is skill, creativity and versatility. Bezalel and Oholiab, the gifted craftsmen and designers whom Moses commissions to lead the team to make the tabernacle, are examples of those who have this sort of wisdom (Exodus 35:30—36:1). NRSV translates the Hebrew word as 'skill' in this passage. This is the wisdom with which God created the world (Proverbs 3:19–20; Jeremiah 10:12).

Wisdom is the shrewd competence and ability which David saw in Solomon when he told him to deal with his old enemies (1 Kings 2:6, 9). He knew that Solomon had the nous to handle that delicate business, the ability to do what needed to be done. We saw this shrewdness, even craftiness, at work in the way Solomon disposed of his rivals to the throne and their supporters. The same ability is displayed in this incident, and verse 28 notes that his reputation for judicial competence begins here. A king is wise if he is a strong and astute ruler, skilled in statecraft and the arts of diplomacy, able to create peace and economic prosperity by his knowledge of the realities of life and politics (see the picture of Joseph in Genesis 41: 37–57, especially verses 33 and 39).

Wisdom is knowledge, the ability to see the meaning of things and to know how everything works. This is the wisdom described in Proverbs, Ecclesiastes and the Wisdom of Solomon in the Apocrypha, all books traditionally attributed to Solomon. He is seen as the patron of wisdom in Israel, as Moses was seen as the patron of Torah (the 'Law') and David of psalmody. These books may look very different— the optimism of Proverbs seems at odds with the pessimism of

Ecclesiastes—but they are doing the same thing. They look at the world and see what is going on. They observe the worlds of nature and of human affairs and draw conclusions about the best way to live. Their basic conviction is that living in accordance with the way things really are leads to harmony, integration and fullness of life for individuals and communities.

Wisdom is also godliness. It is living according to the will and purpose of God. That is why 'the fear of the Lord is the beginning of wisdom' (Proverbs 9:10) echoes and re-echoes like a motto in this literature. To be wise is to take account of God, the ground of all being, the source, guide and goal of all that is. God tends to be in the background in these wisdom writings, but he is not absent. They work on the principle that his will and his ways are to be seen in creation, in the life of nature and of human beings (compare Romans 1:20). His purpose is to be discerned by observation, perception and common sense in the 'orders' or 'regularities' of life.

Wisdom is skill, competence, knowledge and godliness. The wisdom writings suggest that this adds up to a challenge. There are two ways in which to walk: the ways of wisdom and folly (Proverbs 2:1—3:18). To follow the one is to arrive at fullness of life; to follow the other is to end with life's disintegration. The way of wisdom involves developing those values, virtues and attitudes which can be observed in nature and in history to be life-enhancing, such as hard work, sobriety, moderation, a sense of responsibility (especially sexual responsibility), integrity and reliability. The wise observe, reflect and take a long view; they are quick to see, slow to speak. They are successful because they observe what works and avoid what doesn't work.

FOR REFLECTION

Knowledge is more than information.
Wisdom is more than knowledge.

11 1 KINGS 4:1-20

SOLOMON'S BUREAUCRACY

Central government

Verses 1–20 form a single chapter in the Hebrew. It begins with a bold statement which highlights the unity of the two former nations of Israel and Judah under the new king—Solomon is king of 'all Israel'. It ends with a statement of how blessed that kingdom is.

Verses 2–6 introduce us to his central administration. It is double the size of his father's (see 2 Samuel 8:15–18; 20:23–26). According to NRSV and most translations, it consists of:

- two secretaries, who may have been more managers than scribes
- a recorder (the person in charge of the records) or possibly a herald
- the army commander
- a chief administrator who was responsible for the regional officials
- the person in charge of the royal properties
- the person in charge of the forced labour
- four priests

The details of the four priests are confusing. Azariah, son of Zadok, is named first as 'the' priest, which identifies him as the leading priest. Then Zadok, his father, and Abiathar are named together, as they used to be. If this is the Abiathar who was banished to his estates in 1 Kings 2:26–27, his restoration to equality with Zadok (though both are now under the authority of Zadok's son) might be an illustration that Solomon has indeed learned wisdom and changed his ways somewhat. Finally Zabud, son of Nathan (Nathan the prophet?) and the brother of the chief administrator, is named as a priest and 'king's friend'. Whether this means simply that he was close to Solomon or whether it refers to an office of 'royal adviser' is as difficult to decide about Zabud as it was about Hushai who was called David's 'friend' (2 Samuel 15:37; 16:16; 17:5–20).

Even if this list is 'disordered', as the NRSV footnote puts it, it is still impressive. Solomon's Israel is a nation state with a formidable central administration, a far cry from Saul's henchmen and his shoe-string organization of only fifty years before.

It is also possible that some of these officials are foreigners (Elihoreph and Ahishar, for example) and that some of the offices are borrowed from Egypt, for example that of the 'king's friend'.

Regional officials

The organization outlined in verses 7–19 is completely new. There was nothing like it in David's time. It bears little or no relation to any of the tribal boundaries. Nor are any of the tribal leaders involved in it. The whole question of the organization of ancient Israel in tribes and smaller family groups is both a complicated and a controversial one; nevertheless, the arguments for some such groupings are strong. This arrangement ignores them completely, and that may prove ominous. The same is true of the purpose of the arrangement. Neither Saul nor David had taxed the people so blatantly (v. 7), and Solomon's policy will have serious consequences.

Some of the names of the people in both of these lists are interesting as well as being unpronounceable. There is some element of 'keeping it in the family', as one would expect, and that includes two of Solomon's sons-in-law, Ben-abinadab and Ahimaaz.

The second half of verse 19 is a puzzle.

All is well

Despite new taxes and a burgeoning administration, all is well. It is probably reading too much into verse 20 to say that it is picking up the wording of the promise to Abraham in Genesis 22:17, for the expression is used several times in the ongoing story without any such association. The picture is simply that the nation is both very populous and very happy. Solomon had expressed doubts about his ability to rule such a large population (1 Kings 3:8). Verse 20 indicates that God has indeed blessed him with the gifts to do it successfully.

FOR REFLECTION

Happy the one who wisdom gains,
Thrice happy who that guest retains.
Her hands are filled with length of days,
True riches, and immortal praise.

Charles Wesley (1707–88)

SOLOMON *in* ALL HIS GLORY

These verses continue to describe the impressive way Solomon's reign has begun after his dream and his dedication of himself to God when he awoke from it (1 Kings 3:15). If, however, we read them with Deuteronomy 17 and 1 Samuel 8 in mind, there are warning signs to be seen even in the conspicuous wealth which is being described.

Power

Verses 21 and 24 add more to the picture of Solomon's splendour. They portray his political power. He is not only 'king of all Israel' as in verse 1, but he 'rules' over all the small nations from the borders of the great Mesopotamian states in the north to the borders of Philistia in the east and Egypt in the south; from Tiphsah, on the great bend of the Euphrates in the far north-east, to Gaza, on the Mediterranean coast in the far south-west. Nothing is said of an eastern border, the implication being that Solomon controlled everything as far as the edge of the Arabian desert.

The point of this statement of Solomon's dominion is a theological one, that Solomon is marvellously blessed because he trusts in God and recognizes his dependence on God, as in his prayer. The Deuteronomic Historians believed that true faith leads to true blessing. So the picture painted here is of unparalleled power and glory. David had never had such power. Nor would any later king of Israel. The book of Kings will show how Israel loses all of this as loss of faith leads to loss of blessing. The glory of Solomon's early days, however, is painted in such rich colours not only to highlight the extent of the final calamity but also to show that, even in such bright beginnings, the seeds of that calamity are already being sown.

Prosperity

Verses 22–28 concentrate on Solomon's royal splendour seen in the nation's prosperity, but verse 25 also shows the benefits felt by the ordinary people.

Verses 22–23 list the provisions needed daily by the royal establishment, which would include the army and its garrisons as well as the court and the central administration. This would involve a substantial number of people, as can be seen from the quantities required. '30 cors of choice flour' (NJPS—'semolina') is about five tons or 5000 kilos. The thirty beef cattle to be supplied are divided between those which were 'stall-fed' and those which were 'pasture-fed' (NIV, GNB).

Solomon's power is not built on the oppression of the people—at least not yet. Verse 25 paints a lovely picture of a nation safe, secure and happy. In the whole land 'from Dan to Beersheba'—far north to far south—everyone 'sits under their own vines and fig trees'.

Verse 26 reveals both Solomon's wealth and his military power. This is, for Israel, military power on an unprecedented scale. And it is well managed. All appears to be well—but remember the warning of Deuteronomy 17:16.

Prestige

Verses 29–34 extol Solomon's proverbial wisdom and in them we see three more features of 'wisdom'. First, we see that the 'wisdom movement' was an international one. The 'Sayings of the Wise' in Proverbs 22:17—24:22, for example, are taken almost verbatim from an Egyptian wisdom text called the *Instruction of Amen-em-ophet*, and neither Agur nor King Lemuel, whose sayings are quoted in Proverbs 30 and 31, were Israelites. The sons of Mahol in verse 31 may or may not be those mentioned in 1 Chronicles 2:6, but we know nothing of any of them. Second, an important aspect of wisdom was the combination of acute observation and skill with words needed to compose proverbs and songs. 'Song of Songs' is, for example, attributed to Solomon, and Psalms 88 and 89 to Heman and Ethan respectively. Thirdly, we see 'natural history' as another aspect of wisdom (v. 33).

A PRAYER

O God, by whom the meek are guided in judgment, grant us, in all our doubts and uncertainties, the grace to ask what Thou wouldst have us to do; that the spirit of wisdom may save us from all false choices, and that in Thy light we may see light, and in Thy straight path may not stumble, through Jesus Christ our Lord.

William Bright (1600–1670)

13 1 KINGS 5:1–18

The TEMPLE PROJECT

Solomon is remembered for two things—his wisdom and his temple. 1 Kings 5 begins the account of the building of the temple.

The contract

Hiram, previously seen in 2 Samuel 5:11 where he had the contract to build David's palace, returns to the scene. Verse 1 refers to him as a longstanding friend of David, though this probably refers to a political alliance rather than anything more personal. Tyre and its twin, Sidon, were the principal cities of what came to be known as Phoenicia and which we know as Lebanon, a famous trading nation with its ships plying the Mediterranean.

Verses 3–5 introduce us to the important idea of promises and their fulfilment. Solomon sees the temple project as the fulfilment of one of God's promises to David. This promise and fulfilment theme is repeated when the project is completed (1 Kings 8:17–21). Another promise is that Solomon and his descendents will be the true successors of David (v. 5; 1 Kings 8:25–26): see Nathan's words to David in 2 Samuel 7:12–17 and David's response in verses 25–29. Solomon plans to build the temple to express his gratitude to God for blessings received.

Solomon refers to the temple as 'a house for the name of the Lord my God' (vv. 3, 5), a favourite Deuteronomic term which does two things. First, it maintains a proper distance between the Creator and his creation or the Redeemer and the people he has redeemed. Second, it indicates that the temple is the place where this God makes himself accessible. The Old Testament takes it for granted that God is present always and everywhere but that people need special places and special times to recognize his presence and respond to it. We have already seen two such special places—the tent (1 Kings 2:28) and the high place (1 Kings 3:4). The Deuteronomic Historians will increasingly insist that the Jerusalem temple is the only proper place where Israel can honour God and know his blessings (see Deuteronomy 12:5).

Solomon commissions the timber for the project. The precise species of trees cannot be identified. 'Cedar of Lebanon' and cypress (or 'pine' or 'juniper' in different translations) are to be delivered by sea to an unnamed port near Jerusalem and made ready for onward transportation. 2 Chronicles 2:16 names the port as Joppa. It is to be paid for by provisions for Hiram's 'household'. The amounts add up to over 3300 tons of wheat and a thousand gallons of best olive oil per year. Solomon's 'household' needed about 5500 tons of grain annually (see the comment on 4:22). The writer considers this contract to be a good one (v. 12).

Conscription

Verse 13 contains a problem and introduces a sinister new development. In 4:6 Adoniram was named as the official in charge of the 'forced labour'. This is what the Canaanites had been put to when Israel first invaded their 'promised land' (Joshua 17:13), and which Israel had to do in Egypt (Exodus 1:11). David had had such an officer (2 Samuel 20:24) but there is no indication that he was employed forcing Israelites into such serfdom. 1 Kings 9:20–22 indicates that Solomon, likewise, used only Canaanites in his forced labour gangs. Verse 13 in today's passage, however, suggests that the thirty thousand conscripts are Israelites, and 1 Kings 11:28 and 12: 3–4, 18 support this.

Labourers and quarrymen are at work in the 'hill country', the area around Jerusalem, supplying the stone for the project. The actual building is done by a consortium of craftsmen from Israel, Tyre and Gebal, a city on the coast, north of Tyre, later known as Byblos.

FOR REFLECTION

This chapter reminds us of God's promises. It speaks of Solomon's wisdom. It may also refer to his introduction of Israelite forced labour. If this is so, a question is raised in the mind of anyone familiar with the longer story—can the name of the Lord, who brought his people out of slavery in Egypt, be honoured by a project which involves the forced labour of free Israelites? Here is, on the one hand, another fundamental contradiction in Solomon to be added to a growing list (this one exposed by 1 Samuel 8:17–18). On the other hand, here is a king with vision, commitment and ability.

The TEMPLE IS BUILT

The date

Verse 1 gives the date of the start of the building work very precisely. The reign of Solomon is usually dated 961–921BC, which puts the start of work on the temple in the spring of 957BC. The opening words of this verse, however, cause a problem. Taking it literally as an accurate figure puts the date of the exodus from Egypt in the fifteenth century BC, which is two centuries earlier than most other sources indicate. It is probably better to see the '480 years' as a symbolic round figure, perhaps the figure for a generation (forty), multiplied by the traditional number of the tribes (twelve). Is this saying that the building of the temple is the last step in Israel's long walk to freedom —that its construction marks the real end of the exodus and is God's last and best blessing? Whether that is so or not, the details of the dating given to the start of the building indicate the importance and significance of the temple in the nation's life and history.

The building

In terms of size, Solomon's temple was more like a modest Cornish Methodist chapel than an English cathedral. It followed the basic pattern of temples in both Phoenicia and Canaan and was a simple rectangular box—70 cubits long, 20 cubits wide and 30 cubits high. A cubit was six handbreadths, so GNB gives the measurements in metres as 31.5m long by 9m wide by 13.5m high. The equivalent in feet would be 102 by 30 by 45. Inside, it was divided into three—the vestibule (or porch/portico), the nave (the Hekal or sanctuary/main hall) and the inner sanctuary (the Debir or inner shrine, elsewhere called the 'Holy of Holies' or 'Most Holy Place'). There was a three-storey lean-to all around the nave and inner sanctuary containing vestries and storerooms (v. 5). Unlike our churches, of course, it wasn't built to house a congregation. The worshippers stayed outside.

The warning

Verses 11–13 bring us up with a jolt. They are a sharp warning in the middle of all the details about the temple. The 'word of the Lord', last heard in 2 Samuel 24:11, comes to Solomon for the first time. There is no mention of which prophet addresses the king in the name of the Lord, or whether Solomon hears from God directly, but the message is plain. It is the old 'If...' repeated (see 1 Kings 3:14). It is clearly intended to remind Solomon, and all who read the long story, of Deuteronomy 17:18–20.

There are two warnings here—one about the temple and one to Solomon.

The temple must not become a substitute for obedience to God. It will become the focus of Israel's faith, culture and national life. It will symbolize God's presence with his people and his care for them. It will be the place where God's blessings are sought and given. But prophets will insist that the temple and its worship are no substitute for faithful living (Isaiah 1:11–15; Hosea 6:6; Micah 6:6–8), and Jeremiah will roundly denounce both the temple and those who trust in it (Jeremiah 7). The temple and its worship, just like the 'statutes, ordinances and commandments' (v. 12), are God's gifts to his people to help them to enjoy his blessings. They are a means to an end—that the Lord's people may live faithful and holy lives. The warning, all the stronger for being implied rather than clearly stated, is that if these means are abused by becoming a substitute for the ends they are designed to promote, then the future is bleak.

Solomon is warned of his responsibilities. He must walk in God's ways for the sake of his people as well as for his own sake. If he does, the promise of dynasty will be fulfilled (see comments on 1 Kings 5:5). If he fails to do that as king, then the whole nation will share the consequences. There are few passages which point out the responsibility that goes with power more strongly than this one.

A PRAYER

Lord, guide the leaders of this and every nation,
that justice may prevail throughout the world;
let not the needy be forgotten,
nor the hope of the poor be taken away.

INSIDE *the* TEMPLE

The inner sanctuary

The inner sanctuary—'the Holy of Holies'—was partitioned off as a perfect cube twenty cubits (9 metres or 30 feet) square and high. This means that there was either a large roof space above the inner sanctuary or, unlike the picture painted in verses 1–14, that the roof level of the sanctuary was lower than that of the nave.

Interior decoration

The interior of the nave and the inner sanctuary were finished in the same way. All the stone was faced with timber. On this wooden panelling were carvings of gourds and flowers ('rosettes' in NJB) or cherubim, palm trees and flowers (vv. 18, 29). These are usually taken to be symbols of fertility. All of this was then 'overlaid' with gold, although many commentators suggest that the wood panelling was inlaid with gold rather than overlaid by it (compare v. 32). The great doors to the inner sanctuary and the nave featured the same designs as the walls and were covered with gold in the same way (v. 35).

Furnishings and fittings

The inner sanctuary was designed to hold the Ark of the Covenant (v. 19), which GNB prosaically but accurately calls the 'Lord's Covenant Box' (for a full description, see comments on 1 Kings 8:1–21). In it, there was also a wooden altar inlaid with gold (vv. 20, 22), though NRSV prefers to think of a stone altar overlaid with wood and then gold. In addition to the splendid doors, there were also gold chains across the entrance to the inner sanctuary (v. 21). REB adds a detail from the account in 2 Chronicles 3:14 that a veil or curtain was suspended from these chains.

To complete the furnishings of the inner sanctuary were two identical 'cherubs' made of olive wood and either covered with or inlaid with gold (vv. 23–28). These 'winged creatures' stood 15 feet high and had a wingspan of 15 feet. Their outstretched wings touched the side walls of the sanctuary and met in the middle. The Ark would eventually be placed under those touching wings. These 'cherubim'

(-*im* is the plural ending in Hebrew) are much larger versions of the golden ones made to be put in the sacred tent and described in Exodus 25:18–22. The clue to what this is all about is found in 1 Samuel 4:4 and 2 Samuel 6:2 where the Lord is described as being 'enthroned above the cherubim', and in Numbers 7:89 where he speaks to Moses from 'between' them. The cherubim form, as it were, the Lord's throne in the inner sanctuary, much as they form his highly mobile chariot throne in the prophet's vision in Ezekiel 9:3; 10:1–20 and 11:22. These cherubim, then, are rather different from the sphinx-like winged guardians of temples known from elsewhere in the ancient Near East and from the sentry cherubim of Genesis 3:24. Later in Jewish tradition they are seen as one of the higher orders of angels.

Finished

Verse 36 notes that a courtyard was built in front of the temple. It tells how the walls were built (three courses of stone to one of timber) but nothing about how high those walls were or how big the courtyard was.

The temple had taken seven years to build from the laying of the foundation in the spring of 957 to its completion in the autumn of 950BC (v. 37). The temple may have been of modest size, and it may have been dwarfed by Solomon's palace, but the interior must have looked magnificent. Verse 22 says that that was the intention. The gold was used 'so that the whole house might be perfect'.

FOR REFLECTION

Religious people in every age have been divided over the question of church buildings. Some insist that only the best is good enough for God and so applaud the art and splendour of temples such as Solomon's. Others feel that God is better honoured by putting skills and resources to a different use. The debate goes on.

SOLOMON'S PALACE

The palace complex

The account of the building of the temple breaks off at 1 Kings 6:38. The building work is finished, some major furnishings are in place and the walls are decorated; but it is not ready for use. The account of what was done to turn a beautiful shell of a building into a place of worship will begin at verse 13. In between, however, we are told of the building of Solomon's palace, and the way in which 1 Kings 6:38 and 7:1 are put side by side looks far from innocent. One, we are told, took nearly twice as long to build as the other. The ancient storytellers obviously do not approve of the fact that Solomon spent twice as long on his palace as he did on the Lord's. AV brings this out by beginning 7:1 with 'But', and NIV by using 'However'.

One of the reasons why the palace took much longer to build than the temple was that it was a much bigger complex of buildings. For example, the main hall alone occupied twice the floor space of the temple and there were other buildings on the site as well. In addition to the main hall ('The House of the Forest of the Lebanon') there was the Hall of Pillars (or the 'Colonnade' or 'Portico'), the Hall of the Throne (also called 'the Hall of Justice') and two sets of living apartments, one for Solomon and one for his principal queen. Around the complex was a great courtyard in the same style as the courtyard of the temple.

It is possible to draw a picture of what the temple might have looked like, but neither a picture nor a ground plan of the palace is possible on the basis of the data given here. Much effort has been made in the attempt but with little result. What we are given when we read these verses is an impression—an impression of splendour. Verses 9–11 play an important role in creating this impression. These three verses describe the stones used in the building of the foundations and walls of the palace. The word 'costly' occurs three times (though this doesn't come across at all in GNB or NIV). The stones used for the temple had also been described as 'costly', but only once (5:17). Here, again, a contrast is being made.

The House of the Forest of the Lebanon (presumably called that because of the amount of wood in it, not least its 45 cedar pillars) was probably an assembly hall, though it also seems to have been used as a treasury or an armoury (see 1 Kings 10:17, 21; Isaiah 22:8). The purpose of the Hall of Pillars is unknown (v. 6).

The Hall of Justice

We have already seen something of the purpose for which the Hall of Justice (or of 'Judgment') was designed (see 1 Kings 3:16–28). The king played a crucial role in the administration of justice in ancient Israel. It was his responsibility to see that things were put right when they went wrong and to stop them going wrong in the first place.

This is seen very clearly in Psalm 72, which is a prayer that the king will receive God's blessing to do God's work of 'justice' and 'righteousness'. Psalm 72 is also, incidentally, one of only two psalms in the Psalter which are headed 'Of (or For) Solomon'. 'Righteousness', in Psalm 72:1–2 and in the Old Testament generally, means a love which yearns and works to put things right; and 'justice' is love in action to restore things to how they ought to be. So, crucially, when the Old Testament describes God as our 'judge' it doesn't picture him as the impartial and unbending judge of a Roman court but as the one who springs to our aid to sort everything out and make it right again. Likewise, to say that God is 'righteous' is not to suggest that he is hard, stern and unbending but that he is actively concerned to keep things as they should be and to put things right when they have gone wrong. To those who are causing things to go wrong, of course, God's justice and righteousness will have a sharp side.

The king is expected to be and do the same, as Psalm 72 makes plain. The fact that the House of Justice is built as part of the palace complex indicates the importance of this aspect of the king's responsibilities.

FOR MEDITATION

What is displayed here is far more Solomon's
'riches and honour' than his 'wisdom'.
His was undoubtedly the piety of worldly success.

Simon J. DeVries

BRONZE FEATURES

To complete the work on the temple, Solomon hires Hiram, an Israelite master craftsman from Tyre who had learned his trade from his Tyrian father. He is not to be confused with the king of the same name. He is described in similar terms to those used about Bezalel, the craftsman who worked on the holy tent (Exodus 31:3–4). This passage contains a number of terms of uncertain meaning, and much of its detail is obscure.

Two pillars

Hiram's first task was to cast two bronze pillars. The dimensions given here (eight metres high and five metres in circumference and topped with highly decorated capitals 2.2 metres tall) and those given in 2 Chronicles 3:15–17 do not tally. REB follows the Greek in adding that these pillars were hollow. Such pillars are a feature of many temples of the period and these two were erected in the usual place, outside and on either side of the front of the vestibule (v. 21). No doubt they came to symbolize many things as time went on, as religious artefacts do. What they originally symbolized has been the subject of much speculation. Perhaps the clue is in the names they were given: Jachin ('he establishes', see 1 Kings 2:12, 45–46) and Boaz ('in the strength of'), which have been taken to refer to God establishing the Davidic dynasty whose kings ruled in his strength. If that is so, the names may be dynastic inscriptions, shortened forms of statements like Psalm 89:4 and Psalm 21:1. There had been nothing equivalent to these pillars outside the old holy tent.

The 'molten sea'

Next Hiram made the 'molten sea' to stand in the courtyard. This was a huge basin 4.4 metres across and capable of holding about 12,000 gallons of water. It rested on the backs of twelve oxen or bulls. 2 Chronicles 4:6 suggests that it was a replacement for the bronze basin in which the priests did their ablutions (see Exodus 30:18–21), but it is hard to see how they could reach into it as it stood over seven feet off the floor! Some commentaries say that it was a reservoir from which the ten 'water carts' were filled (see vv. 38–39), but that seems impractical. It may have symbolized the victory of God over the cosmic ocean of chaos as in the creation pictures in Psalms 74:12–17; 89:5–11 and Isaiah 51:9–11, which in turn led to the gift of life-giving water (Psalm 104:5–13).

Ten water carts

NRSV's description of these ten 'stands' for the water basins (vv. 27–37) is almost impossible to follow. REB's 'trolleys' and GNB's 'carts' at least make their purpose clear. They were decorated not only with cherubim and palm trees, as were some of the temple walls (see 1 Kings 6:29–35), but also with carvings of lions and oxen, or bulls (vv. 29, 36). The Deuteronomic Historians, who will express disgust at the golden calves which appear later at the new temples at Dan and Bethel, probably because they are symbols of the god Baal (1 Kings 12:28–30), seem to see no conflict between the second commandment in Exodus 20:4 and either the twelve bulls holding up the 'sea' or these 'graven images'.

Having made the carts, Hiram made the bronze basins to go on them, each over five feet across and holding more than 300 gallons. He placed them in the courtyard, for water was essential in most of the acts of worship which would be performed there. Individuals would need to wash their hands, and the priests would need to clean the instruments they used in the sacrifices (see 2 Chronicles 4:6).

We do not understand the symbolism of all these fixtures and fittings, just as future generations of worshippers may not understand the symbols which are precious to us. Without doubt they would have impressed ancient worshippers with a sense of awe and wonder, majesty and mystery, which are essential elements of worship in any age and place.

FOR MEDITATION

O worship the Lord in the beauty of holiness;
Bow down before him, his glory proclaim.

John Samuel Bewley Monsell (1811–75)

BRONZE & GOLD

These verses are like the credits at the end of a film. Hiram's splendid achievements are listed and mention is made of David's contribution too; but the principal credit for the project is given to Solomon.

Bronze

The careful work which has gone into the building and its major fittings is continued in the details—the 'pots' ('ash containers' or 'pails'), the 'shovels' ('scoops' or 'scrapers') and the small 'basins' ('sprinkling-bowls' or 'tossing-bowls') which Hiram made of highest quality bronze. The pots and shovels were used for removing fat and ashes from the altar (see Exodus 27:3), and the small basins were used for sprinkling the blood of the animal sacrifices on the altar and on the worshippers (see Leviticus 7:14).

Verse 46 is an interesting note for industrial archaeologists. The location of these places is not certain, but there is evidence from several places in the Jordan valley of this kind of work using the local clay for moulds. These castings were the work of the royal foundry ('the king cast them').

The meaning of verse 47 is not entirely certain, but the impression it gives of the sheer scale of the enterprise and, by implication, of Solomon's generosity in sponsoring it is clear enough. Hiram might be given due credit for his craftsmanship (which is why his major pieces are listed in verses 41–44) but the emphasis is on Solomon's initiative and overall responsibility.

Gold

Not only was the inside of the temple a splendid display of gold (1 Kings 6:20–22) but all the necessary bits and pieces were gold too. All the credit is Solomon's: there is no craftsman's name mentioned here at all.

The golden altar is the incense altar already mentioned in 1 Kings 6:20, 22 which was put in the inner sanctuary. 'The golden table for the bread of the Presence' (v. 48) was put in the nave. The meaning of this 'shewbread' (AV) or 'loaves of permanent offering' (NJB) can be seen in Leviticus 24:5–8. The twelve loaves are a weekly offering made as a 'commitment' to God and as a sign of the eternal bond ('covenant') between Israel and Lord. The ten golden lampstands are not mentioned in other lists of the furnishings of the holy tent, Solomon's temple or either of its later relacements. What is frequently mentioned is the Menorah, the seven-branched candelabra which has become one of the best-known symbols of Judaism (see Exodus 25:31–40; 37:17–24)—but that is not listed here.

Verses 49–50 give us a glimpse into the working life of the temple with its lamps, snuffers, incense dishes, firepans, tongs (remember Isaiah 6:6) and still more small basins. The 'flowers' are the floral decoration, either on the lampstands or the more general decoration referred to in 1 Kings 6:32 and 35. It is difficult to imagine how useful golden door hinges would be, and there is good sense behind the suggestion that what is meant here is golden panels in the doors. NRSV captures the emphasis of the Hebrew in this listing: '...of pure gold ... of gold ... of pure gold ... of gold'.

It is finished

Solomon's work on the temple is finished and he brings in 'the things that his father David had dedicated' (v. 51). 2 Samuel 8:11 shows what this means. The gold, silver and other articles which David had set aside for the Lord were plunder that he had captured or tribute that he had been given. It was common practice to dedicate such things to the god or gods who had given the victory by which such treasures had been acquired, and temples were the usual strongrooms where such national treasures were kept.

The temple is finished and decorated. It is a magnificent achievement, splendid and impressive. There is no doubt about Solomon's organizational ability or his artistic skill as a designer. It is important at this point, therefore, to remember the word of warning from God which stands over the whole project (1 Kings 6:11–13).

A PRAYER

Lord God, you have made us capable of great things; guard us, we pray, in our achievements, lest we mistake their purpose and, in them, lose our way.

19

The ARK of the COVENANT

The bringing of the Ark into the temple begins the dedication celebrations which are the theme of this chapter.

This most sacred object was a portable chest containing the two tablets of stone on which the ten commandments were written, but its real importance was symbolic. It symbolized the presence and power of the Lord (Exodus 25:10–22; Deuteronomy 10:1–5). It was the sign that the Israelites were the Lord's chosen people and that the Lord was Israel's God. Solomon brings this most potent symbol of Israel's faith and of Israelite nationalism into the temple he has built.

Verse 2 gives the month of this momentous event, though, oddly, not the year. It seems that the official opening was delayed for almost a year until the greatest of all the annual festivals, the feast of Tabernacles, in the autumn of 949BC (see 1 Kings 6:38). In this festival, when the people lived in tents, God's 'dwelling' was moved from tent to temple. The Ark was carried by priests—a dangerous business, as Uzzah had found to his cost when David brought it into Jerusalem (2 Samuel 6:6–11). It was placed in the inner sanctuary, where it served as God's throne or footstool with the cherubim standing guard over it and God 'enthroned' on or above them. Solomon also arranged for the old tent of meeting to be 'brought up' (v. 4). The new temple might make the old tent obsolete, but that doesn't mean it can be thrown away.

There are two difficulties in verse 8. Much ink has been spilled about the Ark's permanent carrying-poles. If they could be seen, it looks as if the Ark was placed parallel to the back wall. The phrase 'to this day' is common in the Deuteronomic History but this is the first time we have met it in 1 Kings. Why it should be used about these poles and nothing else is baffling. It is usually thought that the phrase is an attempt by the writers to assert the reliability of the account they are presenting.

God comes to his temple

When the Ark is in place, the temple is filled with a 'cloud' (v. 10). Here, as often in the Old Testament, when we read of clouds we mustn't simply think of the weather. Cloud marks the presence of

God in his glory, that is, in his power and splendour (for example, Exodus 16:10; 19:9). The point being made here is that the God who comes to dwell in this temple is the God of the exodus who made himself known on Mount Sinai.

Likewise, for the picture of God dwelling in 'thick darkness' see Exodus 20:21 and Deuteronomy 5:22. It is quite inadequate for the NRSV footnote to say that this refers to the fact that the Holy of Holies had no windows! The reference to this darkness is intended to emphasize God's power and splendour.

Solomon addresses the people

Solomon's opening speech in verses 15–21 is a retrospect on how he has reached this point. He blesses (that is, affirms) God as the one who has kept his promises.

Solomon has built the temple as a place for God's 'name'. This expression denotes both God's reputation and his presence. To 'call on God's name' is to seek and find his help and support. To 'praise his name' is to testify to his greatness and to enhance his reputation. NIV shows the importance of this idea here and throughout the Deuteronomic writings by beginning 'Name' with a capital letter. (See also my comments on 1 Kings 5:5, Study 13.)

In verses 15 and 17, the 'Lord' is specifically defined as 'the God of Israel'. As Israel alone knows this name, so Jerusalem alone is the place where this name is made available to Israel.

PRAYER

God reveals his presence:
Let us now adore him, and with awe appear before him.
God is in his temple:
All within keep silence, prostrate lie with deepest reverence.
Him alone, God we own,
Him our God and Saviour:
Praise his name for ever.

Gerhard Tersteegen (1697–1769)

SOLOMON'S PRAYER

One of the techniques of all ancient writers and historians is to put keynote speeches on the lips of key characters at key points in the story. Moses' speech in Deuteronomy 29—31 and Joshua's in Joshua 24:1–25 are two examples, and this prayer of Solomon's is another. The important point for us, as always, is what the prayer as a whole tells us about God, his will and his ways.

Everything in the prayer follows on from what is said about God in verse 23. The Lord, the God of Israel, is unique and his uniqueness lies in his generous faithfulness and steadfast love. Two points are made. The first, that God 'keeps covenant', speaks of his reliability in keeping his promises and standing by his chosen people. The second, that he keeps 'steadfast love', takes us to the heart of the Old Testament's teaching about the love of God, already hinted at in 1 Kings 3:6–7. The Hebrew word is *hesed*. The key text is Exodus 34:6–9, repeated frequently in different strata of the Old Testament and not least in Psalm 103. *Hesed* is that love which greets us new every morning, which seeks us out with generosity and embraces us with kindness and which will not let us go. As F.W. Faber put it in his hymn, 'the heart of the eternal is most wonderfully kind'.

This love is a rigorously committed love, like parental love at its best—committed and tough rather than sentimental. God's commitment to Israel expects a response of committed living from Israel. Such a lifestyle is for Israel's own benefit, for if they 'walk in the good way' (v. 36) they will 'live in the land' (v. 40), creating a society in which fullness of life is available to all. Needless to say, high standards are not always kept (v. 46), but this is forgivable if people recognize wrongdoing for what it is and are genuinely sorry for it.

In verses 24–30, Solomon shares his own experience that God is indeed reliable and trustworthy, and expresses his conviction that God's *hesed* is Israel's hope when things go wrong. Out of God's steadfast love comes the possibility of new beginnings. God cares. God hears. God forgives. God renews. The rest of the prayer gives examples of that sequence.

The purpose of the temple

The prayer is addressed to God, but, like many prayers in public worship, it has something to teach the congregation who are listening. The message in verses 27–30 is, first, that the Lord, this faithful and forgiving God of Israel, is transcendent. He is beyond and above everything he has made. He cannot be domesticated and will not be manipulated. Those who think the temple can be used to do that must think again. Second, the prayer contains the assurance that God wants the best for his people. They will find that he is near them when he is needed.

The temple stands as a symbol—a reminder and a sign—of the generous faithfulness and steadfast love of God. The prayer acknowledges that people need signs and symbols, and even turning towards the temple to pray is a help if it strengthens them in their faith in a God who hears and forgives.

Seven examples

Solomon is sure that God hears, forgives and renews. Much of the temple liturgy will be concerned with sin and forgiveness, and much of the theology involved is complex and confusing; but at heart there is a radical simplicity—that God hears, forgives and renews. The rest of the prayer (vv. 31–53) gives seven examples. Some of the circumstances described reflect beliefs and attitudes very different to ours and which many of us today cannot accept (for example, that drought and famine are God's punishment for sin). These difficulties should not blind us to the underlying message, which is that our sins, failures and mistakes do not have the last word. Israel, rescued from slavery in Egypt but eventually ending up in exile in Babylon, is to remember that.

For the moment, the temple is their reminder because 'here in newness and renewal, God the Spirit comes to each' (F. Pratt Green). Before the end of the story, however, the temple will have been destroyed and the situation envisaged in verses 46–53 will have become fact. But even in that self-inflicted catastrophe, the prayer insists, Israel can rely on the generous faithfulness and steadfast love of God to make a future possible.

MEDITATION

Read Psalm 103, for there is no clearer presentation of the hesed *of God in the Old Testament than in that psalm.*

21

COME & JOIN *the* CELEBRATION

Solomon finishes his prayer and gets up off his knees to address the congregation. The sermon is a powerful summary of the theology which underpins the book of Kings. There is one God, and one alone, the Lord. He has made himself known to Israel, and called them to be his people so that, through them, eventually, all the world might come to believe in him, him alone. Through Moses he has blessed them with instructions about how to live life at its best, and if his people live in this way they will be blessed indeed and fulfil their vocation. The Lord is a God of promise and blessing. The Lord's people, Israel, are very privileged, but with that privilege comes responsibility and challenge as well as joy and blessing.

Following the sermon, the temple is dedicated with sacrifices.

Sacrificing to the Lord

The sacrificial system in ancient Israel was very complex, and what follows is an over-simplification, but the basic thing to grasp is that sacrifice was the normal way of worship in the temple. Two parallels come to mind—the Mass in the Roman Catholic Church and hymn-singing in Methodism. For the Roman Catholic, the Mass is the normal form of worship—to worship is to say Mass and to say Mass is to worship. For Methodists, to worship is to sing and to sing is to worship. In the temple, to worship was to sacrifice and to sacrifice was to worship. All worship was expressed through sacrifice, and therefore there were different sacrifices for different acts of worship.

If we think about sacrifice at all, however, we tend to think of two things—blood and sin. We assume that all sacrifice involved blood and that all sacrifice was to do with sin; but neither was the case. There were sacrifices which did not involve animals, like the 'grain offerings' in this passage; and the sacrifices which they offered in such great abundance here were all sacrifices of praise. None of the 'sacrifices for sin' were offered on this occasion. This was neither the time nor the place.

Sacrifice of praise

In the 'sacrifice of well-being', part of the animal was burnt on the altar, part was given to the priests and the rest was taken away by the worshippers and used for a feast. Such a sacrifice was a huge celebration of joy and thanksgiving in which families and friends got together and enjoyed each other's company. These were sacrifices which promoted and encouraged fellowship, solidarity and community—which is why the AV called them 'peace offerings'. The dedication of the temple was therefore a celebration of community togetherness, in which everyone had a place as they rejoiced together in their corporate faith. For the instructions for this type of sacrifice, see Leviticus 3.

The 'burnt offering' was the sacrifice in which the whole animal, after it had been skinned, was burnt on the altar. There were so many of these on this occasion that the altar of burnt offerings in the main courtyard—an item not mentioned in the temple fittings listed so far—was inadequate and the floor of the courtyard had to be consecrated and used instead. This was the 'standard' form of regular sacrifice, offered night and morning daily in the temple, a kind of multi-purpose morning and evening prayers. (For the instructions for this type of sacrifice, see Exodus 29:38–42 and Leviticus 1.)

'Grain offerings' of corn and olive oil, sometimes in the form of cakes, could be offered separately but were often used with other sacrifices, as they are here. They too were completely burnt. (For the instructions about them, see Leviticus 2.)

Keeping the feast

Even allowing for the fact that the celebrations lasted a week, the number of animals killed may well be exaggerated. The purpose of the exaggeration is worth exploring. Is it expressing the intensity of Israel's dedication and commitment? Or highlighting Israel's gratitude? Or showing how prosperous and blessed the nation is in having all this wealth to offer? Or pointing up how wonderfully happy and united a society Israel is, sharing this feasting together? The picture is of all Israel, from far north to deep south, united in celebration. It was not always so, as we have seen. Nor would it always be so, as we shall see.

A PRAYER

Eternal God, may our worship declare your praise
and our living glorify your name.

Another WARNING

The by-now-familiar message is repeated in God's warning to Solomon in this second vision, after Solomon had finished building the temple. The first vision in Gibeon (see 1 Kings 3:5–14 and our discussion of it in Study 9) came to Solomon when he had successfully gained the throne. It ended with an 'If…'. This second vision comes to him after his great building feats are finished. He is at the height of his power. This vision has hardly begun, however, when the 'If…' appears (v. 4).

Walking in the way

There were two sides to being God's covenant partner. In Study 20, we focused on the privileges and blessings that it brought. God had taken the initiative in rescuing Israel, he had offered his generous help to the young nation, and his reliable, steadfast love had sustained his people. 1 Kings 8:56–61 spells out the responsibility involved. In 1 Kings 2:3; 3:14 and 6:12, we saw how Solomon was reminded of that personal responsibility which was the other side of his privilege of being God's chosen and blessed king. He is to rule in God's way. If he does that, he and his people will find that their life together is blessed. Solomon had preached that message at the dedication of the temple. If they walk in God's way by keeping his 'commandments, statutes and ordinances' (see 1 Kings 2:3–4 and our discussion of it in Study 6) they will find his promises of blessing so abundantly fulfilled that even their international neighbours will recognize that there is no God but the Lord, the God of Israel. He had reminded them that the best way to preserve their nation and to make progress in freedom and prosperity is to listen to the good advice God has given them and to put it into practice. Now in this vision the Lord gives the same warning to Solomon that he had given to the people.

What could happen to the temple

So far, so good. God has heard Solomon's prayer and answered it. The temple has been built and blessed. But Solomon should not be misled by the 'for ever' and 'for all time' of verse 3, for the first 'If…'

follows immediately. If Solomon behaves, his throne will be secured not only for himself but for the line of David after him. The implication is that if not, not even God himself is in a position to keep the promise he made first to David. That promise was conditional on human faithfulness. It is not that God is fickle or helpless, but that he has taken the great risk of trusting humankind with moral responsibility. The shape of the future lies with human decision. Solomon is plainly told here that the future is his and his people's to make. This is what is meant in Genesis 1:26–28 by God's decision to make humanity 'in his own image'. To be made in the image of God means that God entrusts us with the ongoing stewardship of creation. He gives us power and responsibility to act as his agents and representatives in shaping the future. What is given to every human being in that creation story is focused here in Solomon. As king he exercises this responsibility *par excellence*.

Verses 6–9 point out the consequences of not walking in God's way, and begin by showing the source of such failure. It is to 'go and serve other gods and worship them'. This is the first mention of this key crime against God in Kings. It will not be the last (see 1 Kings 11:4, 10; 14:9; 2 Kings 5:17; 17:7, 35–38; 22:17). Two consequences of this ultimate misbehaviour are mentioned: the nation will be 'cut off' from the land and the temple will be 'cast out of God's sight'. This is unthinkable, but the unthinkable happened. Here, for the first time in Kings, there is a warning of the end of the story. And with the hint comes the explanation. The king (and the people) didn't listen to the 'If...'. The destruction of the temple is a sign of the Lord's power, not his weakness. He has destroyed his own temple. Why? Verse 9 repeats the reason, that his people had forsaken the God who brought them out of Egypt—and the consequence for those who do that is to find themselves exiled from their land and back in slavery. That is the warning given in Deuteronomy 29:24–28.

A PRAYER

Grant us, O Lord our God,
to walk in your ways.

23   1 KINGS 9:10–28

MISCELLANEOUS NOTES

1 Kings 9:9 marks the end of the long and sustained narrative of Solomon's rise to power. 1 Kings 10:1 begins another sustained narrative which will tell of his decline. In between are these verses which read like a collection of jottings. They are, however, very revealing. Is Solomon's wisdom laced with folly? Is his glory only a veneer? We shall see. Reread Deuteronomy 17:14–20 before you go any further, for that is the text on which Kings is the sermon.

Financial straits?

In verses 10–14 we see that Solomon has to make a deal with his business partner, King Hiram of Tyre. Solomon has overreached himself and is in need of cash. Twenty 'cities' in Galilee for four and a half tons of gold must have seemed fair on paper, but when Hiram sees the land in question he is in no doubt about who got the better half of the bargain. 'Cabul' doesn't appear in any dictionary, but we are left in no doubt about what it means. Do not be confused by verse 11, for these cities are not to pay Hiram for the materials used in building the temple and the palace; that had already been paid for (see 1 Kings 5:11). This note, somewhat confused as it is, sends out a warning. In the longer story, the point has already been made that the land is God's. He has given it to the Israelites as their 'inheritance'. Such things as the Jubilee laws in Leviticus 25 and the complex inheritance rules in Deuteronomy 25 are built on the understanding that ancestral land is not a commodity which can be sold off, and Naboth will make that very point against one of Solomon's successors in 1 Kings 21:3.

Building projects

Verses 15–23 contain an impressive list of Solomon's building schemes. Verse 22 defends Solomon against any suggestion that he used Israelites to provide forced labour for these projects, but this verse must be read alongside the accusations in 1 Kings 5:13 and 12:4 that he did so. In addition to the temple and the palace, he built a new city wall in Jerusalem and the 'Millo'. NJPS calls this a citadel; NIV thinks it was a set of 'supporting terraces' and GNB sees it as a major landfill project. The list of extensive nationwide building work is impressive.

Verse 19 says a lot. The references to 'Lebanon' and to 'all the land of his dominion' show that Solomon is now an important player among the smaller nations of the eastern Mediterranean region. The mention of cities for storage, cavalry and chariots points to his extensive military facilities. The understated comment that whatever Solomon desires to build he can build speaks volumes.

We might regard it as unjust for Solomon to use the remaining Canaanites as forced labour (vv. 20–21), but the writers of Kings thought differently. This is their first mention of such people, and their very existence is a sign that Solomon, like his predecessors, had failed to do what God required. The Canaanites should have been destroyed in dedication to God. Obviously we have a problem with such a view because our values are so different, but the point made by referring to this situation is clear enough. It is that there are flaws in Solomon's reign.

Other ventures

Verse 24 highlights another issue. This political marriage, already mentioned in 1 Kings 3:1, had benefited Solomon (see v. 16) but the writers believe that no good will come of such foreign entanglements.

And yet Solomon is also a devout and pious king. He leads the worship at the three great annual festivals, as the kings in Jerusalem would continue to do for many years. The meaning of the final sentence in verse 25 is uncertain. NRSV's reference to completing the house seems out of place. 'And so fulfilled the temple obligations' (NIV) and 'he kept the house in repair' (NJPS) make more sense.

The fact that King Hiram felt that Solomon had cheated him in the Galilee deal didn't stop him from co-operating with Solomon in some merchant venturing (vv. 26–28). The lure was gold from Ophir—whose location is unknown. The quantities were enormous, about sixteen tons. This will not be the last mention of Solomon and the enormous quantities of his gold.

A PRAYER

Grant us, O Lord our God,
the gifts of faith and faithfulness.

The QUEEN *of* SHEBA

Here is the stuff of legend. Handel wrote a famous piece of music about it. Hollywood made a movie out of it. The arrival of the Queen of Sheba has all the right ingredients. An exotic and mysterious queen travels to meet the king whose fabulous wealth and wisdom have become legendary in his own lifetime. She is overwhelmed and dazzled by everything she finds. He gives her 'everything she desires' (v. 13).

Two ways to read the story

We can read this story as a straightforward account of Solomon's wisdom and wealth. The Queen of Sheba travels to see if all that she has heard about him is true and discovers that she has not heard the half of it. For the second time he is tested with hard questions brought by women (see 1 Kings 3:16–28) and she learns that everything she has heard about his wisdom is true. When she sees the magnificence of his court she learns that everything she has heard about his wealth is also true. She is overcome by it all (v. 5). Solomon's international reputation is fully justified. He brings honour to Israel and glory to Israel's God.

Or we can read the story differently. We don't know where Sheba was—possibly in Yemen—but this queen is the second foreign woman to weave a spell over Solomon. He more than matches her gifts and presents and does indeed impress her with his wealth: but an Israelite looking at the splendour of his table and his liveried servants would be more worried than impressed. Solomon's extravagance and his eagerness to please his royal visitor call his wisdom seriously into question.

Here are two points for those interested in odd details:

• The AV translation of verse 7 is the origin of such English slang expressions as 'you don't know the half of it' and 'not 'arf'.

• The reference in verse 13 to King Solomon giving the queen everything she desired has inspired a number of legends that he gave her a son and heir. The best known is the claim of the now deposed royal house of Ethiopia to be directly descended from the son born to Solomon and the Queen of Sheba.

Making an impression

The writer of the story makes his view quite clear. He wants us to read the story the second way, so he reminds us that the fame which the queen has heard about is 'fame due to the name of the Lord' (v. 1). The queen, on the other hand, never gives the Lord any of the credit for Solomon's accomplishments and wisdom. Instead she seems to think that Solomon's throne and royal power are God's due reward to this outstanding man (vv. 8–9).

Perhaps at this point we should remind ourselves about how and where this royal dynasty began; then we might be able to see more clearly what is actually being said about Solomon in this passage. Israel's first king was Saul, at first a humble and reluctant king but one who eventually lost his throne because, according to the prophet Samuel, he overstepped the mark (1 Samuel 15:17–19). A new king is to be found and Samuel is sent to a particular family in Bethlehem, where the old prophet himself learns a lesson. The sons of Jesse appear before him and the eldest, Eliab, tall and impressive, is not the Lord's chosen one. Neither is the next; nor the next. The Lord's choice is the youngest, David; and although he's a handsome boy, that's all he is—little brother doing the menial job of looking after the sheep. In that story in 1 Samuel 16:6–13, the message is plain: appearances can be deceptive.

Temptation

As we read this story, we must remember that chapter 10 comes after chapter 9 and before chapter 11. Chapter 9 contained a warning to Solomon about what God expected of him, followed by a set of jottings which showed that he was ignoring what he had been told. Chapter 11 begins with an accusation that Solomon has gone badly wrong and continues with descriptions of the consequences of that failure. In the light of chapters 9 and 11, there is little doubt about how to read chapter 10. On the face of it, judged by worldly standards, Solomon is the epitome of success; but God's standards are very different and, judged by them, Solomon's position is becoming precarious.

FOR MEDITATION

The Lord looks on the heart.

1 Samuel 16:7

KING SOLOMON'S WEALTH

Here are more notes emphasizing Solomon's great wealth. A number of them contain words, phrases or details whose meaning is at best uncertain and at worst completely unknown, but the overall impression is abundantly clear as well as being explicitly stated in verse 23.

Wealth

Solomon controls a huge network of trade and business. We have already seen his partnership in a trading fleet with King Hiram of Tyre; now we read of his own fleet of 'ships of Tarshish' importing gold and luxury goods. 'Ships of Tarshish' seems to have been a name for large, ocean-going vessels as distinct from local coasters, just as our maritime forebears might refer to 'East Indiamen' (see 1 Kings 22:48; Isaiah 23:1; Psalm 48:7). Tarshish itself was a port in Spain (see Jonah 1:3).

Solomon clearly profited from Israel's strategic position controlling major land trade routes. Verse 15 points to Solomon's income from taxes and customs dues, from Israelite traders and merchants on the one hand and from those of neighbouring kings and rulers on the other. Verses 28-29 refer to income from importing and exporting horses and chariots, but the details are very confused. NRSV says that Solomon imported horses from Egypt and Kue, which is the area around Tarsus on the south-east coast of modern Turkey, formerly known as Cilicia; and we know that Egypt was a market leader in chariots and that Cilicia was famous for its horses.

It is possible that Solomon bought horses from the north, selling them to Egypt, and chariots from Egypt which he sold to the northerners—the Hittites who occupied much of what is now Turkey, and the kings of Aram, which we now call Syria. The exchange rate was four horses for a chariot.

Wisdom

Wealth does not completely overshadow wisdom in this passage. Solomon's wisdom is internationally famous and God is still given the credit for it, though this too is turned into a source of profit as international dignitaries shower Solomon with presents (or tribute, as this word is translated in 1 Kings 4:21) on their annual visits (vv. 23-25).

Conspicuous wealth

Solomon's income, in gold alone, is enormous—25 tons per year (v. 14). Much of it is used to beautify the main hall of the palace (the 'House of the Cedars of Lebanon'—see 1 Kings 7:2). There are 200 large golden shields and 600 smaller ones on the wall, and a magnificent ivory throne overlaid with gold occupying centre stage. Even the drinking cups and tableware are gold. Count how many times the word 'gold' occurs in this passage! Such is the luxury, splendour and prosperity that silver counts for nothing in Solomon's Jerusalem, a point made twice (vv. 21, 27). His wealth invested in his own horses and chariots is not insignificant either. Assyrian sources say that King Ahab fielded two thousand chariots against them at Qarqar in 853BC—unless they are exaggerating—so it is not impossible for Solomon to have had 1400.

Where is all this leading?

This passage repeats much of what has already been said of Solomon in 1 Kings 4:20–34. At that point, it was easy to read the accounts of his wealth and wisdom and to take them at their face value. By this time, it is almost impossible to forget the warnings of Deuteronomy 17:14–20. If the statement in verse 23 marks the pinnacle of Solomon's greatness, his fall away from it begins almost immediately. His many horses (v. 26) are a sign of his downfall, as Deuteronomy 17:16 says they would be.

A PRAYER

Lord God,
the protector of all who trust in you,
without whom nothing is strong, nothing is holy:
increase and multiply upon us your mercy,
that you being our ruler and guide,
we may so pass through things temporal
that we finally lose not the things eternal.

26

1 KINGS 11:1–13

FOREIGN WOMEN

The rules for kings

Deuteronomy 17:14–20 contains five simple rules to follow:

- The king must be a native Israelite and not a foreigner.
- He must not acquire many horses.
- He must not acquire many wives.
- He must not acquire much silver and gold.
- He must have a copy of the Torah written for him and read to him daily.

So far, the criticism of Solomon has been implicit, audible only to those with an ear attuned to this statute. Now it becomes explicit. After the multiplying of gold and horses comes the multiplying of women, and God's disapproval is loud.

The indictment of Solomon

Solomon loves his wives (v. 1), but the key command to Israel had been to love the Lord (Deuteronomy 6:5; 10:12; 11:1 and so on). He clings to his wives (v. 2), but an important part of loving the Lord was to hold fast to him (Deuteronomy 10:20; 11:22; 13:4 and so on). His heart is not true to the Lord any longer (v. 4), though he himself had told the people to devote themselves completely to the Lord (1 Kings 8:61).

Solomon loves his many foreign wives. The Old Testament permits a man to have several wives. Deuteronomy 17:17 warns against the king having many of them because his 'heart will turn away', though it doesn't say why this will happen. The indictment shows precisely how Solomon's many wives turned his heart away. They were foreign women and he 'followed' their gods and built them shrines in and around Jerusalem. It is quite a list. The writers detest them and call them 'the abomination of...' or the 'loathsome god of...' (REB). Verse 2 reminds us that it is not only the ruling in Deuteronomy 17 which Solomon has broken but the general command to all the Israelites that they were not to intermarry with the people of the land (Deuteronomy 7:3–4). Why not? Because their hearts will follow these other gods!

Solomon now loves and clings to his many foreign wives and the result is that he no longer 'completely follows' the Lord (v. 6).

The punishment to follow

NRSV does not say how many foreign wives Solomon has, only that among them are 700 princesses and 300 concubines. A concubine was a slave woman married to a free man—a proper and legal wife, though lower in status to any wife who was a free woman. To his many horses and vast quantities of gold he adds a huge harem. In loving them, Solomon is led to the ultimate betrayal (vv. 3–4).

Verse 6 delivers the verdict in what will become a key phrase for reading the rest of Kings. The explanation of the utter catastrophe of the exile 300 years or so later is that Solomon and his successors 'did what was evil in the sight of the Lord'.

The immediate consequence of this in verse 9 was that the Lord was angry with Solomon. Not only had he appeared to Solomon twice (1 Kings 3:5; 9:2) but Solomon had been fully instructed about what was right. The result of his disobedience is that he will have the kingdom 'torn out of his hands' and the kingdom will be divided—but not in his own lifetime, because God does not wish to dishonour the memory of his father. It will happen in the lifetime of his son, whom we have yet to meet. This son will find himself left as king of a tiny remnant consisting of only one of the twelve tribes, and that will be left to him for the sake of David and Jerusalem. He will have nothing whatsoever for which to thank his father. The rest of the kingdom will go out of the family and into the hands of one of his subordinates.

A PRAYER

'You shall love the Lord your God
with all your heart
and with all your soul
and with all your might.'

Lord, have mercy upon us, and incline our hearts to keep this law.

The END

Three adversaries

The threat made in 11:11–13 materializes immediately in the shape of Hadad the Edomite from the south and Rezon the Aramean from the north, who pay off old scores (see 2 Samuel 8:3–6; 10:15–19), plus Jeroboam from Israel itself. Solomon, who once had no adversaries (1 Kings 5:4), now has three. Jeroboam is the one to note. He is the 'servant of Solomon' we have been told to expect (v. 11). He is introduced as the next key player on the scene, designated by the prophet Ahijah as the one to whom the torn-away kingdom will be given. Here is another prophet and king-maker. As Samuel had anointed Saul and David, and as Nathan had championed Solomon's cause, so Ahijah commissions Jeroboam by this dramatic action of tearing up his coat, which both demonstrates and shapes the new future (vv. 30–31). This illustrates what is meant by saying that 'the Lord raised up' these adversaries. God is involved with us in shaping the future. History is not pre-programmed: there is space for freedom and choice, both for us and for God.

Much the same is said to Jeroboam (vv. 31–39) as had been said to Solomon (1 Kings 3:14; 8:56–61; 9:6–9; 11:9–13): the same 'If...' applies. If he is faithful to God, he will prosper; if not...

From the mention of these adversaries and this glimpse into the future, the story moves quickly and with minimal comment to note Solomon's death (vv. 41–43). Two very different obituaries could be written.

Obituary—*Jerusalem Royal Post*

'We join with the whole nation and his many admirers from around the world to mourn the death in Jerusalem yesterday of Solomon bar-David, king of Israel. During his forty-year reign, the united state of Israel became a major player on the international scene and Jerusalem one of the most splendid and most visited capitals in the world. The temple of the Lord and its magnificent neighbour, the palace, will stand as eternal achievements crowning his extensive building projects in the city and throughout the land. The splendour of his court had already become legendary in his own lifetime and the whole nation shared in unparalleled economic prosperity during his reign. Like his wealth, his wisdom is already proverbial. He died in the palace in the early hours of yesterday morning, surrounded by his leading wives. Burial took place late yesterday afternoon in the Old City following a sacrifice of praise in the temple of the Lord. Funerary offerings were also made at shrines throughout the city. He is succeeded by his son, Rehoboam. Thanks be to God for the glories he gave to Solomon his king and to Israel his people.'

Obituary—*Prophetic Voice*

'The king died yesterday in the luxury of his royal apartments and surrounded by his foreign wives. Though they and those who have grown wealthy in his service might grieve his passing, he will not be mourned by many in Israel. Jerusalem has become a magnet for the rich and famous from around the world, but a snare for the Lord's faithful and an abomination in his eyes. The glory of the temple is defiled by shrines to loathsome gods in the Holy City. The great ideals of one nation under God have disappeared under the hewn stones of palaces and new cities. The price of Solomon's ambition has been paid in foreign bureaucrats and royal armies. He began well, looking to the Lord for wisdom, but wisdom can be vaunted and then what is it but folly? So in his ambition he multiplied horses, gold and wives. May the Lord have mercy on him and on us.'

Evaluation

How shall we evaluate the reign of Solomon? The truth probably lies somewhere between these two obituaries. There is no reason to doubt that there was much that was magnificent about Solomon and his reign, no matter how much our stories may exaggerate. There was enough for him to be seen in later imagination as the epitome of wisdom ('the wisdom of Solomon') and wealth ('Solomon in all his glory'—Luke 12:27); but the fact that the kingdom fell apart on his death, as we shall read, shows that all had not been well.

A PRAYER

Almighty God,
give us grace to live as you command,
that others may rejoice in the legacy of our lives.

28   1 KINGS 12:1–24

REHOBOAM *of* JUDAH (932–916)

Rehoboam's folly?

All the tribes assemble at Shechem, and Rehoboam goes there to be made king. This time there is no doubt about which of the old king's sons should succeed him, if the tribal assembly should so choose. We get the clear impression of a power struggle. The tribal assembly want Rehoboam to understand where the power really lies. If he wants to be king, he must travel to meet 'all the tribes' in old Shechem with its association with Joshua and democratic choices (v. 1; see Joshua 24). On the other hand, if they want to negotiate terms, he insists that they must come to him (v. 3). So Rehoboam faces a delegation which includes Jeroboam, who has returned from asylum in Egypt. Their complaint is simple. Free Israelites have been treated like slaves. They want assurances that it will not happen again.

There is an ominous sound to Rehoboam's reference to 'this people' (v. 6). Set apart by birth and upbringing, the prospective king is distanced from the people and despises them.

The old democratic traditions are seen again in the phraseology of verse 12. Jeroboam and 'all the people' assemble and when they do we see which advice Rehoboam has decided to hear. His wrong choice leads to a split. The old coalition between Israel and Judah falls apart and two kingdoms appear. In the north, the 'ten tribes' with Jeroboam as king emerge as the nation of Israel. In the south, with its capital in Jerusalem, the Davidic line continues to rule over the 'two tribe' kingdom of Judah. 'To your tents, O Israel' is an old cry (see 2 Samuel 20:1)—Jeroboam and the northerners will have nothing more to do with David's dynasty.

The strength of feeling against Rehoboam, a sign of the hurts and repressed anger of many years, shows itself in the killing of Adoram, who had controlled the hated levy (v. 18). Even before Jeroboam is made king, the Israelites will have no more of Rehoboam's rule, even in towns in Judah. He is forced to flee in his chariot even from parts of Judah itself.

In verse 19 we see the viewpoint of the Deuteronomic Historians. They write from a Judean perspective and support the Davidic dynasty, despite all their suspicions of it and reservations about it. From where they stand, Israel is in rebellion, at fault, in the wrong. We shall see why they feel this so strongly later, in 1 Kings 12 and in the difficult chapter 13.

Or Solomon's?

Verse 15 shows that this is not a simple story of the youthful and crass Rehoboam living out the folly of his privileged upbringing with disastrous results all round. It suggests that we cannot blame everything that happens on the stupidity of Rehoboam.

By this point in 1 Kings, we have become very familiar with the basic theology of the writers that life and faith are about choices and that choices have consequences (what I have referred to as the 'If…' facing each king in several previous studies). Solomon has chosen wrongly and so would forfeit the kingdom to God's new man Jeroboam, though not immediately and not entirely. His son will keep Judah 'for David's sake' (1 Kings 11:29–37). It is because Israel's existence as a separate nation is the result of the outworking of this principle, and therefore part of the will of God, that Rehoboam's plan to bring the rebels to heel is thwarted by another prophet. Shemaiah tells him that 'this thing is from God' (v. 24), and so the army returns home.

Verse 15 shows that Rehoboam is the victim of his father's folly, as God blights his kingdom as a consequence of his father's wrong choices. Of course it was hard on Rehoboam—though we might feel that he deserved it—but that is not the point. Wrong acts have consequences and it is often the innocent who have to bear them.

FOR MEDITATION

And evils wrought by human pride
Recoil on unrepentant heads.

From the hymn 'Creator of the earth and skies' by Donald Hughes

JEROBOAM *of* ISRAEL (932–911)

Apostasy

Solomon's folly led to the break-up of the united kingdom. Jeroboam's first act as king of the new northern state seems sensible enough. A new state needs a capital and a new king establishes his reign and his reputation by his building schemes, so Jeroboam of Israel follows the example of Solomon and fortifies Shechem and then Penuel. There is a certain ambiguity about the choice of Shechem. To its credit was its association with Joshua, as we saw in the last chapter; but on the debit side it had been the centre of an earlier attempt at monarchy which had destroyed itself in intrigues and conflict (see Judges 9). Penuel is usually located east of the Jordan and the move there is sometimes associated with the invasion of the area by Pharaoh Shishak of Egypt around 922BC (see 1 Kings 14:25–28).

Jeroboam is astute enough to recognize that any new kingdom needs a religious centre and that Israel in particular needs something to counteract the pull of Jerusalem. But in meeting that need, he acts with unprecedented folly. He commits the greatest possible breach of the very conditions of his reign as set out in 1 Kings 11:31–39. He makes two 'golden calves' and erects them in Dan in the far north of the kingdom and in the old holy place of Bethel in the south. Verse 30 gives the verdict: 'And this thing became a sin.' This, as far as the Deuteronomic Historians are concerned, was the unforgivable sin.

For readers of the longer story from Exodus onwards, any mention of 'golden calves' must seem like asking for trouble, and that is exactly what the writers want us to recognize. 'Here are your gods, O Israel, who brought you up out of the land of Egypt' (v. 28) is an almost verbatim quotation of Exodus 32:4. Jeroboam is repeating the great sin of Aaron. He may have thought that he was doing the same sort of thing that Solomon had done when he made the two golden cherubim for the temple in Jerusalem, making a throne for God (see 1 Kings 6:23–28). And were there not twelve bronze oxen supporting the molten sea in the courtyard of the temple in Jerusalem (see 1 Kings 7:25)? But the writers of Kings will not let him get away with either of these comparisons. Not only was the bull a symbol of the

Canaanite god, Baal, but golden calves had been the sign and cause of the greatest apostasy in the history of God's people so far. And Jeroboam was repeating it.

Compared with that, the fact that he also built shrines on the 'high places' (though verse 31 might mean that he built a temple at the old sacred site in Bethel), appointed priests who were not of the official line and instituted a rival festival not in the official calendar seem like minor blemishes. They do, however, add up. Notice the emphasis throughout this passage on Jeroboam's relentless activity to ensure that no one in Israel will look to Jerusalem and its temple. In the comment in verse 33 about the festival which 'he alone had devised', we are intended to see how far all this activity is from what he should have been doing, which was to trust in God and pay proper attention to the 'statutes and ordinances' about these things.

This is much worse than any of Solomon's follies. He had led the nation astray by worshipping foreign gods and the nation had suffered for it. Much worse, Jeroboam makes two idols, for that is what the writers clearly intend us to see that these two golden calves really are, and says that they are Israel's god or gods 'who brought you up out of Egypt' (v. 28). Notice that even in this extraordinary act of idolatry, the exodus remains the event which defines the God of Israel. Aaron had made one golden calf and said, 'This is your God'. Jeroboam makes two and says, 'Behold, your gods!' In so doing he both breaks the second commandment which forbids idols (Exodus 20:4–5; Deuteronomy 5:8–9) and undermines the *Shema* which insists that the Lord is one (Deuteronomy 6:4).

He too had heeded bad advice (v. 28). The new nation is already doomed and it is Jeroboam's sin which is always cited as the reason for it (for example, 1 Kings 15:26; 2 Kings 17:21–23).

FOR MEDITATION

The writers of Kings portray Jeroboam as an apostate,
one who worshipped false gods. Perhaps all Christians should
ask themselves, now and again, what false gods we might
set up and worship?

30

A WORD *from* GOD

1 Kings 13 begins and ends with Jeroboam, and is uncompromising. The altars he has built and everything associated with them are wrong. His new kingdom is fated. What had begun in obedience has become disobedience, for Jeroboam has gone far beyond the mandate God had given him in 1 Kings 11:31–39. In his very act of emulating Solomon and standing to dedicate his new altar, a southern prophet appears with a message from God condemning the whole enterprise. At first Jeroboam scorns the message and, not for the first or last time in the story of Kings or in the history of God's people, one of God's faithful and outspoken messengers is abused.

This chapter contains the first miracle in Kings. Jeroboam's hand is withered or paralysed and then healed. This is one of three signs given to Jeroboam by which he can know that the prophet is speaking from God. The first is that the altar collapses as the prophet said it would (v. 5). The second is that his arm is healed when the prophet prays. He has been shown, twice and clearly, that this prophet is to be listened to, and Jeroboam can't, at first, do enough to mollify the prophet he was ready to treat so roughly a few moments before. The third sign will be the death of this same prophet (13:24). None of them, however, will make Jeroboam change his mind in a way that really matters.

In verse 6 we see the role of the prophet in intercession, speaking to God and asking for help for Jeroboam—an important part of the task of prophets (for other examples, see 1 Samuel 7:8; 1 Kings 17:20–24; Amos 7:1–6).

Prophets and 'the word of the Lord'

This unnamed prophet brings the number of prophets in these accounts of the beginnings of the two new kingdoms to three (the other two are Ahijah from Shiloh in 11:29 and Shemaiah in 12:22), and another unnamed one will appear in verse 11. The northern pair are called 'prophets' and the southern pair 'men of God' but they play the same key role in the drama. The kings may have the leading parts, but it is the prophets who are producing the play—which might have had a happier ending if the actors had followed the script.

The script is 'the word of the Lord', a phrase which occurs eight times in 1 Kings 13 and frequently in the book as a whole. Sometimes, as in GNB's translation of verse 1, it refers to the command given to a prophet to speak or to act: 'At the Lord's command a prophet from Judah...' More often it refers to what the prophet is commanded to say, as in verse 2, where the message from God is introduced by the standard formula, 'Thus says the Lord'. Behind this lies the idea that God has a plan for his people and that the prophets are his agents in making this known and seeing it through.

Hospitality refused

The Old Testament comes from a culture in which hospitality was important. Meals were not simply occasions of satisfying one's hunger. Meals with people were symbolic occasions. If you ate with someone, that was a sign that you were friends and that you were bonded together. To refuse to eat with someone was a powerful sign that you had nothing to do with that person; you were not in communion with them; you wanted no covenant or bond with them. So when this southern prophet refuses to accept the hospitality offered by the king, a powerful message is being sent (vv. 7–10). It is not simply that the king is being insulted or rebuffed, though he is, but that Jeroboam is being given another version of God's message that he has already heard. The prophet explains that he is acting as God has commanded him to act and the message in the action is that God no longer wants anything to do with this new king of Israel. The covenant between them is in jeopardy. By word and action, that message is given to Jeroboam.

A PRAYER

Let the wicked forsake their way, and the unrighteous their thoughts; let them return to the Lord, that he may have mercy upon them, and to our God, for he will abundantly pardon.

Isaiah 55:7

A TALE *of* TWO PROPHETS

Verses 11–32 tell a story of two anonymous prophets, one of whom is tricked by the other and then killed by a lion. The southern prophet was obedient in fulfilling the hard and dangerous task that God had given him to do. He had gone to Bethel and told Jeroboam what God had given him to say. He was, however, disobedient in a tiny detail, even though it was a fellow prophet who tricked him into it. There was still a chance and he should have turned away from it as soon as it was pointed out to him. He did not and the result was death. Had he repented, he might have got home safely after all. If this summary of a rather bizarre story is on the right lines, we might see the message to Jeroboam—and the story is intended as a message for Jeroboam—as something like this:

> *You have obediently done the big and dangerous thing which God asked of you. You have led Israel to independence. You have, however, followed wrong advice and that has led you into this evil with the golden calves. There is still time to pull back from this. If you don't, you are doomed.*

The final note in verses 33–34 concludes that Jeroboam failed to 'turn' from his evil way. All through the chapter, the storyteller plays with that word, though it isn't always obvious in our translations. The implication is clear. Had he done so, the situation could have been redeemed.

A detail

Verse 19 says bluntly that the northerner was lying. He would, wouldn't he? As a northerner, working in the old holy place of Bethel, he wouldn't have welcomed this southern upstart with his damning message. He rushes off to see what he can do to stop his message coming about. There are several examples of prophets disagreeing with each other in the Old Testament and it is clear that there was a real problem in deciding which prophets were 'true' and which were 'false'. Only during the meal does the northerner learn that the southerner had spoken truly from God.

Believable or unbelievable?

Some readers will have trouble believing this lion story (vv. 24–28). Others will not. I said in the Introduction that in 1 and 2 Kings the question, 'Did this or that actually happen?' is not a very helpful question to ask. Everything we have read so far in 1 Kings could have happened. It has all been about our real worlds of politics and power, architecture and ambition, or religion and rivalry. We have been reading about the same kind of world that we live in. Now, for the first time, we read about a stranger world in which animals do the will of God. We will see more of this later with Elijah's ravens (1 Kings 17:4–6) and Elisha's bears (2 Kings 2:24), though neither really compare with Balaam's talking donkey or Jonah's fish. Some commentators call this sort of literature 'midrash', a Jewish way of telling a story with a moral or theological message in it. The term may not be quite accurate but some readers might find it helpful, for here is a story with a message, and the important thing is that all who read it should get the message.

Obedience

It is a question of obedience. The southern prophet was obedient in delivering his message, but his obedience was compromised when he accepted the northerner's hospitality. The sharing of hospitality created lasting bonds of friendship and support. The prophet should not receive any northern hospitality at all, because that would be to support Jeroboam— it would mean that the prophet himself would be caught up in the punishment which was to be Jeroboam's fate. The consequence of his disobedience, even though he was deceived into it, is fatal. Even prophets have to be obedient in the details, and if a prophet cannot escape the consequences of disobedience, then neither can a king.

The prophet's death is the final sign for Jeroboam. The grave of these prophets will feature later in 2 Kings 23:15–20 when the corruption of this altar at Bethel is finally eradicated by Josiah.

FOR REFLECTION

To obey is better than sacrifice, and to heed than the fat of rams.
For rebellion is no less a sin than divination, and stubbornness is
like iniquity and idolatry.

1 Samuel 15:22–23

Jeroboam's End

From hope to horror

In 1 Kings 11:29–39, Ahijah of Shiloh had announced to one of Solomon's most able administrators that the Lord had decided that he would rule the kingdom which Solomon was about to forfeit. He had told him that Solomon's sons and heirs would be left with only a fragment of the nation which Solomon had inherited from David. He had told him why. He had advised him about the ways in which he should live as God's newly chosen one. Now, old and blind, Ahijah appears again with another message for the same man.

Jeroboam's son is seriously ill and he sends his wife in disguise to ask the old prophet what the future is to be. Many years have passed since that first meeting, and the old man's message for her to take back to her husband is devastatingly harsh. Jeroboam has been worse than Solomon. He had been told that the kingdom was being torn from Solomon's grasp because he had introduced into it the worship of foreign gods. Jeroboam is now told that because he has done worse, his people will be torn from their land and sent into exile beyond the Euphrates. He had been told that, for David's sake, a son of Solomon would succeed him and continue to rule over what was left of David's kingdom. He is now told that no son of his will survive and that only one of them—the one his wife has been sent to enquire about—will even be given a proper burial.

Reading 1 Kings 11:29–39 and 14:1–20 side by side we see the move from hope to horror, both for Ahijah to speak and for Jeroboam to hear. Jeroboam had been promised an enduring dynasty (1 Kings 11:38), we readers have been told of the end of his house (13:33–34) and now Ahijah announces to Jeroboam that this is what will be. It happens in the first year of the reign of his son (see 15:27–30).

Other gods and images

So far, the two main accusations against Jeroboam are that he made the golden calves (1 Kings 12:28–29) and ordained as priests those who were not eligible (12:31; 13:33–34), followed by enhancing the facilities at the 'high places' (12:31) and devising a new festival (12:33). We see another in 14:15, that under his leadership Israel has made 'sacred poles'. These *asherim* are sacred poles or trees erected as symbols of Asherah, the main Canaanite goddess.

The kernel of God's rejection of Jeroboam is seen in verse 9. Jeroboam has 'thrust God behind his back'. He has done to God what Jesus did to Satan (Mark 8:33). Pushing God behind him, he has 'made' other gods for Israel and manufactured images (1 Kings 12:28). He has, above all else, broken the first and second commandments and not only sinned himself but caused the nation to sin. The writers of Kings will remark constantly that future generations will be caught up in Jeroboam's sin as they continue to patronize the golden calves at Dan and Bethel (for example, 1 Kings 16:26; 22:52; 2 Kings 10:29; 17:22).

David my servant

Time and again in Kings, David is cited as the example that failed kings, of both nations, ought to have followed. Despite the troubles of his reign and the errors of his ways, he is God's 'servant' *par excellence*. Far from perfect though he was, he is the model king who kept the basic conditions set out by God (v. 8).

Obituary

Verses 19–20 present Jeroboam's obituary. As with Solomon's, it makes reference to where a fuller account of his reign can be found, though we know nothing more of these Annals. The phrase 'how he warred and how he reigned' reminds us just how little of Jeroboam's 22 years we have actually been told about. Attention has focused on his conduct of the religious affairs of his nation to the total exclusion of everything else. That, as we shall see, is usually the case, and we will look at why it might be so in Study 37 when we consider King Omri, and in Study 45 when we read of Naboth and his vineyard.

A PRAYER

Lord of all power and might,
graft in our hearts the love of your name,
increase in us true religion,
nourish us in all goodness,
and of your great mercy keep us in the same.

REHOBOAM'S FAILURE

Jeroboam of Israel and Rehoboam of Judah have much in common, at least according to the brief summaries of their reigns in Kings. In both of their reigns, the Lord was angry with what went on in the name of religion. In both countries, the situation was seriously sinful. But the consequences of this for the two kings were quite different. Jeroboam, as we saw, was told that his dynasty had no future at all. It would be annihilated in a very bloody way. Rehoboam, on the other hand, is told nothing of the sort because he is of the house and lineage of David, and his dynasty in Judah is covered by the old promise to David (2 Samuel 7). There were, of course, conditions attached, so that if the kings of Judah did wrong they would be punished, but that punishment would never be total. And even though Rehoboam's mother is an Ammonite, as we are told twice—one of Solomon's many foreign wives—the promise to David still holds. Remember the reason behind the writing of Joshua to 2 Kings and you will appreciate the significance of this reassuring contrast between the fates of Jeroboam and Rehoboam.

The reference to Jerusalem in the second part of verse 21 is the key to that difference. Jerusalem is the one and only city where the Lord has 'put his name'. It is the one place where the Lord is to be worshipped. The heart of Jeroboam's sin was that he had set up two places in opposition to Jerusalem. Religious affairs might go seriously wrong in Rehoboam's reign, as verses 22–24 show, but at least the temple in Jerusalem is still there.

The sins they committed

Verses 23–24 list the religious malpractices which were prevalent in Judah during Rehoboam's reign. The 'high places' (that is, the outdoor sacred sites) were renovated and refurbished, or new ones were set up, or both. Pillars and *asherim* multiplied, though it is difficult to see quite what the difference between these two symbols might be. Male temple prostitutes are mentioned here for the first time in Kings, although GNB might possibly be right in saying that temple prostitutes were of both sexes. These, as with everything else in this list, were features of local Canaanite religion which was much concerned with the fertility of the land and its families. 'On every high hill and under every green tree' denotes the prevalence of these old religious rites and customs which the developing nations of Israel and Judah, with their different approach to religion, had been unable to eradicate.

These practices or 'abominations' provoked the Lord to jealousy (v. 22). The Old Testament believes that God is passionately involved with his people and has no hesitation in talking about his feelings either of love (the classic text here is Hosea 11, especially v. 8) or anger (as with Solomon in 1 Kings 11:9). The second commandment sees God as a 'jealous God' (Exodus 20:5) who expects the total loyalty of his people just as he offers himself totally to them.

The consequences

Sin is followed by punishment, as always for the writers of Joshua to Kings, and the punishment takes the form of the invasion of Judah by Pharaoh Shishak, who pillages the temple and the palace. An inscription in the temple in Karnak refers to this campaign in Palestine, although it gives no date and no details. Solomon's splendour and the faithfulness of the past cannot guarantee immunity from the consequences of present wrongs. Neither will God defend his own temple (see 1 Kings 9:8–9). Shishak might have led the invasion but it is Judah itself which is to blame for the fact that Solomon's gold has been replaced with Rehoboam's bronze (vv. 26–27).

Rehoboam's brief obituary notes, in contrast to 1 Kings 11:24, that Rehoboam and Jeroboam had been at war throughout their reigns, though it draws no conclusions from the fact. It may be that we should observe here another consequence of Judah's sins—that Solomon's peace has been replaced by Rehoboam's constant war (1 Kings 5:4).

One point is becoming clear in the treatment of these two reigns. It is that faithfulness to the Lord is the one thing that matters, either for the king (as in the case of Jeroboam) or for the nation, as in the case of Judah.

FOR MEDITATION

You shall worship the Lord your God.
Him only shall you serve.

Deuteronomy 6:13; Matthew 4:10 (RSV)

Two More Judeans

Abijam of Judah (916–914)

Abijam succeeded his father, Rehoboam, but the evil that the father had done continued through the son (v. 3). Note again that allowances are made, 'for David's sake', to Judean kings who go wrong. In the case of Abijam, it is that his son can succeed him, which is expressed in a delightful little phrase that 'God gave him a lamp in Jerusalem' (as in 1 Kings 11:36).

Asa of Judah (914–874)

Asa, Abijam's son, was different. He 'did what was right in the sight of the Lord' (v. 11) and his reign was a long one. He instituted a religious reform which included the removal of the male temple prostitutes and of the 'idols' (the pillars and the *asherim*) as well as removing Maacah from the position of queen mother because she had promoted the worship of Asherah, the principal Canaanite goddess, by erecting some kind of 'abominable image'. He did nothing about the high places but he did bring the offerings his father had given to them into the temple, which is where he made his own offerings (vv. 9–15).

'Maacah' presents a puzzle guaranteed to intrigue all those interested in family trees, and those wishing to solve the problem of father and son having the same mother (Abijam in verse 3 and Asa in verse 10) should consult a more technical commentary. Some other translations read verse 10 to say that Maacah is Asa's grandmother and not his mother, and that may be the most likely solution.

Verse 6 perhaps means that all this time the old 'war' between Judah and Israel was still going on, though some manuscripts read 'Abijam' instead of 'Rehoboam', which makes more sense. Some commentators suggest that the verse has slipped in here by mistake. The war was probably little more than border skirmishing, with the occasional bigger raid.

With the advent of Baasha as king of Israel, there was an escalation in the fighting as Baasha advanced into Judah and started to build a major fort at Ramah, a highly strategic site only five miles north of Jerusalem, so that he could blockade the city. Asa appealed to Ben-

Hadad of Aram (or Syria, as it is called in many translations), who invaded the north of Israel, thus drawing Baasha away and confining him in Tirzah, which served as the capital of Israel in this period. In his absence, Asa demolished Ramah and enrolled all the able-bodied men to move the materials to build two city fortresses of his own. Note the reversal of fortune here: Solomon had received tribute from Aram, but Asa has to buy Aram's help (vv. 18–20).

Aches and pains

In Asa's obituary (vv. 23–24), we are told, as usual, where the details of his reign can be found, but we also find a fascinating detail about the old king's bad feet. We can, I suppose, read all sorts of things into this detail. Is it a sign of things going wrong in Asa's old age as they did in Solomon's? Is it a sign of God's judgment because he was not entirely faithful? Or is it a touch of humour, that even faithful old kings get gout? I would invite you to smile at this note, as long as you remember that you too will get old, and to read it as a theological comment. The writers of Kings are often accused of having too simplistic a view on life—that righteousness is rewarded and sin is punished—but where do the chances and changes of life fit in? Its minor aches and pains? Its little niggles and frustrations? No amount of faithfulness can exempt you from these. Or is that too simple too?

A PRAYER

O Lord,
support us all the day long of this troublous life,
until the shades lengthen and the evening comes,
and the busy world is hushed,
and the fever of life is over
and our work is done.
Then, Lord, in thy mercy,
grant us safe lodging,
a holy rest
and peace at the last.

After J.H. Newman

The FIRST BLOODY COUP

Nadab of Israel (911–910)

Nadab's short reign is briefly covered and quickly dismissed (15:25–26, 31–32). Israel continues in the wrong ways into which Jeroboam has led it and the friction between the two states continues too.

Baasha of Israel (910–887)

In marked contrast to the settled and secure dynasty in Judah, Israel will experience a series of bloody coups, and verse 27 introduces the first of them. The end of Jeroboam's line takes place as the prophet Ahijah proclaimed it should; but no prophet authorizes or commissions Baasha to take power. He assassinates Nadab during a military campaign and then kills all his family. Others will follow that example later.

1 Kings 16:4 repeats the idea of 14:11, and we can visualize something of the utter horror involved. Baasha is doing the obvious thing, eradicating any possible opposition to the new regime, and we are familiar enough with that practice in our own era. What is more difficult for us is to share the belief of the writers of Kings that this is the will of God. Here is another one of those instances in which we see that our values are different from those of these ancient writers. No doubt future believers will look equally askance at some of our views and practices. The 'house of Jeroboam' is no more (see 1 Kings 14:10). It had survived his own death by a mere two years. Baasha's father is, confusingly, also called Ahijah.

A new king changes nothing. The same sin is perpetuated and the conflict with Judah continues (as we saw in 1 Kings 15:17–21). Baasha's reign is condemned in exactly the same way Nadab's had been (compare vv. 26 and 34). A prophet appears, Jehu son of Hanani (16:1), to announce that Baasha is to suffer the same fate as Jeroboam and for the same reason. Baasha dies and his obituary is printed (vv. 5–6); but then, unusually, a final word is added from the prophet who had announced his fate. This repeats the first and general charge against Baasha and adds a second, which is that he had destroyed 'the house of Jeroboam'.

This second charge in the last phrase in verse 7 sounds odd because the story has emphasized that the destruction of Jeroboam's family is exactly what God wanted. Why, then, should Baasha be penalized for doing it? Is it that he had not been the one authorized to do it? That is one suggestion offered by commentators, but that is at odds with verse 2, which says that God had brought Baasha to power. Another is that although God had destined him to do it, he was still accountable for his action. In fact, the Hebrew syntax is not clear and verse 7 could be translated like this:

'But the word of the Lord had come through the prophet Jehu son of Hanani against Baasha and against his house, that it would fare like the House of Jeroboam—which he himself had struck down—because of all the evil he did which was displeasing to the Lord, vexing him with his deeds' (NJPS).

Listening to the prophets

Apart from 1 Kings 15:17–21, which recounts the fighting with Asa of Judah, thirteen verses are devoted to Baasha's 24-year reign. Of those verses, five are given over to the words of the prophet Jehu ben Hanani, the fifth prophet to appear so far in the story of the divided kingdoms. A pattern is beginning to emerge. We are being invited to focus our attention not on the doings of the kings but on the sayings of the prophets. Their place in the story is to explain the plot as we read. They explain what is happening and why. The explanation they give, we are invited to believe, is not theirs but God's. We shall soon encounter the two great prophets Elijah and Elisha and read stories of their encounters with kings, but it is already becoming clear why the overall title for the books of Joshua, Judges, Samuel and Kings in the Hebrew Bible is 'The Former Prophets' (that is, the 'Earlier' ones) and not 'The History of Israel'.

A PRAYER

Lord, help us to discern your will and purpose for human life and society today, and to live and work to make it happen.

The SECOND BLOODY COUP

Elah of Israel (887–886)

Elah's short-lived reign ended with his murder while he was 'drinking himself drunk' (v. 9). In the summary of his and his father's reigns in verse 13, AV describes Jeroboam's golden calves as 'vanities', that is, things without weight or substance—worthless, pointless things (it is the same Hebrew word found in the famous opening of Ecclesiastes). The word captures the scorn that is being poured out on these things.

Zimri of Israel (886)

Zimri, one of Elah's senior military staff, was the murderer and he then proceeded, as Baasha had done, to eliminate not only all the males of Baasha's family but of all his friends as well (v. 11). Everything has happened to Baasha's house as the prophet Jehu proclaimed it should. Zimri's reign is the shortest of all. The army are again engaged against the Philistine city of Gibbethon—the very place where Baasha had staged the first coup nearly thirty years before —and as soon as they hear what has happened they elect Omri, the army commander, as king. Whatever Zimri's motives may have been (and note that there has been no prophet encouraging him to act), the army sees his action as treason, a word used three times about what he had done ('conspired' and 'conspiracy' in NRSV, vv. 9, 16, 20). This is the first time for fifty years that anything like the old northern tradition of the people electing the king has happened. Omri and the army beseige Tirzah and Zimri commits suicide in a spectacularly horrible way, burning the palace down with himself inside it (v. 18).

North and south

The story has been told of the first fifty years of the separated kingdoms of Israel and Judah, focusing first on one state and then on the other. Mention has been made of the ongoing struggle between them but only once have we seen any of the skirmishing (in 1 Kings 15:17–21). What has become obvious is that the settled dynastic succession in Judah is very different from the chaotic changes in leadership in Israel. 870BC is, near enough, the jubilee of the death of Solomon. In Judah, the reign of Asa, his great-grandson, is drawing to a close and he will die in his bed like his forebears in David's dynasty. In Israel, Omri's son is king. Three of his six predecessors have met violent deaths and he is a member of the fourth dynasty to have claimed the throne.

We can sum up the theology underlying the accounts of these kings like this:

- 'Choice' is the buzz-word in the Deuteronomic way of looking at things.
- The vital choice to be made is for or against God.
- Choice against God leads to death and disintegration, not always for the person who makes the wrong choice, but sometimes for others or the next generation.
- Choice for God leads to life and integration, though it is not always easy and it requires continually renewed commitment.
- Prophets play an important role in offering the choice and in pointing out the consequences of failing to maintain it.

Jeroboam and Baasha illustrate the fourth point well. They were called to the high vocation of leadership in Israel and they chose for God, but they did not maintain that commitment. Vocation brings with it ongoing challenge and the continual need to make the right choices.

The possibility of anarchy

Leadership in Judah was by inheritance. In Israel it was by vocation, which had meant the election of their king on the nomination of a prophet, although that had fallen by the wayside. Without procedures, choice and freedom bring with them the danger of anarchy, which is what we see in Zimri. He was self-appointed, without call or authorization. Fortunately for Israel, the army recognized him for what he was and remembered the old way of doing things (vv. 15–16).

FOR PRAYER

*Pray for those parts of our world where there is
no peace, security or stability.*

The HOUSE of OMRI

Omri of Israel (886–875)

Omri's election by the army does not meet with universal approval, and Israel descends into four years of civil strife, if not civil war, which end with the death of Omri's rival. His reign is treated in much the same way as his predecessors', with the additional note that he is the worst king so far. Only one detail is given, that he moved the capital from Tirzah to the new city of Samaria which he built and fortified (v. 24). It was to become a magnificent city (see Isaiah 8:4; Amos 6:1–7; 3:15) which would serve as Israel's capital until the Assyrians destroyed both city and nation in 722BC, and after that would give its name to a new state.

Omri was, as far as historians are concerned, one of Israel's greatest kings. Such was his reputation that Israel was known in Assyrian records as the 'Land of Omri' well after his long dynasty had come to an end. The Moabite Stone, which King Mesha of Moab commissioned about forty years after Omri's death to celebrate his victory over Omri's son or grandson, shows that he had subjugated the northern part of Moab. You would guess none of that from this brief account. This dismissal of his reign is the strongest example yet of the fact that the Deuteronomic Historians were working to a different agenda.

The reign of every king so far has ended with a note referring those readers who are interested in facts and details to the appropriate State Annals. The focus of the account of each reign has been, as we have seen, on the religious affairs of the nations under the king in question. Part of the reason for that is the writers' view that Israel and Judah owe an obligation of total obedience to the Lord. This may be because he is the one who rescued them from Egypt and so is the only God for them, or it may be because he is the only true God there is. In the first case, to worship and value anything less than the Lord is to risk forfeiting your inheritance in the land he has given you. In the second, it is to jeopardize your life by exchanging commitment to truth for commitment to falsehood. Either way, the saying of Jesus in Mark 8:36 ('What will it profit someone to gain the whole world but forfeit their life?') is one that the Deuteronomists would approve. The other part of the reason, we shall see in Study 45 when we read of Naboth and his vineyard.

Ahab of Israel (875–854)

We shall hear much more of Ahab than of any of his predecessors because the next five chapters feature his conflict with the prophet Elijah. The introduction in verse 30 indicates that Ahab was even worse than his father, and verses 31–33 say why. He married Jezebel, a foreign princess, imported her god into Israel and built a temple for him in Samaria (echoes of Solomon's last days here: see 1 Kings 11:1–8).

The word *baal* means 'lord', 'master' or 'husband' and it was used widely in Canaan as a title for various gods. One of these, the 'Baal of Tyre', was the god Jezebel worshipped and for whom Ahab built a temple in Samaria. 'Baal' was also the name of the great storm-god in the Canaanite pantheon. In the Old Testament, the identities of these gods tend to merge with that of the storm-god into a single figure— Baal—who is portrayed as the chief rival to the Lord for the allegiance of the people. Alongside this worship of Baal, Ahab either erected an *asherim* symbol or introduced the worship of Baal's consort, Asherah (v. 33 can be taken either way).

The meaning of verse 34 is not certain, though it is obviously intended to illustrate how bad things were in Ahab's reign. It might mean that Hiel offered his children as human sacrifices when he was building a new city at Jericho, or that he chose to ignore Joshua's ancient curse and two of his children died because of it. The fact that Hiel was from Bethel is significant. Bethel was one of Jeroboam's two centres, from which sin and evil are spreading everywhere! Verse 34 quotes Joshua 6:26 in which the great old leader had warned about rebuilding Jericho at all. Ahab chose not to listen to what God had said through Joshua, and the stage is now set for his confrontation with God's great contemporary messenger, Elijah.

A PRAYER

Lord, help us to remain faithful to you
through all the changes of life and history.

ELIJAH

The story in 1 Kings now changes gear. From snippets covering a decade in a verse or two and alternating between the kings of Israel and Judah, the story slows right down to focus on two reigns and two prophets.

Who controls the rain?

Elijah, the northern prophet, confronts Ahab, the northern king. Ahab has given his public support to Baal, the storm-god, the lord and giver of life who controls the rain in a dry and thirsty land. Elijah stands before him as the representative of the Lord and challenges Ahab and his god on this very point. The Lord, the true God of Israel, is the one who gives the life-giving rain, and to prove it there will be no more until the Lord says so.

Elijah doesn't run and hide because he is scared of Ahab—that comes later. God commands him to go and hide himself in the Wadi Cherith. Although we don't know where that was, both places mentioned in this chapter are significant. It is a dangerous thing to camp out in a wadi. These seasonal water courses might contain a gentle stream in the dry season or they might dry up completely, but after a storm they would be subject to dangerous flash-floods. Elijah can camp in the wadi in safety because there will be no storm to cause it to flood!

How does he survive? The ravens feed him night and morning, just as Moses and the Israelites had been fed in their desert wanderings (Exodus 16:8). Some commentators take most of the sense of the miraculous out of this by translating the word as 'bedouin' or 'Arabs', but whilst the words are similar this misses the point. Again it is important to ask the right question. Why did the writers tell it like this? First, to emphasize the power of the Lord, the true God. This note in the NRSV margin puts it well: 'The element of the miraculous in the stories is an integral part of the writer's intent to dramatize the power of God through the prophet's words and actions.'

There is a second reason too, which is to show that Elijah and all God's people and prophets with him can rely on God's support and care. Elijah's vocation as a prophet will be a hard and demanding one, but through all its trials and tribulations he can rely on God to sustain him.

Who helps the widow in Sidon?

The 'word of the Lord' moves Elijah on to Zarephath (vv. 8–9), a town in Sidon. Elijah travels to Jezebel's father's country. He is now in the land where Baal is the official god. The scene is set for another sign of the power of the Lord, and we are given two.

The first is to do with Elijah and the widow. The Old Testament portrays God as being particularly concerned for 'the widow, the orphan and the poor', that is, the vulnerable and marginalized in society (for example, Deuteronomy 14:29; Psalm 94:6; Zechariah 7:10). Here we see the Lord demonstrating care for a vulnerable foreigner whose own god is no help to her and her son. He feeds them daily.

The second sign is to do with her son (v. 17). The story does not suggest that God caused the son to die so that his power could be demonstrated. The boy's death is a natural event. It is 'one of those things', one of the chances and changes of life; but the widow's re-action is absolutely typical. She blames God's representative and she blames God. She sees this premature death as some sort of punishment for sin. Elijah does not argue, but takes her son upstairs, lets God know exactly what he feels about all of this and prays that her son may be restored to life. This second sign demonstrates the life-giving power of the Lord and also authenticates Elijah as a genuine prophet.

Even on his home ground, Baal is no match for the Lord.

FOR MEDITATION

Elijah's name means 'My God is the Lord' or 'The Lord is my God.' Elijah himself, as well as his words and deeds, is God's sign to Ahab, and Ahab must choose between the Lord and Baal.

TROUBLERS *of* ISRAEL

Act I of the drama

1 Kings 18 is a drama in three acts. Act I prepares for the contest on Mount Carmel and has five scenes:

Scene 1: Elijah is sent back to Ahab (vv. 1–2).

Scene 2: Ahab sends Obadiah to look for water (vv. 3–6).

Scene 3: Elijah and Obadiah meet on the road (vv. 7–15).

Scene 4: Obadiah reports to Ahab (v. 16).

Scene 5: Ahab and Elijah meet (vv. 17–19).

Scene 3 contains a very well-scripted dialogue which evokes our sympathy for Obadiah. He is already in danger because he has helped the Lord's prophets, and Elijah's instruction is a risk too far. This is a very human scene, equalling the dialogues between Elijah and the widow of Zarephath for pathos.

The threat from Jezebel

Nothing that we have heard about Jezebel so far prepares us for what we are told in this passage. From 1 Kings 16:31–32 we might imagine her to be another foreign princess exercising an unhealthy hold over the king and leading him astray, much like Solomon's wives had done. It is much worse. The statement in verse 4 shocks. In case we are thinking it is just too unbelievable to be true, verse 13 repeats the bare fact. Jezebel has been killing the Lord's prophets.

We have encountered nothing like this in the story so far. We have seen Solomon permitting the worship of foreign gods in Jerusalem and the northern kings making idols and erecting pagan symbols, but there has been nothing about the northerners worshipping other gods in place of the Lord. To achieve that, however, is Jezebel's mission, and so she is persecuting the Lord's prophets. This is an unheard-of and unprecedented situation about which Ahab must have known.

Hundreds of prophets

So far in Kings, we have met prophets in ones and twos. The only reference in the longer story to a large number of them is to the band of prophets whom Saul met near Gibeah (see 1 Samuel 10:10–13). Here, however, they are numbered in hundreds. Obadiah had rescued a hundred but there were others he had not been able to save; and Elijah tells Ahab to assemble the 450 prophets of Baal and the 400 prophets of Asherah whom Jezebel sponsors and maintains.

Prophets were not confined to ancient Israel or Judah. Canaanite religion had its prophets too, as did the other religions of the ancient Near East. They came in various different forms but the phenomenon of these visionaries, charismatics and holy men and women who were in touch with the gods and through whom the gods spoke was widespread. The account of their antics around the altar on Mount Carmel is obviously written to ridicule the prophets of Baal and Asherah, but comparison of 1 Kings 18:26–29 with the story of Saul and the prophets of Gibeah reveals that both groups had much in common. It was not their methods, styles or organization that differentiated the prophets of the Lord from those of other gods. It was their theology and their God.

Verse 15 introduces us to a new version of the Lord's name not used in Kings so far—'the Lord of Hosts'—an ancient title which honours God either as Lord of the Israelite armies or, more likely, as the king of the heavenly host, which may be the heavenly beings that surround his throne or the sun, moon and stars.

Who is the real nuisance in Israel?

Ahab, completely oblivious of the true cause of the nation's suffering, accuses Elijah of bringing the drought upon them (v. 17). Elijah turns the name-calling back on to the king and spells out the root cause of the trouble (v. 18). The time has now come to see who is right, so Elijah instructs Ahab to set up a contest. Mount Carmel was very near the border with Tyre and would make the ideal place to teach Jezebel and her Baal a lesson.

A PRAYER

Give thanks to God for those who stand firm when persecuted for their faith, and for those who put their lives at risk to protect them.

ELIJAH & *the* PROPHETS *of* BAAL

Standing alone, Elijah challenges the 450 prophets of Baal to a public contest to decide who will be Israel's God—the Lord or Baal. Verses 20–40 must be one of the best-known scenes in the Old Testament. There is drama, colour, tension, action, humour and suspense; but we must not allow this to blind us to the seriousness of the point at issue. That is set out in verse 21. The people of God have to make a choice—not just those of Ahab's day, but all the people of God in every time and place.

Act II of the drama

Act II has six scenes:

Scene 1: Ahab assembles the prophets (v. 20).
Scene 2: Elijah issues the challenge (vv. 21–24).
Scene 3: The prophets of Baal attempt the challenge (vv. 25–29).
Scene 4: Elijah prepares his altar (vv. 30–35).
Scene 5: Elijah prays and successfully attempts the challenge (vv. 36–39).
Scene 6: Elijah kills the prophets of Baal (v. 40).

The prophets of Baal, despite their numbers and their frenzied religious zeal, are powerless. The translations of verse 26 make some interesting suggestions. The verb used is the one found in verse 21 and correctly translated there as 'limping' or 'wavering'. But in verse 26 an intensive form of it is used which denotes vigorous action, so NRSV's 'limped' is quite inadequate. NIV and GNB have 'dancing' but REB's 'dancing wildly' is best of all.

Verse 29 is interesting too. After midday Elijah leaves them to their 'ranting and raving' (GNB, REB), which NIV translates as 'frantic prophesying' while AV is best of all with 'prophesying'. They were only doing the sort of things that prophets did, though Israelite prophets would not have have cut themselves in their rituals because that was forbidden (Leviticus 19:28; Deuteronomy 14:1). This type of ecstatic behaviour is exactly what Saul was caught up in with the prophets at Gibeah (see also 1 Samuel 19:20–24).

Elijah calls the people over to watch him as he rebuilds the altar to the Lord which, presumably, Jezebel had desecrated. Mount Carmel had been one of the many 'high places' where the Lord was worshipped. He prepares his sacrifice and douses it with water, despite the continuing drought. His quiet prayer is answered. The contrast with the other prophets is deliberate.

'The Lord indeed is God!'

In verse 31, Elijah had reminded the Israelites about who they were. They were 'Israelites', members of the twelve tribes of the sons of Jacob. Had they forgotten why God had given him a new name? In verse 36, Elijah calls on the Lord and names him explicitly as the God of their ancestors Abraham, Isaac and Israel, using the third patriarch's new name of 'Israel'. We cannot be precise about the meaning of 'Israel' but Jacob had been given that new name because he had fought or struggled and won (see Genesis 32:27–28; 35:10). Here is a new struggle between God and his people.

The acclamation by the people in verse 39 is the climax of the drama. The assembled people acknowledge that the Lord, not Baal, is God.

Act III of the drama

Now that the main point is proved, Elijah informs Ahab that the rain is coming. He can go up from the wadi and eat. After Elijah's intense prayer (v. 42), the rain comes. Empowered by God ('the hand of the Lord was upon him'), Elijah runs before Ahab's chariot the 17 miles to the entrance of Jezreel (v. 46).

In all of this Ahab remains silent, as silent as the people had been at the beginning (v. 21). They have seen what he has seen and made their vocal response to it. His silence is ominous: when he does speak, it will be to Jezebel, and he will not say what the people have said (see 1 Kings 19:1).

A PRAYER

Read Psalm 100, which is a celebration psalm affirming that the Lord—the Lord alone—is God. Its theology matches this passage magnificently.

ELIJAH FLEES *from* JEZEBEL

Ahab had said nothing to Elijah after the defeat of the prophets of Baal on Mount Carmel, but when he speaks to Jezebel he holds nothing back. For him, however, the last word is not that the Lord proved himself to be the true God for Israel, but that Elijah had killed all Jezebel's prophets (v. 1).

Jezebel has been a threatening presence in the background since her name was first mentioned. Now she speaks for the first time and her threat sends a terrified Elijah fleeing south for his life (v. 3). If Ahab has told her that the Lord has been proved to be the true God, she has taken no notice of it. She still believes in the gods, swears on them that Elijah will die and sends a messenger to tell him so. Elijah might have championed the Lord's cause yesterday, but today he flees from Jezebel's anger and the oath she swears to her gods.

He arrives at Beer-sheba in the far south of Judah, 130 miles from Jezreel, leaves his servant there and travels on another ten miles into the wilderness. Empty and despairing, he wants to give up.

The angel of the Lord

As he sleeps, another messenger appears. This one is from the Lord and most translations have 'angel', though the word is the same one used for Jezebel's messenger. 'Angels' in the Old Testament are usually members of the 'heavenly host' sent to deliver a message, but they can be human messengers such as a prophet. Elijah has already been fed by ravens (1 Kings 17:6); now he is fed by this mysterious messenger from God.

The mountain and the cave

The parallel with Moses becomes clear in verse 8 when Elijah's destination is revealed. He is to journey to the holy mountain which the northerners called Horeb and the southerners called Sinai. The journey will take 'forty days', another symbolic figure rich in associations with the story of Moses (Exodus 24:18; Numbers 14:33–34).

Elijah arrives at Horeb and spends the night in a cave, another possible association with the Moses stories (see Exodus 33:22). Next day he hears the 'word of the Lord' again. The last time that the 'word of the Lord' had come to him, it had put him in this jeopardy by commanding him to confront Ahab (1 Kings 18:1). Now it asks him to account for himself (v. 9). He begins by summing up the nation's parlous state. 'They have forsaken God's covenant' (v. 10; see 1 Kings 11:11 where Solomon was accused of failing to keep God's covenant). Then he repeats what he has said before (1 Kings 18:18, 22). But notice what he doesn't say. There is not a word about the victory on Mount Carmel. Nor is there anything very personal. He doesn't say that he has run away because he was terrified.

Faithfulness and fear

There is something very human about Elijah in this story. We can feel for him and recognize bits of our experience in his. He has been faithful to God and has stood up for God at considerable risk and considerable cost. He has been exiled from home for several years. He has been hunted. He has done what has been asked of him, and mostly without question. He has known both exultation and despair. The way that the one follows the other so quickly in this passage should not surprise us; indeed, it shows that our storytellers knew their psychology. Despite all the positive things, he sums up his life as a failure. Notice how he has magnified Jezebel into a 'they' in verse 10. He has, sadly, no faith in the people who have just acclaimed that the Lord is God. Nor, even more sadly, is he capable any longer of trusting in the Lord in whom he was so confident so recently. He wants to die.

A PRAYER

Lord, sustain those today who know Elijah's despair.

The STILL, SMALL VOICE

If the scene on the top of Mount Carmel is one of the best-known pictures from Kings, its best-known phrase must be 'the still, small voice of calm', from the AV translation of verse 12 via John Greenleaf Whittier's famous hymn, 'Dear Lord and Father of mankind'. It is a splendid hymn, but the beauty and peace of its words have an undesirable side-effect. They lead us to sentimentalize this story of Elijah's meeting with God outside the cave by taking the phrase completely out of context. The same is true about how we usually use this reading in church. We read from verse 1 but rarely read beyond verse 14. If we do proceed beyond that verse, we see that the second thing that this still, small voice does is to instruct Elijah to stage a coup and arrange a massacre!

Elijah is instructed to go out of the cave, for God is about to pass by (shades of Exodus 33:17–23 here). Once outside, there is a terrible wind, an earthquake and a fire—though Mr Whittier puts them in a different order in his hymn to help his rhythm. Then there is the quiet. The wind and fire are good examples of 'theophany' language which elsewhere in the Old Testament speaks of the Lord appearing in a terrifying storm (for example, Exodus 19:16–20; Judges 5:4–5; Psalm 97:1–5). Here, however, he is not present in these terrifying sights but in what follows. Commentators puzzle over what the 'still, small voice' means but don't agree on its significance. Neither do the translations agree on how the Hebrew phrase should be translated. NRSV gives us 'a sound of sheer silence'. God, Elijah learns, can make himself known in various ways, but what is important is to listen and to obey.

New instructions

A voice repeats the question posed in verse 9 and Elijah makes the same answer, which is again ignored (v. 14). He is given a new commission, much as the servant of God who complains about his failures is ignored and given an even bigger task in Isaiah 49:3–6. The Lord instructs him to go home and to anoint two new kings and his own successor. They will purge the nation of the worship of Baal, and then Elijah will see that he is not alone as a faithful worshipper of the

Lord. The numbers are frightening: only 7000 men will remain alive, such has been the extent of the national apostasy under Ahab. Nothing like this purging in fact took place at the time, but after the Assyrians overran the nation in 722BC the Israelites as an ethnic and religious group virtually disappeared from history. The writers intend us to see that catastrophe as God's judgment on Ahab.

There are two other things to note here. Elijah is to anoint Hazael as the new king of Aram (Syria), an unprecedented thing for an Israelite prophet to do. It is, however, part of God's traditional method of working to use foreign nations to punish his own people when such correction is needed. Many examples of that can be seen in the cycles of stories in Judges (for example, Judges 3:12–14; 4:1–3; 6:1), and will be seen in the use to which he later puts the Assyrians (2 Kings 17:1–7; Isaiah 7:17; 10:5) and then the Babylonians (for example, 2 Kings 24:1–4). Secondly, this idea of a remnant of faithful people within the nation is an idea which will become increasingly important (see Amos 5:15; Isaiah 10:20).

The commissioning of Elisha

Verses 19–21 tell an odd story. Elijah carries out the third instruction first, and doesn't in fact carry out the first two at all. He leaves Elisha to do that. He commissions Elisha to be his successor by throwing his cloak over him. This may be another deliberate parallel with Moses, who appointed Joshua to succeed him (Deuteronomy 34:9). Elijah's enigmatic reply to Elisha's natural request to go home and say goodbye reminds us of Jesus and the would-be follower in Luke 9:59–60. The meal of boiled beef cooked over a fire of the wood of the oxen's yoke was a costly gesture. Elisha has 'burned his boats' and moves into a new future as he becomes Elijah's 'servant'.

A PRAYER

Speak through the earthquake, wind and fire,
O still small voice of calm.

John Greenleaf Whittier (1807–92)

BEN-HADAD LAYS SIEGE *to* SAMARIA

A Ben-hadad of Aram was mentioned in 1 Kings 15:18 where Asa of Judah bribed him to invade northern Israel to draw Baasha away from blockading Jerusalem. That one was probably the father of the king in this chapter. Here, Ben-hadad II gathers his army and 32 'kings' and beseiges Samaria (v. 1). At first Ahab is prepared to submit and pay tribute, but when Ben-hadad increases the terms he calls an assembly of elders who support him and encourage resistance (vv. 2–12). An unnamed prophet appears and tells Ahab that the Lord will give him victory. He must take the initiative and use the 'young men who serve the provincial governors' to lead the attack (vv. 13–15). These young men lead the small army of 7000 Israelites and they rout the Syrians, though Ben-hadad himself escapes (vv. 16–21). The prophet returns and warns Ahab that they will be back next spring (v. 22), which is exactly what Ben-hadad's officers are planning to do (vv. 23–25).

Out of place? Or not?

Some commentators point out that 1 Kings 20 interrupts the sequence of stories about Elijah. They also say that it feels quite out of place and seems to have little relation to what else is happening in the story. They note, too, that Jezebel is also completely absent here. They conclude that this was a story about Ahab which the Deuteronomic Historians wanted to include, so they took the opportunity offered by the mention of Aram in 1 Kings 19:15–17 to insert it at this point. Some add that their reason for wanting to include this story at all becomes clearer late in the chapter.

Much of this may be true, but there are at least three themes which are common to this chapter and the stories about Elijah. One is that the unnamed prophet of verse 13 points out that what will happen will happen so that Ahab will 'know' that the Lord is God; while in 1 Kings 18:36 Elijah prayed that the outcome of the contest on Mount Carmel would be such that it would be 'known' that the Lord was indeed God in Israel. The second theme is that in both stories the king is at odds with the prophets of the Lord. The third is that both stories end with Ahab facing God's punishment. In both stories too, the odds are stacked against Israel and Israel's God. Is there any significance in the fact that the figure of 7000 also features twice?

As it is, we can see the sad story of Ahab unfolding. Having learnt nothing from his confrontation with Elijah, will he learn anything from this victory over Aram and from this anonymous prophet who tries his best to encourage him?

Five details

The 32 'kings' of verse 1 are probably local tribal or town leaders. There is a possibility, however, that this passage contains a memory of the coalition of Canaanite states which fought the Assyrians at the Battle of Qarqar in 853BC. Records show that Ben-hadad and Ahab fought in that coalition, and it may be that Ahab fought as one of Ben-hadad's vassals.

Note the exchange in verses 10–11 where Ben-hadad's threat is countered by Ahab's 'Real soldiers boast after a battle, not before' (GNB). This is a very different Ahab from the one who hardly dared to face Elijah and whose wife seemed to be the real king of Israel.

The dialogue between Ahab and the prophet in verses 13–15 shows the same reluctance to believe as Moses had displayed in that scene at the burning bush which ought to be entitled, 'Here I am, send Aaron' (count his excuses for yourself in Exodus 3:1—4:17). The prophet insists that Ahab will know that the Lord is God by the coming victory.

In verses 23–25, the defeated Syrian officers are quick to make excuses and then to point the finger of blame. First, they rationalize their defeat theologically—somebody should have known that their lowland gods were at a disadvantage in the hills. Second, they remove the 'civilians' from control of the army and put in military personnel instead.

And finally, as a teetotaller, may I point out that twice now in Kings we have been alerted to the dangers of alcohol (here in verses 12 and 16 and previously in 1 Kings 16:9).

FOR REFLECTION

We should not be too quick to smile at the Arameans in verse 23. Although J.B. Phillips' famous little book, Your God is Too Small, *is now years out of print, its title can still give all of us food for thought.*

BEN-HADAD IS SPARED

The spring arrives and the expected campaign takes place. The Arameans attack in huge numbers and the odds, as ever, are stacked against the Israelites who only look like 'two little flocks of goats'. Another prophet tells Ahab, who from verse 13 to the end of the chapter is never named but always called by his title, that the Lord will give him victory. He also tells him why. It is so that Ahab will understand ('know') that the Lord is God, which he was also supposed to have learnt from the victory at Samaria (v. 13) and from the outcome of the contest on Mount Carmel (1 Kings 18:36–37). The Arameans are routed. The numbers are exaggerated as usual. The seven days of waiting and the city wall which falls down remind us of the battle of Jericho (see Joshua 6). The message ought to be clear to Ahab.

An act of mercy?

Ben-hadad escapes alive from the fighting but is trapped in the city (v. 30). Eventually, after checking everything out, he surrenders to Ahab and his appeal for clemency is granted (v. 34). In response to the very public submission of his officers and in return for significant concessions, Ahab lets him go. What the Arameans had heard about the kings of Israel had proved, in this instance at least, to be true.

Or of disobedience?

At verse 35 the Lord reappears in the story. He does not approve of Ahab's leniency—not at all. The message is conveyed to Ahab by another unnamed prophet following a dramatic gesture at the roadside. We readers are given the background, which involved two or possibly three prophets who were members of the same 'company' or 'guild'. Our sympathy goes out to the one who was killed by a lion, whose only offence was to refuse to hit his fellow prophet, but we have met a lion before (1 Kings 13:24–25, 28). Lions are obviously reminders that if you disobey God even with the best of motives, it is still disobedience. The second person told to hit the first prophet doesn't need telling twice.

Verses 35–42 are very difficult, but our difficulty doesn't lie with the fanciful nature of this incident, which is a dramatic piece of entertaining storytelling. Our difficulty lies with the underlying theology. Ahab is condemned because Ben-hadad's life was 'devoted to destruction', though he had not been explicitly told that this is a 'holy war' in which these terms apply. His life should have been 'put to the ban', destroyed as an offering to God (v. 42).

Ahab is guilty both of the sin of Achan, who had kept something for himself after the battle of Jericho which should have been totally destroyed in devotion to God (Joshua 7), and of the sin of King Saul, who had been too lenient with his defeated opponent, King Agag (1 Samuel 15:8–33). The prophet Samuel condemned Saul and 'hewed Agag in pieces before the Lord', and Joshua exposed Achan and punished him and his whole family. Readers of the longer story will therefore know what Ahab can expect and why his reaction was as it was.

'But I say to you...'

The end of the twentieth century brought the phrase 'ethnic cleansing' into our vocabulary, though the practice was an ancient one. 'Holy war' is also a phrase we sometimes hear. For the writers of Kings, both of these are acceptable ideas: doing these things demonstrates true commitment to God and brings honour to him. The teaching of Jesus in Matthew 5:44 that we should love our enemies and in 5:39 that we should 'turn the other cheek'—and that these are the actions which demonstrate real faith in God and bring true honour to him—must, however, be set against the Old Testament way of looking at things. Jesus recognizes that in the past God's people saw things differently, but that God's new word is the one that *he* speaks. According to Jesus, the voices of the prophets in this chapter are addressed to their day and age. God's new word is that we should love our enemies.

A PRAYER

Lord, help us to hear what you say to us through Jesus
and to live by it.

NABOTH'S VINEYARD

We have frequently noted that the writers of Kings focus their attention on the religious policies of the kings. In Study 37 we saw one of the main reasons why. Here we see the other. Religion, so they believed, was not a private matter unconnected with everyday life, because what people believed expressed itself in what they did and how they did it. The religious views of a king have public and practical repercussions.

Ancient Israel, so they taught, was not a society in which religion and politics could be kept separate, as some today insist they should be. It was a society in which, they believed, God's will and purpose were to be worked out in every part of life. It was essential, for them, to get the religious question right because values and lifestyle and, in the case of a king, public policy followed on from it. This story of Jezebel and Naboth illustrates exactly what was at stake. Jezebel and her Baal are such a threat because they bring alien values into Israelite society which threaten Israel's values and lifestyle.

A fair exchange?

Ahab's request in verse 2 seems perfectly reasonable. Naboth's reply in verse 3 indicates that it is not. There is more at stake here than an odd acre of vines.

Underlying this incident—and much of the tension in modern Israel too—is the fact that the land is one of the most potent symbols in Israel's religious faith. The Torah and the land are God's great gifts to his people, the twin pillars of his covenant with them. Abraham had left home to journey to a land of promise (Genesis 12:1; 17:8), Moses had guided his descendents to its borders and Joshua had led the Israelites into it to claim their 'inheritance' and 'inheritances' (Joshua 24:1–28; note especially vv. 13, 28). Throughout Deuteronomy it is emphasized that God has given them the land to 'possess'. Because this land was their special possession, there were rules for what could be done with it; and because Israel was a society of free people, there were rules to ensure that the land was safeguarded for everyone (see the 'Jubilee' law in Leviticus 25:8–12, the law of female inheritance in Numbers 27:5–11 and the law of 'levirate marriage' in

Deuteronomy 25:5–10). That is why Naboth reacts as he does.

There is other symbolism at work here too. Naboth has a 'vineyard'—is not Israel the Lord's vineyard (for example, Isaiah 3:13–15; 5:1–10)? Ahab wants to turn it into a 'vegetable garden' (v. 2). The only other time this phrase is used in the Old Testament is at Deuteronomy 11:10 where Egypt is called a 'vegetable garden' which has to be irrigated and slaved over, in contrast to the fertile land of Canaan which will be God's gift to his people. What is at stake is nothing less than a 'return to Egypt'.

Note the repetition in verse 4 of the two adjectives from 1 Kings 20:43. Naboth has no reason to fear the resentful and sullen Ahab. All he does is take to his bed and sulk. Once Jezebel's name is mentioned, the atmosphere changes completely.

Robbery with violence

Jezebel comes from a country where kings rule, not where they let ideas of accountability, equality and stewardship render them impotent. She cares nothing for this notion of 'ancestral inheritance', nor for the idea that kings must obey the laws of God. In her country the king speaks in the name of god. His word is law. She tells her faction among the leading citizens of Jezreel what to do and they do it. The ninth commandment against bearing false witness does not detain her for a moment (Exodus 20:16; Deuteronomy 5:20). Jezebel, as we have come to expect, has no respect for Israel's laws or its religion: her god does things differently. Naboth falls victim to a clash of ideologies.

When Jezebel tells Ahab what has happened, he makes no comment and does what he is told to do (vv. 15–16). There is no law giving the king the right to confiscate anyone's land in circumstances such as these, but Jezebel hardly needs one. She speaks to Ahab in the same language that God had used to speak to Joshua (compare v. 15 and Joshua 1:2): she is giving him that vineyard land to 'possess'. The contest for the soul of Israel is not over.

FOR PRAYER

Pray for today's victims of injustice.

46   1 KINGS 21:17–29

ELIJAH'S CURSE

Elijah, who has had no contact with Ahab and Jezebel since 1 Kings 19:3 and who has been absent from the scene since 1 Kings 19:21, reappears in the story and receives another command from God to go on a mission and to deliver a message (vv. 17–19). He is to meet Ahab in Naboth's vineyard and confront him with the atrocity that he has committed in order to stand where he is standing. Elijah is given two words to say. First, that Ahab has 'murdered' in order to 'possess' (v. 19). The first verb is the one used in the sixth commandment (Exodus 20:13; Deuteronomy 5:17). Ahab can add that one to the other five which he and his wife have broken. The second verb is the one used frequently in Deuteronomy about Israel 'possessing' the land of Canaan. Ahab has 'possessed' a fellow Israelite's 'possession'. The second word Elijah is given to say is that Ahab will die on the spot on which Naboth died (v. 19).

The confrontation takes place and the initial sparring reminds us of their encounter in 1 Kings 18:17. After the briefest opening shot from Ahab, Elijah launches into his condemnation. Ahab knows from whom he has come and on whose behalf he speaks, so there is no need for Elijah to preface his words with the usual, 'Thus says the Lord'. The Lord will bring the same total disaster upon Ahab's house that has already come on that of Jeroboam (1 Kings 14:11; 15:29–30) and Baasha (1 Kings 16:4, 11). In this case, however, the Lord has a special word for the queen too. She has been the cause of much of the evil that has been done, and she will die because of it.

Verses 25–26 read like part of the standard obituaries which the northern kings receive, noting that Ahab was, in fact, the worst of them all. Others had permitted or encouraged the use of idols in the worship of the Lord, or had permitted or promoted the worship of other gods. Ahab has been so bad that he is compared with the Amorites, one of the main ethnic groups occupying Canaan before the Israelites. The NRSV puts these verses in brackets and calls them an evaluation by the writer which breaks the connection between verses 24 and 27. That is not necessary. These verses serve to point out that Elijah's curse on Ahab and Jezebel is completely justified and to prepare for the unexpected turn of events in verses 27–29.

'Repentance' and 'forgiveness'

Most religions recognize a distinction between right and wrong and have ways of dealing with wrongdoing. These will include a variety of preventative measures and means to neutralize the power of evil. There will be ways to give a new start to those who see the error of their ways and a system of sanctions against those who do not.

Ahab, either because he recognizes the truth about himself in what Elijah says or because he is terrified by the sanctions about to come into force, 'humbles himself' before God. He is penitent and expresses his penitence in fasting and in wearing a sackcloth undershirt and sleeping between sackcloth sheets. Fasting and the use of sackcloth are two ways of expressing penitence for wrongdoing, but the final phrase in verse 27 indicates that something inward is required as well. The translations vary considerably but the point is that Ahab feels remorse or regret. He is sorry, though the phraseology in verse 29 rather suggests that Elijah needs to be convinced that this sorrow is genuine.

We are told that because of this repentance the threatened disaster will now take place in Ahab's son's reign instead of in his own. The punishment on Jeroboam and Baasha had not, in fact, taken effect in their lifetime but in that of their sons, but there is a precedent for Ahab actually being told this in the case of Solomon (1 Kings 11:12).

Some might wonder, however, why the disaster should now take place at all. Has not Ahab been forgiven? Does not forgiveness mean a new start with the slate wiped clean? The Deuteronomic response to that question would be to say that it is not as simple as that. We might answer the question by pointing out that acts have consequences and that for some forms of wrongdoing at least, although forgiveness can and does take away the guilt involved, it cannot take away the consequences. That is a hard lesson which Kings, in its own way, insists that we must learn.

A PRAYER

Lord, we thank you for new beginnings.
Grant us also the courage and strength
to live with the consequences of our past.

ISRAEL & JUDAH *in* ALLIANCE

The struggles between Elijah (and the Lord) and Jezebel (and Baal) for the soul of Israel have concentrated our attention on the house of Omri and the northern kingdom. 1 Kings 22 continues to focus on northern affairs, but in verse 2 the new king of Judah, Jehoshaphat—who had succeeded his father as long ago as 1 Kings 15:24—comes on the scene.

Israel and its northern neighbour, Aram/Syria, have enjoyed three years of peace, and the rumbling skirmishings and tensions between Israel and Judah appear also to have come to an end. Jehoshaphat visits Samaria, and Ahab proposes an alliance to reclaim the town of Ramoth-Gilead which Aram had annexed some years before and which Ben-hadad had not returned as he had promised (1 Kings 20:34). Jehoshaphat pledges his total support (v. 4).

Historical interlude

Historians suggest that this short period of 'peace' between these small squabbling states may have been due to the invasion of the Assyrians, the superpower from the north. This came to a stop at the battle of Qarqar in 853, an incident not mentioned in the Old Testament. Assyrian records show that they were opposed by an alliance of ten local states led by Aram, in which Ahab supplied over half of the 4000 chariots that took to the field, plus 10,000 of the 50,000 infantry. Even allowing for the customary exaggeration in such things, Ahab's role is impressive. The same records claim it as an Assyrian victory, but the alliance must have fought well enough because the Assyrians did not advance further into the region.

Seeking the will of the Lord

Verses 5–12 illustrate the role of prophets as political and military advisers, but note that it is Jehoshaphat who has to suggest to Ahab that, before any action is taken against Syria, it would be wise to see if it has the Lord's approval.

Ahab gathers 400 prophets together. This is the third time we have seen prophets in this number or one very like it, which rather suggests that '400' really means 'a large number'.

There are real difficulties here. Where do these 400 prophets of the Lord suddenly come from? Elijah—whose name is not mentioned at all in this major incident—had complained that he was the one loyal servant of the Lord left (1 Kings 19:10, 14), so are we to understand that these are 'false prophets'? But God had told Elijah that he wasn't the only one left (1 Kings 19:18), so are these part of the faithful remnant? As this incident unfolds, we see that one prophet is prepared to take a stand against the majority, so how do we decide between true and false prophecy? Last but by no means least, what are we to make of 'lying spirits' sent by God to deceive?

The fact that Jehoshaphat asks for a second opinion is significant (v. 7). Does he have sufficient of his great-great-grandad's wisdom to know that even equally sincere religious people can come to different conclusions? Is he simply weighing all the options and wanting to hear every side? Or does he suspect that these prophets are not the Lord's prophets at all? NRSV, NJPS and NJB are wrong to put 'Lord' in capitals in verse 6, for these other prophets speak in the name of the 'Lord', but not in the special name of the LORD, Israel's God. (Remember that in most English translations LORD, or occasionally LORD GOD, in capitals, represents the special divine name usually rendered as 'Yahweh'. 'Lord' or 'God' in lower-case letters translate the Hebrew terms for Lord or God, which is what we have in verse 6). Jehoshaphat has noticed an ambiguity which has escaped these modern translators, so he asks, 'Is there not a prophet of the LORD we can ask?'

The prophets assemble outdoors and begin their 'prophesying' in the square at the city's main gate just as the prophets of Baal did on Mount Carmel (the same word is used). The place is called a 'threshing floor' in many translations but that is inappropriate here: it is a bit like calling one of the parks in central London a 'village green'. Zedekiah's gesture in verse 11 is another example of the sort of prophetic action or drama we saw Ahijah perform (1 Kings 11:29–31). It is designed to reinforce the spoken message.

A PRAYER

Lord, at a time when many claim to speak and act in your name, grant us Jehoshaphat's caution and discernment.

MICAIAH ben IMLAH

Micaiah ben Imlah is the prophet who never has a good word to say to Ahab (22:8). The messenger the king has sent to fetch him tells him about what has happened and what has been said, and advises him (for everybody's sake?) to say the same. Micaiah is uncompromising (vv. 13–14).

When they meet, Ahab asks him a direct question but Micaiah spars with him until finally he tells Ahab what he has really seen— Israel is a leaderless army, scattered like sheep without a shepherd. This vivid metaphor is also used in Numbers 27:17, Ezekiel 34:5 and Zechariah 13:7, and in the Gospels, in Mark 6:34 and 14:27 and parallels. Ezekiel 34 uses the picture of the king as shepherd to launch a devasting attack on the later kings of Judah and to express a hope for a new shepherd like David. Ahab's response is to turn to Jehoshaphat and say, 'I told you so' (v. 18).

Micaiah then reports that in his vision he had seen the Lord seated on a throne surrounded by the 'host of heaven'. This is a similar picture to the familiar one in Isaiah 6, though there the heavenly council is gathered in worship and here it is gathered for debate. We also find this picture in Psalm 82 and Job 1—2 and it lies behind the 'us' in Genesis 1:26. The various members of this heavenly council are 'seraphs' in Isaiah, 'gods' in Psalm 82 and 'sons of God' or 'heavenly beings' in Job, one of whom was the 'Satan' (the Adversary, the Accuser). Angels belong here too. In Micaiah's vision of this 'heavenly host', the key role is played by a 'spirit'. Later writings develop this scenario with gusto, producing graphic descriptions of the different heavenly beings, often in great detail (for example, Revelation 4:6–11; 5:6–14). These imaginative depictions need not cause us any difficulty. They remind us that reality is infinitely more complex than the human mind can recognize, describe or define. They are an attempt to recognize that there are dimensions of reality away and above those in which we live and which defy description. We shall return to this in Study 60 when we read 2 Kings 6:1–19. Whatever we do, we must not let our impoverished Western imaginations limit us here.

A lying spirit from God

Micaiah explains how these other prophets have spoken as they have. He refers to them as 'these your prophets' (v. 23) and it is not clear whether he accepts them as genuine prophets of the Lord. He explains that they have deceived Ahab because God had 'put a lying spirit' into them so that his judgment on Ahab could take effect.

The scene is a session of the heavenly council. The item on the agenda is how Ahab is to meet his end. There is no doubt about his end: he has brought that upon himself by his wrong choices and, in good Deuteronomic theology, he must reap what he has sown. The only question is how and when. God had already delayed his end when Ahab recognized the error of his ways (1 Kings 21:29) but it has to come sometime. God has decided that it will happen at Ramoth-gilead, but the question is how to get Ahab there. Various possibilities are discussed, until one of the members of the council makes the suggestion that Ahab can be enticed to Ramoth-gilead if his prophets tell him to go. The Lord recognizes the merit of this suggestion and tells the one who made it to go ahead. But why is Micaiah putting the whole plan in jeopardy by spilling the beans? Then we recognize that Micaiah is God's fall-back strategy. God knows that if Micaiah tells Ahab not to go, Ahab is all the more sure to go. The total plan is foolproof.

Micaiah's explanation of his vision leads to a confrontation with Zedekiah, followed by his imprisonment until Ahab should return safely. He insists both to the king and the crowd that that is the acid test. They will see which prophets have been speaking the truth from God by whether or not Ahab does return (vv. 24–28).

Micaiah insists on telling the truth, no matter what it costs. Doing so puts him in prison on reduced rations of bread and water. Integrity has a cost.

A PRAYER

Lord, at a time when words are cheap and image counts for much, grant us Micaiah's integrity.

49 1 KINGS 22:29-40

The END *of* KING AHAB

The battle for Ramoth-gilead

Why does Ahab insist on disguising himself? Is he worried that perhaps Micaiah was right after all? But does he think a disguise can outwit the Lord? The king of Aram is not named here and neither is the king of Israel. Jehoshaphat of Judah is, but his part in events is quite marginal. The Arameans, who have re-equipped the 32 units of their army since their defeat at Aphek, are only looking for the king of Israel. They find him and they kill him, but it is not their doing. Ahab's disguise did work. The Arameans did not recognize him, but that did not save him. He was shot by a bowman who did not know who he was. Some might call it a lucky shot at that, finding its way through the armour as it did. Readers know, however, that Ahab was doomed as soon as he 'went up to Ramoth-gilead' (v. 29).

He bleeds to death, and even in his death there is an ambiguity about the way Ahab is presented to us. He commands his driver to take him off the battlefield, but he stays all day, propped up in his chariot. Is he a coward or is he brave?

The battle ends at sunset when the Israelites realize that their king is dead. Micaiah's words about everyone returning home leaderless have been proved true.

Obituary

Ahab gets a fuller obituary than usual (v. 39). Mention is made of his splendid ivory palace. Excavations at Samaria, Hazor and Megiddo have revealed examples of ivory inlay on major buildings, much of which appears to date from Ahab's time (compare 1 Kings 10:22; Amos 3:15; 6:4; Psalm 45:8).

Ahab died at Ramoth-gilead and the dogs licked his blood in Samaria. The announcement in 1 Kings 21:19 had been that this would happen in Naboth's vineyard in Jezreel. That will happen to Ahab's son (2 Kings 9:25-26).

The reference in verse 38 to the prostitutes washing themselves in Ahab's blood is curious. Nothing has been said to lead us to expect anything like this and it is not clear what it means. Perhaps the clue

114

is to be found in Deuteronomy 23:17–18 which condemns both female and male temple prostitutes and refers to the male ones as 'dogs'. Among his other failings, Ahab had encouraged this kind of religious practice in the temples and this verse, rather obscurely to us, shows the writer's abhorrence of it.

The main point, however, is that his fate was as it had been announced by the prophets. It was 'according to the word of the Lord' (v. 38). The simple and basic Deuteronomic viewpoint is being reinforced all the time as we read through the lives of these kings: death and disaster do not happen by chance but by choice. If the nation chooses wrongly, it must face the inevitable consequences of that wrong choice.

Ahab is dead. More space has been given to his reign than to any king since Solomon, and it is not hard to see why. Ahab has been, in two ways at least, a repeat of Solomon. Two of Solomon's failings have been duplicated in Ahab and one of the two has been magnified. 1 Kings 11:1–4 pointed out how Solomon's many foreign wives had led him astray. Ahab had only one foreign wife, Jezebel, but she had not only led him astray, she had also dominated the kingdom and imposed her alien religion and ideology upon it. Or at least she had tried to, and, had it not been for Elijah, she might have succeeded. That story has been told at length because its application is timeless. Israel's true religion has a unique set of values inherent in it and they must not be compromised. If they are, society falls apart, then as now. The other comparison between Solomon and Ahab is that they were both builders (v. 39) and that they both built to display their wealth. With Ahab, as with Solomon and with us, wealth contains an insidious threat to the core values of faith.

A PRAYER

Lord, may the legacy our lives leave behind bring glory to you and blessing to others.

TWO KINGS

Jehoshaphat of Judah (874–850)

Judah appears centre stage here for the first time since 1 Kings 15:24. The long reigns of Asa and Jehoshaphat have been uneventful, entirely without the dramas and traumas that Israel has experienced.

Verses 47–49 are a curious jumble of detail. Solomon had lost control of Edom (1 Kings 11:14–25) but it had apparently been regained by one of his successors and was still subject to Judah at this time—it would gain independence in the reign of Jehoshaphat's son (see 2 Kings 8:22). A change in the verse division and in a detail of the Hebrew enables REB and GNB to say that Jehoshaphat appointed the deputy or viceroy (the word is the one used for Solomon's local governors in 1 Kings 4:5). The attempt to renew Solomon's trading enterprise is shipwrecked (see 1 Kings 10:11–12, 22) and Jehoshaphat refuses to let Israel join the enterprise. No reason is given.

Jehoshaphat receives the same general note of approval as his father had done. The removal of the remainder of the male temple prostitutes indicates that he had been continuing his father's firm line on local Canaanite religious practices (see 1 Kings 15:12), in contrast to Ahab in the north who had been actively promoting them. He had done little, however, to centralize the worship of the Lord, and the 'high places', regarded as centres of corrupt and syncretistic worship, still flourished.

Ahaziah of Israel (854–853)

Ahaziah's short reign is discussed briefly and dismissed immediately in verses 51–53. Not only does he continue the utterly wrong forms of the worship of the Lord which Jeroboam had introduced, but he also serves and worships Baal, as Ahab and Jezebel had done. Note the addition of 'and mother' in this case in verse 52. We are not allowed to forget the influence of Jezebel. She is still on the scene and we must wait until 2 Kings 9 before we see her fate.

Contrast

The contrast between these two kings and their two kingdoms is seen if you put verses 43 and 52 side by side. Both kings 'walked in the way' of their forebears but the one 'did what was right in the eyes of the Lord' and the other 'did evil in the sight of the Lord'. Here again is the basic Deuteronomic metaphor of 'walking' and the choice of going in two different directions.

End of Part One

Although the break between the two volumes of Kings is entirely artificial, it exists and provides us with a moment to stop and recap.

1 Kings began with the aged David and the intrigues which led to Solomon becoming king after him. Solomon's reign saw the proper unification of the nation, the building of the temple and Israel recognized as a powerful, prosperous and significant nation in the region. At the same time, we also saw that this monarchy was failing in exactly the way that Deuteronomy 17:14–20 warned that monarchy would fail. On Solomon's death, the opportunity to put things right was not taken and the kingdom was divided into two feuding parts. In the south, Judah preserved the Davidic monarchy and with it a measure of stability and of faithfulness to David's God. In the north, the more powerful and prosperous Israel was ruled by a succession of dynasties which seized power in bloody coups and which continued the worst side of Solomon's dallying with other religions, despite all the efforts of the prophets sent to warn them.

There is no hiding the viewpoint of the storytellers. Suspicious of monarchy in general, they are emphatically opposed to the northern kings, because these kings maintain Israel's corrupt religious practices centred on the golden calves at Dan and Bethel and, worse still, actively promote the worship of Baal. The storytellers' verdicts on each reign have become monotonously predictable and, unless there is a major change of heart on the part of Israel's kings, we can see that the future is looking bleak.

A PRAYER

Lord, as we reach this point in a story which is turning into a tragedy, help us to reflect on its lessons for our life and faith.

ELIJAH & *the* DEATH *of* AHAZIAH

Ahaziah's life had been summed up in 1 Kings 22:53. The consequences of serving Baal and provoking the Lord to anger are given in detail in this chapter, where Elijah appears again.

The chapter begins, however, on a different note. Without any introduction, verse 1 notes the rebellion of Moab on the death of Ahab. No further comment is made about this until 3:4. It may be that here again we are invited to see a north/south contrast. The faithful south retains control of Edom; the unfaithful north loses control of Moab. The consequences of Ahab's apostasy are not merely personal but also national.

Ahaziah is a minor figure among Israel's kings, yet his death is treated at great length. He has fallen off the balcony in his palace and lies injured. He sends messengers to seek an oracle from Baal-zebub, the god of Ekron, to find out if he will recover (vv. 2–4).

Baal-zebub is mentioned in the Bible only here. He is referred to as the local deity of the Philistine city of Ekron. 'Baal-zebub' can be translated as 'lord of the flies' (as used by William Golding in the title of his book), a 'fly-god' with the power to send or avert plagues. The footnote in NJB suggests that the name is a mocking pun on the god's real name which was Baal-Zebul (Baal the Prince). This name is known from the Ras Shamra texts as the principal god of Syria and is found also in the New Testament (Matthew 10:25; Mark 3:22 and parallels, especially Luke 11:14–23). If this is correct, he would have been widely worshipped in the western Mediterranean area, and Ekron would have been the site of one of many shrines to him.

Nothing so blatant has happened before. Jeroboam might have sent his wife in disguise but at least he wanted to consult an Israelite prophet about his son's prospects for recovery (1 Kings 14:1–18). Things must be bad for a king of Israel to send to one of the Philistine states for a decision from one of their gods—so bad that Elijah reappears, commanded by an angel, and sends the king's messengers back with a message that is repeated three times in the chapter (vv. 3–4, 6, 16). From the description, Ahaziah recognizes Elijah (just as readers of the New Testament are expected to see John the Baptist as the new Elijah from the mention of his leather belt in the description in Mark 1:6 and Matthew 3:4). Quite what Elijah was wearing is not, however, entirely clear. Was it a leather belt (as in most translations) or a leather loincloth (NJB)? NRSV says that he was 'hairy', which can mean either that he had long hair and a beard or that he was wearing a coat of hair or a cloak of animal skin. Zechariah 13:4 suggests that such a coat was a kind of uniform for prophets.

The king sends troops to arrest Elijah who is 'sitting on the top of a hill' (v. 9). That tells us immediately how to read what follows. This is another confrontation between the Lord and Baal like that on the last hilltop in 1 Kings 18. Sure enough, 'fire' comes down from heaven and 'consumes' the soldiers. Three platoons of soldiers are sent in all. The first captain had made a request to Elijah, the second issues a command and, sensibly, the third is very careful how he pleads with Elijah to meet the king. There is a play on words in these exchanges: 'man of God' is *'ish 'elohim* and 'fire of God' is *'esh 'elohim* (v. 12).

Elijah, obedient to the divine messenger again, goes to Ahaziah and repeats his message. Verse 17 pointedly follows verse 16 without a pause. The Deuteronomic Historians cannot make their point any plainer.

Ahaziah has died childless, so is succeeded by his brother Jehoram (who is not to be confused with Jehoram son of Jehoshaphat, who has just succeeded his father on the throne of Judah). The dating in verse 17 cannot be synchronized with the dating in 3:1. This leads those commentators who are interested in such details to say either that verse 17 has got it wrong (and/or that it is a later insertion) or that there was a co-regency between Jehoshaphat and his son for a year or two.

FOR REFLECTION

What does the Lord have to do to convince Ahab and his house?

ELIJAH IS TAKEN UP *into* HEAVEN

2 Kings 2—9 and 13 is a cycle of stories about the prophet Elisha, who is Elijah's nominated successor, and chapter 2 deals with the handover from the one to the other. The Elijah stories focused on the battle between Elijah and Jezebel for the soul of the nation, but these stories range more widely. There is another significant difference too. The element of the dramatic, the supernatural and the miraculous which was present in many of the Elijah stories is much more prominent in the stories about his successor, as we see immediately in verse 1, which introduces the story of Elijah being 'taken up to heaven by a whirlwind'.

Farewells

Elijah would have preferred to have made his farewell journey alone but Elisha insists on accompanying him. The itinerary is curious. They travel from Gilgal, the ancient sanctuary near Jericho where Joshua had celebrated the crossing of the Jordan (Joshua 4:19–24), up (not 'down') to Bethel, then back to Jericho and down to the Jordan. In Bethel and Jericho, Elisha is met by the official prophets who give him the same message—that his master will be taken away that day. Fifty of the prophets from Gilgal meet them at Jericho to go with them to watch—fifty supporters in contrast to the fifty soldiers sent to arrest Elijah in the previous chapter (v. 7).

Elijah and Elisha arrive at the Jordan and Elijah parts its waters, just as Moses had done with those of the Reed Sea and Joshua had done with the waters of the Jordan here or hereabouts (Exodus 14:21–31; Joshua 3). Those watching and those reading are to get the message about Elijah's status and authority. That status is clearly seen in the transfiguration scene in the Gospels (Mark 9:2–8 and parallels) where Moses and Elijah appear together.

As the time is drawing near, Elijah offers Elisha a last request (v. 9). Elisha asks for the share that by law a firstborn son would inherit from his father (Deuteronomy 21:17), a 'double share' of Elijah's spirit or power. The purpose of the story is not simply to authenticate Elijah as the greatest prophet since Moses, it is also to authenticate Elisha as his successor as 1 Kings 19:19–21 had designated him to be. As Joshua was Moses' chosen successor, so is Elisha to Elijah.

Elisha's leadership has been earned. He has served his apprentice-ship to his predecessor and proved his worth to succeed his master as the recognized leader of the prophets of Israel. That leadership, however, is not simply taken or assumed. It is formally handed over and God's part in the process is not forgotten. Called to this task, Elisha is both recognized and equipped for it.

The chariot and the whirlwind

Elijah is taken up to heaven, ascending in a whirlwind, with a chariot and horses of fire (we will return to these in Study 60 when we look at 2 Kings 6:17). For another powerful picture of a heavenly chariot, see Ezekiel's commissioning vision in Ezekiel 1.

Elijah does not share the usual fate of mortals, good and bad, which was to die and be gathered to their ancestors in the grave. Remember that there is no belief in life after death at this time in the development of Israel's faith—that came later. Instead he is taken up alive into heaven, as only Enoch had been before (Genesis 5:24). This gave rise to the expectation that Elijah would return (see Malachi 4:5; Mark 9:11 and parallels). To this day, a vacant seat is kept ready for him at every Passover meal.

Elisha's exclamation in verse 12 is difficult. It is repeated at 2 Kings 13:14 where the distraught king uses it about the dying Elisha. NRSV is typical of most modern translations with 'Father, father! The chariots of Israel and its horsemen', which follows the Hebrew closely even though the resulting expression makes little sense. Is it that Elisha sees the heavenly army coming to collect his master? GNB offers something different with 'My father, my father! Mighty defender of Israel! You are gone!' which takes the phrase about chariots and horsemen to be an exclamation depicting Elijah as the great defender of Israel's faith.

A PRAYER

Pray for those called to leadership among God's people today, that in their many responsibilities they may be strengthened and equipped by God's Spirit.

ELISHA & HIS MIRACLES

Elisha is recognized as Elijah's successor

Elisha picks up Elijah's dropped mantle, calls on the Lord in the name of Elijah and the river parts for him too. The onlooking prophets accept this as proof that he is Elijah's successor, but still want to mount a search for Elijah just in case. They seek him but do not find him, just as Elisha had said it would be (vv. 16–18).

Elisha is now recognized as the leader of the official prophets (note v. 15 and the reference to 'servants' in v. 16). We have met these groups or companies of prophets attached to local sanctuaries before, and there have been suggestions that they are not all that they might be. Here there is no indication that these prophets, even those from Bethel, are anything other than true prophets of the Lord or that they are in any way suspect.

Two miracles

The local people bring their problem to the new prophet and he solves it by a miracle. The same word is used in verses 19 and 21, which some translations render by 'unproductive' or 'sterile' and others by 'miscarriage'. There is more to it than that, however, for this city is Jericho, cursed by Joshua (Joshua 6:26) and the site of Hiel's evil sacrifices (1 Kings 16:34). Elisha, in the name of the Lord, is offering new beginnings. The people of Bethel are treated to a much less edifying proof of the power of Elisha's words (vv. 23–24). He has the power to bless or curse, just as everyone has the power to choose between good and evil. He revisits the scene of Elijah's greatest triumph and then 'returns to Samaria'. We wait to see how he will deal with what he finds in the capital.

The miraculous

We have read much about the supernatural in Kings so far—from encounters with angels (1 Kings 13:18; 19:5, 7; 2 Kings 1:3, 15) to the divine presence filling the temple (1 Kings 8:10–11). We have also read some miracle stories, particularly in the narratives about Elijah (1 Kings 17:16, 21–24; 18:37–39; 2 Kings 1:10). In the longer story, the drama of Moses and the exodus, in particular, was punctuated with miracle. It is clear that to all who wrote about them they were momentous, never-to-be-forgotten times. The miracles in those stories impress upon the reader the importance of those events and illustrate the fact that Israel owes everything to the power and generosity of God. To put it another way, the real miracle is not that God parted the waters of the Reed Sea but that he chose, protected and brought Israel to free nationhood. The miraculous stories in 2 Kings 2:1–12 can be understood in the same way. They also impress upon us the importance of Elijah and illustrate the fact that his life and ministry were the work of Israel's true God.

The element of the miraculous increases in the stories of Elisha, although we sometimes seek in vain to see anything of deeper meaning and purpose behind these stories in which the storytellers seem to delight. It is hard to see the incident of the bears in this chapter, for example, as bringing credit on either this prophet or his God.

Miracles used to be seen as one of the most important proofs that the Bible's message was true, but to many people they are an obstacle to belief rather than an asset. Some commentators spend much effort in insisting that these miracles happened, others in showing that they could not have done; while others still offer 'explanations'. These are important questions and discussion of them needs to go on. All commentators agree, however, that miracle stories are important in themselves. Telling such stories testifies to a fundamental conviction that life and faith depend on God. The two miracle stories here show that. The first reminds Elisha's contemporaries that their land is a gift from God who parted the waters for them. The second shows them that God's purposes for them are life and health and that every victory of life over death is to be seen as his gift.

A PRAYER

*Give thanks to God for his generous and sustaining love
at the heart of all life and faith.*

MOAB REBELS

Jehoram of Israel (853–842)

2 Kings 3:1 returns to the analysis of the reigns of the kings. Without melting down the golden bulls at Dan and Bethel, there is nothing Jehoram (who is called 'Joram' in NIV and GNB) could do to avoid the accusation of continuing in the evil ways of Jeroboam. It is noted to his credit, however, that he did remove the 'pillar of Baal' that Ahab and Jezebel had erected and Ahaziah had left in place (v. 2).

Moab rebels

Verses 4–27 tell of Israel's ineffective response to Moab's rebellion mentioned in 2 Kings 1:1. Ahab had supported Jehoshaphat of Judah against Aram at the cost of his life (1 Kings 22). Jehoram of Israel now asks for Jehoshaphat's support against Moab. It is given in the same words as Ahab's had been (compare v. 7 and 1 Kings 22:4).

The decision is made to march south into Judah, east into Edom and then north to attack the south-eastern border of Moab. Edom is still subject to Judah so the support of Edom's king can be commanded. They find themselves in the wilderness without water, and complain, exactly as their ancestors had done (Exodus 17:1–3). Again it is Jehoshaphat who suggests that a prophet of the Lord should be consulted (v. 11), as he had in 1 Kings 22:5. And it is a servant or 'officer' who has to enlighten Jehoram that Elisha is with them. So Elisha enters the frame as a new Moses. The three kings have to go to him!

The Moabite Stone

In 1868 an inscribed stone was found on the site of Dibon, thirteen miles east of the Dead Sea. Now in the Louvre in Paris, it gives Mesha's version of these times.

> I am Mesha, son of the god Chemosh, king of Moab... I made this high place for Chemosh at Qrchh... for he saved me from all the kings and let me see my desire upon my adversaries. Omri, king of Israel, oppressed Moab for many days, for Chemosh was angry with his land. And his son succeeded him and he too said, 'I will oppress Moab.' ...

> Omri had taken possession of the land of Medeba and Israel dwelt in it
> in his days and half the days of his son... but I fought against it and took
> it and slew the people of the town, a spectacle for Chemosh and Moab. And
> I brought back from there the altar-hearth of David and I dragged it before
> Chemosh at Qeriyoth...
>
> And Chemosh said to me, 'Go, take Nebo from Israel.' And I went by
> night and fought against it from dawn till noon, and I took it and slew all:
> seven thousand men, boys, women, girls and female slaves, for I had conse-
> crated it to Ashtar-Chemosh...
>
> And the king of Israel had built Jahaz and he dwelt in it while fighting
> against me: but Chemosh drove him out before me...

Apart from the intrinsic interest of this ancient inscription, I quote it
because it is interesting to compare its outlook with that of Kings
itself. There are, on the one hand, striking similarities. Mesha's explanation for Israel's long dominion over Moab is that Chemosh, the god
of Moab, has been angry with his land. Kings will explain the exile in
587 in precisely the same way. Mesha speaks of Chemosh fighting for
Moab, just as Kings ascribes some of the victories it reports as due to
the Lord fighting for Israel. Finally, the practice of 'consecrating' the
people captured at Nebo is exactly the one which the unnamed
prophet in 1 Kings 20:42 complained that Ahab had failed to do.
There is, on the other hand, one clear and major difference. No king
of Israel or Judah, however bad, would call themselves a son of God.

These similarities should not surprise us, for the people of Israel and
Judah began on their pilgrimage of faith with the same worldview as
their neighbours. The differences should not surprise us either, for by
the guidance of God's Spirit they came to see things radically differently. The writers of Kings still had much in common with the theolo-
gians of their neighbouring faiths, as we see from the Moabite Stone,
but they were already moving in a different direction which would lead
to the belief in one God so beautifully expressed by the anonymous
prophet of the exile whose words are preserved in Isaiah 40—55.

FOR PRAYER

*The anonymous 'servant' in verse 11 is the first of several such
people who play important roles in these stories. Give thanks to
God for such faithful people, then and now.*

ISRAEL WITHDRAWS

Elisha is consulted

Elisha is the leading Israelite prophet from Samaria (2 Kings 2:25) but Jehoram had not even known that he was accompanying them. It was the king of Judah who, albeit belatedly, suggested that they seek the Lord's guidance via a prophet and it was Jehoshaphat who recognized Elisha as a true prophet of the Lord as soon as his name was mentioned (v. 12). It is not surprising, therefore, that when Jehoram and Elisha meet, the conversation is strained. Elisha only co-operates at all for Jehoshaphat's sake.

Elisha calls for a musician, and under the influence of the music is overcome by the 'power (or 'hand') of the Lord'. This is the second of only two instances in the Old Testament where music is used to induce a trance in which a prophet can see or hear the message of God. The other involved Saul and the prophets from Gibeah (see 1 Samuel 10:1–13). Elisha receives two messages from God. The first is a mere trifle (v. 18). The nearby wadi will soon be full of water (v. 17, NRSV) or they must dig ditches ready to be filled (as in some other translations). The second is that they will be victorious over Moab. Next day, at the time of the morning offering, the wadi is as full of water as Elijah's trenches had been on Mount Carmel at the time of the evening offering.

A victory?

The scene moves immediately to the Moabites massed on their border ready to repel the invasion (vv. 21–23). The water, provided by the Lord to save the Israelites, contributes directly to the rout of the Moabites. The Israelites are coming from the south-east or east, and the reflection of the rising sun on the water makes it look like blood on the ground. There is a play on words in the Hebrew here— 'Edom' and the Hebrew term for 'red' are very similar words (for the country was named after the colour of its red soil), and the word for blood is *dam*.

The invading troops pursue the Moabites and employ a scorched-earth policy. Spoiling the best fields with stones (v. 25) is curious: it would take as much effort for the coalition to do that as it would for the Moabites to undo it later. Even these ancient writers recognized the importance of trees, for in Deuteronomy 20:19–20 they were expressly forbidden to cut down trees when they invaded the promised land. It is for the same reason that they are commanded to do it in Moab. The land is to be devastated.

The battle halts at the walls of the capital, Kirhareseth. The coalition's slingers are brought into action and the Moabites make a desperate sortie, either against the Edomite troops, who they may have seen as their enemies' weakest link, or to go for help to the king of Aram. The words for Edom and Aram are very similar in Hebrew and only one small change makes 'Aram' possible. For the king to lead a desperate sortie against the Edomite troops looks much more likely as a battle tactic. Neither slingers nor swordsmen are successful.

In desperation, Mesha offers his firstborn son as a sacifice in full view of the besieging army (vv. 26–27). Human sacrifice is not unknown in the Old Testament, though it is forbidden in Deuteronomy 18:10, where it is included in a list of the evil practices of their new neighbours which they are not to copy when they enter the promised land. The same point is made in the difficult story of Abraham and Isaac in Genesis 22. It was the fate of Jephthah's daughter (Judges 11:30–39) and of the sons of two later kings of Judah, Ahaz (2 Kings 16:3) and Manasseh (2 Kings 21:6), as well as the two children of Hiel (1 Kings 16:34).

The reaction of the Israelites to Mesha's human sacrifice can be understood in a variety of ways. NRSV gives a literal translation: 'great wrath came upon Israel'. Other translations interpret this to mean that the Israelites were very frightened by what Mesha did, or that there was 'great consternation' among the Israelites. The Greek version speaks of great repentance or regret coming on Israel. NIV sees it differently, that there was great 'fury against Israel', though whether this is from the Lord or from the Moabites or their god is not clear. What is clear is that the coalition disbands and that Moab's rebellion is not ended.

PRAYER

Lord, your gift of faith is intended to make us sane and humane.
Forgive our abuses of it, ancient or modern,
which make us less of both.

A CHAPTER *of* MIRACLES (I)

2 Kings 4 is an 'interlude of miracles' in which Elijah performs four miracles, each one to do with helping people through a crisis.

The prophet's widow

One of the ways in which Elisha differs from his predecessor is that Elijah usually acted alone whereas Elisha often operates with the members of the prophetic guilds who are associated with the different local sanctuaries. The widow of one such prophet appeals to Elisha for help (vv. 1–7). She is in debt and, as the law permits, because she cannot pay her debts her creditor has come to claim her two children as slaves in payment instead. The main ground for appeal to Elisha is that her husband had been a true prophet of the Lord. Elisha solves her problem in a similar way to that in which Elijah had helped the widow and her son in Zarephath to survive (1 Kings 17:14–16).

In verse 1, NRSV renders the Hebrew literally and says that her dead husband had 'feared the Lord'. We might say that he had been 'genuinely religious'.

Slaves/slavery is one of those things which both Testaments of the Bible take completely for granted, as did almost every culture in the ancient world. Our understanding of slavery has been shaped significantly by the slave trade from Africa to the Americas in the 17th and 18th centuries. No doubt that kind of slavery existed in the ancient world too, especially where slaves were taken in war. There were, however, other forms of slavery which were much less traumatic, and most slaves in ancient Israel would have been domestic slaves, living and working as the lowest members of an extended family. The Old Testament contains regulations for slavery as it does for many other aspects of life, and these regulations make a distinction between Israelite slaves and foreign slaves. Israelites could not be enslaved for life, unless they were born in slavery or voluntarily offered themselves in certain circumstances (see Exodus 21:1–11; Deuteronomy 15:12–18; Leviticus 25:39–46). Whether the provisions for release after six years ever worked in practice is an open question (on that, see Jeremiah 34:8–16). Debt was, as with this widow, one of the main reasons for Israelites becoming slaves.

The wealthy Shunammite woman

The parallel between Elisha bringing the wealthy Shunammite woman's only son back from the dead (vv. 8–37) and Elijah doing the same for the widow of Zarephath is obvious (see 1 Kings 17:17–24), but the Elisha story is considerably longer. It also has links with a number of other Old Testament themes, not least that of the elderly childless couple conceiving a son in their old age (Sarah and Abraham, the unnamed wife and Manoah, Hannah and Elkanah and, in the New Testament, Elizabeth and Zechariah). The phrase 'in due time' in verses 16 and 17 makes a clear link with the story of Sarah in Genesis 18:10 and 14.

The wealthy woman of Shunem—the town from which Abishag had come (1 Kings 1:1–4)—first provides hospitality for Elisha as he passes through the town and then extends this hospitality into the provision of an overnight room, built on the flat roof of the house. She does not simply honour him as a prophet (a 'man of God') but recognizes that he is a particularly special or important prophet ('holy'). That may explain why Elisha communicates with her via Gehazi. There are other curious elements in verses 12–16. What exactly is Elisha offering to do for her? Her reply about living among her own people probably means that she has everything she needs. She is happy and secure as she is. Notice that these verses take Elisha's authority and influence with the king and the army for granted.

Gehazi offers a suggestion to which Elisha responds positively, but the woman is sceptical. What Elisha had said, however, takes place (v. 17).

FOR REFLECTION

Gehazi is only a minor character in the story,
but he is the one who sees the heartache under the rich woman's
'I have everything I want.'

A Chapter *of* Miracles (II)

The child and his mother

The story in verses 18–37 poses few difficulties. The woman does not tell her husband that their young son is dead, and brushes aside his surprise that she is going to see a prophet on such an ordinary day. Likewise she brushes aside Gehazi's questions. The death is to be kept secret until the prophet is told. Perhaps he can do something. The woman who had previously kept a respectful distance from the holy prophet now falls before him, grabs his legs and insists that he must go with her. As Moses had performed miracles with his staff (see Exodus 4:1–4; 17:8–13), so Gehazi is despatched with all speed with Elisha's staff. It fails to have the desired effect. Verse 31 is terse: 'There was no sound or response' (NIV), as in 1 Kings 18:29. Gehazi is as ineffective as the prophets of Baal had been. Elisha arrives and, accompanied only by his servant, he prays and lies on the boy, repeating his action seven times. The posture is the one Elijah had adopted on Mount Carmel while waiting for the rain (1 Kings 18:42). There is silence when the Shunammite woman receives her son back, just as there had been when Elisha had spoken of his conception.

Hungry prophets

Presiding at a meeting of the guild of prophets in Gilgal, Elisha instructs his servant to prepare them a meal (v. 39). Because of the famine, he has to go scavenging in the countryside and unknowingly brings back a poisonous plant. In a miracle reminiscent of Elijah cleansing the spring at Jericho (2 Kings 2:19–22) and Moses the one at Marah (Exodus 15:23–25), Elisha makes the bad meal edible (vv. 38–44).

Notice that the prophets too were suffering in the famine. If we take the famine to be a consequence of the wrongdoing of the nation, the suffering is experienced by both the good and the bad, the innocent and the guilty. In the Old Testament a great deal of emphasis is placed on the idea of corporate responsibility and solidarity. 'We are all in this together' would be the usual way of looking at things. The downside of this is that individuals can become demoralized ('It's not our fault but we're suffering all the same') and individual action for change can be discouraged ('What's the point? There's nothing we can do about it'). It is that downside which Ezekiel addresses in his outburst from a more individualistic position (Ezekiel 18). Individualism too has its downside, as much of today's Western society knows to its cost.

Multiplying the loaves

The instruction for offering the 'first fruits' of the harvest to God can be found in Exodus 23:16 and 19. This was a costly sacrifice. Food would be scarce in the weeks before the harvest, often resulting in a short-term local famine as in verse 38. The first of the new crop would therefore be welcome either to feed the farmer's hungry family or to make the highest price in the market. Neither is permitted. It must be given to God as a gesture of gratitude. Ezekiel 44:30 says that it must be given to the priests, but 2 Kings 4:42–44 reflects an older tradition which permitted it to be given to any of God's representatives.

Generally speaking, the names of people and places in Kings do not seem to play any significant role. Few commentators deal with the place from which this man comes, apart from attempting to identify the location of Baal-shalishah. The meaning of the name is unknown. It is possible that in this detail, in which a man from a village containing the name of Baal brings his first fruits to Elisha, we are being reminded that it is the Lord alone who is the true Lord of the harvest.

Both of these stories have parallels in the Gospels, the first in the raising of Jairus' daughter in Mark 5:21–43 and the second in the multiplying of the loaves and the collecting up of the leftovers in Mark 6:30–44 and 8:1–10. The Gospel writers clearly saw in these old stories that God was the Lord of life and the conqueror of death, a truth which they also saw lived out in the life and ministry of Jesus.

A PRAYER

Lord of life and conqueror of death, give to us and all your people the gifts of compassion and care.

2 KINGS 5:1–14

NAAMAN *the* SYRIAN

2 Kings 5 contains a sudden and totally unexpected change of scene. We find ourselves somewhere in Aram (Syria) and we are introduced to Naaman, the commander of the Syrian army (v. 1). As Elijah had helped a foreigner, the widow in Zarephath, so does Elisha. The last time that Aram and its army featured in the story was in 1 Kings 22. There we saw Ahab, king of Israel, propped up in his chariot and dying on the battlefield at Ramoth-gilead. The day had ended with the Israelites routed. Naaman, verse 1 implies, was the Syrian commander in that battle, the Lord's agent in defeating Israel for the sins of Ahab and Jezebel. This passage does not argue that the Lord is the only God, the one God of the whole earth; it simply assumes it. The defeat of the Israelites at Ramoth-gilead was not the work of the Aramean gods but of the Lord. The gods of Aram are not able to help this Aramean VIP but the Lord can and does.

Leprosy

Naaman was, however, a victim of a serious skin disease. Biblical 'leprosy' was probably not the full-blown disease we mean by the term today. The word used for it covers a variety of skin diseases, major and minor. According to the regulations in the Old Testament, these made people ritually unclean, with all the serious social consequences that that implied, although they would not necessarily be seriously ill (see especially Leviticus 13:1–46).

Small is beautiful

Next we meet one of those unnamed minor characters in the story who play such a crucial role. A captured Israelite slave girl casually says to her mistress how sorry she feels for her master and what a pity it is that he can't meet the prophet from Samaria (vv. 2–3). Many things flow from that conversation.

The Syrian king sends Naaman to the king of Israel with a covering letter and an extraordinary set of presents. Seven hundredweight of silver (five times what Omri had paid for the land on which to build his capital—see 1 Kings 16:24) and 150lb of gold was a fortune, and no wonder the king of Israel sees it all as some kind of plot (v. 7). No name has been mentioned since 2 Kings 3:6 but we must presume that the king who finds himself in this quandary is Jehoram. He is the one who didn't know that Elisha was accompanying them in the campaign to retake Edom (2 Kings 3:11–12) and here too he does not think of consulting any of the Lord's representatives. What he says echoes Deuteronomy 32:39 and 1 Samuel 2:6. Elisha hears of this and sends the king a curt message. If Naaman comes to him, he will know that there is a prophet in Israel, even if the king doesn't (v. 8).

Elisha didn't speak personally to the Shunammite woman at first, and neither does he to Naaman. Naaman storms off, muttering about rivers. Again it is the minor characters who save the day. Naaman listens to his servants and bathes in the River Jordan as instructed, seven times, as laid down in the leprosy rules in Leviticus 14:7–9. He is made 'clean' as promised (vv. 10, 14). The other translations which only talk about his skin becoming clean and healthy miss the important point being made here, that not only is his skin healed but his 'impurity' or 'uncleanness' is dealt with too.

The distinction between 'clean' (that is, ritually pure) and 'unclean' is an important distinction in the Old Testament. It is seen at its clearest in the food laws, though how and why some animals are considered 'clean' and therefore eatable, while others are deemed 'unclean' and therefore not, remains a mystery. Naaman is not only healed but also made ritually pure again. The Hebrew of verse 14 contains a clear reminder of the role of the young Israelite slave girl in beginning this process when it says that Naaman's skin is now like that of a 'little boy'. The Hebrew phrase is the masculine equivalent of the one used of her in verse 2.

A PRAYER

Lord, grant us the humility to listen and to learn.

GEHAZI *the* LEPER

Naaman shows his gratitude

A grateful Naaman returns to thank the prophet, who refuses to take any reward for his work. Naaman then makes two requests. The first is that he can take some of Israel's soil back home so that, on it, he can worship the one true God—which rather shows that he has not quite grasped what is implied in believing that there is no God in all the earth except the Lord. The second request is that the prophet will understand if ceremonial duties mean that he must still worship in the temples of other gods. Elisha wishes him well on both counts, extending him the forgiveness he requests and which is part of God's will (compare v. 18 and 1 Kings 8:41–43). Rimmon was another name for Hadad, the chief god of Syria, whose temple was in the capital, Damascus.

This exchange takes on greater significance if we remember that the purpose of the writers of this history is to explain the exile and, presumably, to enable the people of God to live through it. They need to remember that if the Lord is the only God on earth, then he is accessible to his people always and everywhere. If it is not possible to worship him in his sacred place in Jerusalem, that does not mean that he cannot be worshipped at all. Does Elisha's ready acceptance of the second point—which runs quite counter to the whole tenor of 1 and 2 Kings—imply that in the very difficult circumstances of the exile the Lord himself will understand if his people are sometimes forced into compromising situations?

Naaman joins the Old Testament's short list of faithful and perceptive foreigners in whom God's third promise to Abraham is fulfilled, that all the world will be blessed by Israel's faith (see Genesis 12:3).

Gehazi

Gehazi, who up to this point has appeared as Elisha's faithful servant, sees an opportunity not to be missed and takes it (vv. 20–24). Naaman, gladly taking this opportunity to express his gratitude, gives him double the money he asked for. One would not expect someone of Naaman's rank to 'jump down from his chariot' to talk to a messenger. Gehazi hides the silver in the 'citadel'. The Greek reads 'in the darkness', a reading which involves only the tiniest of vowel changes at the beginning of the word. If it were justified, it would be a neat and effective way of expressing the evil Gehazi had done.

The curse of leprosy

Elisha, already aware of what has happened, asks Gehazi where he has been (v. 25). We do not know what might have happened had he told the truth, but he chooses not to. Elisha curses him with Naaman's leprosy in its most acute form. The curse will be on his descendents too, another sign of that corporate rather than individualistic outlook of the Old Testament. Gehazi is more than a lone individual. As his life is bound up with that of his family, so are they involved in his misdeed and have to live with the consequences. The classic picture of that is the effect which Achan's greed caused for his family in Joshua 7.

We need not speculate on how Elisha knew what he knew. In the culture of the time, prophets were expected to know what others could not know, from mundane things like the whereabouts of lost asses (1 Samuel 9:6) to the possibility of a sick child's recovery (1 Kings 14:3) or details of things talked about in private conversations (2 Kings 6:12). It was thought to be their gift from God to know such things.

Elisha knows full well what Gehazi has taken but the long list in verse 26, with its clear allusion to the tenth commandment (see Exodus 20:17), is intended to expose the core of his wrongdoing. He has been guilty of the sin of covetousness. He has 'set his heart on' things that he shouldn't. Gehazi's old-fashioned sin began with greed (v. 20), continued with deceit (v. 22) and ended in terrible disgrace (v. 27). The Old Testament regards 'covetousness' as sin. Jesus warns strongly that 'life does not consist in the abundance of possessions' (Luke 12:15). Much in modern society disagrees. This passage shows what damage is done to those individuals who are taken in by the 'lure of wealth' (Mark 4:19).

A PRAYER

Lord, grant us Naaman's gratitude and forgive us Gehazi's greed.

A GLIMPSE *into the* REAL WORLD

From the 'ridiculous'

The resident community of prophets need more living space. In the course of cutting the timber for their new buildings from the thick forest beside the Jordan, a butter-fingered prophet drops his borrowed axe into the river. To save him from the lender's ire, Elisha retrieves it by a spot of 'magic' (vv. 1–7).

This is the sort of miracle which gives miracles a bad name, not least because it appears so utterly trivial. Readers who are suspicious of miracles and embarrassed by the very word have all their worst fears confirmed here. They insist that iron axe-heads just do not float! But readers who relish miracles and see them as the clearest pointers of all to the power of God are delighted by this one. For them, the more impossible the better! Some commentators try to compromise by finding ingenious ways of explaining how an axe-head might float. Others exploit the miraculous. Others deny it.

I suggest that most of these arguments miss the point. There is no doubt that the writer of this story believed in miracles and that a good number of his readers did—and still do—too. This means that they did not come to this story with the inevitable question which many modern readers bring to it. They did not ask if it 'really happened'. They took that for granted and so they looked at what the story said. If we do the same, verses 1–7 become a touching little story of a national leader who takes time to help a careless junior out of a spot.

To the 'sublime'

Verses 8–23 tell another miracle story with a happy ending. This one is full of drama. Elisha wakes one morning to find himself trapped in Dothan, surrounded by the professional army of Syria and protected only by the village militia and the town wall. But are things quite what they seem? That is the question.

Applying the same principle to this miracle story as we did to the last, we see that the key lies in the dialogue between master and servant. The servant is terrified when he sees the Syrian army. The master reassures him in the wonderful words of verse 16. Hearing this, the servant thinks that his master has finally flipped, for what he says is nonsense. The master sees the look on his face and prays. The prayer is answered and the servant sees what the master has seen all the time—themselves, the Syrian army, plus the horses and chariots of fire (as in 2:11). The serious problem remains—the Syrians are still there—but around and beyond and above them are the horses and chariots of fire, the army of the living God.

The obvious question is, which of them saw things as they really were, the master or the servant before the prayer? Was it that the boy saw the situation as it really was, whereas Elisha was dreaming and his vision was only wishful thinking? Or was it that the boy only saw things as they seemed to be, whereas Elisha saw them the way they really were? The story answers that question emphatically. The 'real world' is not the world as it appears to be. The master was seeing right, not the servant. The story hinges on Elisha's prayer and demonstrates that faith sees the world differently but sees it correctly. Before his eyes were opened, the servant saw things only as they appeared to be; afterwards he saw them as they really were.

Or is it?

The two stories in this chapter show God's concern to save the life of the great prophet and Elisha's concern to save the embarrassment of his butter-fingered junior. It is immensely difficult at times to believe that God is and that he cares. The evidence is often massed against it. These two stories insist, however, against all the odds, that that is the case, whether it looks that way or not. Sometimes it is impossible to see beyond the Syrian army or even a lost axe-head. These two stories not only reassure us of the 'real world' beyond such things, but also remind us that God has given us Elisha and his successors to make us aware at such times of the 'horses and chariots of fire all around'.

A PRAYER

Lo, to faith's enlightened sight,
All the mountain flames with light!
Hell is nigh, but God is nigher,
Circling us with hosts of fire.

Charles Wesley

Thanks be to God!

61

FAMINE *in the* CITY

A terrible time

The peace and goodwill between Syria and Israel established by Elisha's clemency (vv. 22–23) is ended when Ben-hadad lays siege to Samaria. The result is a terrible famine, much worse than in his previous siege (1 Kings 20). Inedible food fetches amazing prices and the city's inhabitants resort to cannibalism, not unknown in such circumstances (for example, Deuteronomy 28:54–57; Lamentations 2:20; 4:10). A donkey's head is sold for a pound's weight of silver and a half-pint of dove's droppings for an ounce of silver, though this one defies the explanation of even the most ingenious of commentators. Some translations avoid this obvious difficulty by suggesting other foods, for example, 'wild onions' (NJB), 'seed pods' (NIV), 'locust beans' (REB). NJPS adds a footnote that 'dove's dung' was a popular term for carob pods.

The king is not named in the chapter, but it is still Jehoram, son of Ahab and Jezebel. He wears his regal gowns to reassure the population, but under them he is wearing sackcloth as an expression of his sorrow and in appeal to God (as his father had done in 1 Kings 21:27). His outburst to the woman in verse 27 shows his anguish and despair. Unlike Solomon, he has no answer which will bring justice to the woman whose son is dead. All he can do is lash out in his despair and call for Elisha's head, just as his mother had threatened Elijah (1 Kings 19:2). Why he should blame Elisha is not clear. Is it that Elisha had let the Syrian army go when the Israelites had had it at their mercy (vv. 22–23)?

Elisha is blamed and threatened

Elisha knows exactly what the king intends, as the Syrian officer had said he did (6:12). He takes sensible precautions but he is neither cowed nor daunted by the king's threat. The elders in verse 32 may be the senior members of the prophets' guild of which Elisha is the head, or else the leading citizens of the capital. Elisha's reference to the king as 'this murderer' is strange. He has been dismissive of Jehoram before (see 2 Kings 3:13–14; 5:8) but has said nothing as strong as this to him or about him. Does he blame Jehoram for the deaths in the famine?

Whether the question at the end of verse 33 is voiced by the king or the messenger, it is one that demands an answer. It is also, remember, a question directly relevant to the situation addressed by 1 and 2 Kings as a whole. Where was God when Jerusalem was destroyed by the Babylonians, and why should anyone continue to put their faith in him?

The question is asked in two subtly different ways in modern translations. Why should the king 'hope in' the Lord (NRSV)? That is, why should he worship him, serve him and give him his allegiance? This is a deep question about God's very existence and nature. Is the Lord the true and only God, the one who is worthy of our worship and service? On the other hand, other translations frame the question more narrowly. Why, the king asks, should he 'wait for' the Lord to act? Here the implication is that if the Lord cannot or does not deliver what he has promised, then that is sufficient ground for worshippers to change their religious allegiance. Many people today, it seems, 'shop around' for a religion which offers what they want. The king, in this translation, is their role model.

Elisha pronounces God's word to the situation and it is a promise of immediate relief for Samaria. The scepticism of the equerry is met with an immediate response from the prophet which will work itself out in due course (see 7:17–29).

FOR MEDITATION

It is a real temptation to modern religion to promise much.
The words of Shadrach, Meshach and Abednego in
Daniel 3:16–18 are much more profound.

62

2 KINGS 7:3–20

The CITY IS SAVED

As the prophet said it would be

Elisha, speaking as the Lord's messenger, had promised that the famine would end and the city be saved in 24 hours (7:1). This chapter tells how those words were proved true. The story begins with four unlikely heroes with nothing to lose and ends happily for all except the sceptical officer. The chapter emphasizes that the 'word of the Lord' spoken by Elisha is proved to be entirely accurate: food is available when he said it would be and at precisely the price he quoted (compare v. 16 and v. 1) and the fate of the sceptical officer is exactly as Elisha had indicated (compare vv. 17–20 and v. 2). Apart from some detail in verse 13, there are no technical difficulties in the chapter.

Elisha had given no word about how it would all be done, and no one could possibly have guessed. The four lepers could hardly believe their luck. The king and his officer rightly suspected a trick. Even the scepticism of the cursed officer was justified. He had been right to say that it was impossible for the 'windows' of heaven to open and the needed rain to fall in the time indicated. His fault had been to fail to consider other possibilities.

The Aramean army had been tricked by God and had fled (vv. 6–7). It is a familiar theme in the Deuteronomic History that the God of Israel is able to fight for his people. This victory which the Lord has engineered is the seventh such victory in that History. He had thrown the Amorites into a panic at the time of Joshua (Joshua 10:10–12), defeated Sisera and his army at the time of Deborah and Barak (Judges 4:15), enabled Gideon to terrorize the Midianites (Judges 7:19–23), caused panic in the Philistine cities which had captured the sacred Ark (1 Samuel 5:9), thundered against the Philistines at 'Ebenezer' (1 Samuel 7:10) and led the Arameans away blind from Dothan (2 Kings 6:18–23). This time he panics them with noises in the twilight and the city is saved—and we are reminded of those other 'horses and chariots' in 2:11 and 6:17.

The writers have shown, time and again, that the Lord could also give others victory over his own people. We will soon read that the next time Samaria is besieged there will be no salvation, for then the besieging Assyrians will be doing what the Lord requires (2 Kings 17:5–7, 18). The long-term lesson is not, however, about Samaria but about Jerusalem. As the Arameans have disappeared from around Samaria during the night, so the Lord's next great victory will be a night-time one over the Assyrians as they besiege Jerusalem (2 Kings 19:32–36), but the next siege of Jerusalem by the Babylonians will have a very different outcome.

The key to this story lies in 7:1. The Lord has spoken via a prophet—a word of hope to the city and of doom to the sceptic. What he said has taken place. This is another major theme of Kings. God speaks to his people through his prophets. Elijah and Elisha feature large in the overall story, but messages have been given by many others, named and unnamed. Prophets are to be listened to. There may be difficulties in deciding between those who truly speak from God and those who do not, but that problem should not be used to dismiss the prophets wholesale. The outcome of their words may not be as immediate as this one—in fact, so far in the story we are still awaiting the fulfilment of Elijah's words of doom on Ahab's son in 1 Kings 21:29 (repeated by Micaiah in 22:23)—but that does not mean they can be ignored either. The overall message is that if Israel had listened to the prophets in the past, then things would have been different. They are the key interpreters of present events. Therefore the prophets' explanation of the exile is to be believed and their guidance about the future is to be heeded!

FOR REFLECTION

Look at the four lepers. They are outcasts with nothing to lose. They have a struggle with their consciences. What tips the balance, sadly, is the fear of punishment.

PICKING UP THREE THREADS

The wealthy Shunammite woman

Verses 1–6 pick up the story we left in 2 Kings 4:8–37. Seven years have passed and the woman and her household have survived the famine by living in Philistine territory. It appears that her husband, who had been described as 'old' the last time he was mentioned, is now dead. It is therefore left to the woman to take all the initiative as she returns to her old home.

As we saw in the note about the widow in Sidon in Study 38, widows were vulnerable, especially those whose fathers were dead and who had no male relatives to take responsibility for them. Unlike many other widows, however, this one has both money and, thanks to Elisha, a son who will eventually be able to look after her in old age.

There are some other interesting glimpses into social realities in these verses too. Local famines lead to population movements and produce 'economic refugees'. 'Ancestral land' can be lost either by default or by appropriation by others. Appeal can be made to the king, but how real was this for those without any wealth, status or connection? Incidental information in passages like this is very useful to historical sociologists in their work to build up a picture of life in ancient Israel.

Famines and the number seven are both regular features in Old Testament stories. (For the most famous seven-year famine, see Genesis 41:1–36.) Verse 1 points out that God had 'called for' this one, though there is no reason given here or in 2 Kings 4:38. In the Deuteronomic way of looking at things, famine is either a punishment for disobedience or a consequence of it, and this note may be seen as a reminder to forgetful readers that Jehoram, though a distinct improvement on his parents, is still a flawed king (see 2 Kings 3:1–3).

Gehazi

There are two strange things about Gehazi in these verses. The one is his reappearance at all, for we last saw him as a doubly disgraced outcast (2 Kings 5:27). The other is the nature of the question he is asked by the king. At their first meeting, Elisha had been downright rude to the new king (2 Kings 3:13–14) and that tone had been repeated on at least two other occasions (2 Kings 5:8 and 6:21–22). Little wonder that the king had finally lost his temper and tried to kill Elisha (2 Kings 6:31–32). Given that history, the king's question in verse 4 is odd.

Hazael of Damascus

The terrifying message of the 'still small voice' which Elisha's master had heard outside the cave was that he should legitimate two bloody coups to be staged by Jehu in Israel and Hazael in Aram (1 Kings 19:15–18). No mention has been made of either of those commissions until now.

The deference in Ben-hadad's welcome to Elisha ('your son') and the lavishness of the presents he gives him indicate the prophet's prestige. Elisha had cured Naaman, the commander of the Aramean army (2 Kings 5:1–14), and he had tricked that army at Dothan and then let them go (2 Kings 6:1–23). Readers of the story also know that he had had a hand in the Aramean flight from Samaria, and might infer that Ben-hadad would have thought so too. Unlike some of Israel's own kings, this foreigner recognizes both the Lord and his prophet (v. 8).

The irony is that Ben-hadad sends Hazael to Elisha. Elisha clearly sees what the future holds when Hazael becomes king of Aram and it makes him weep, yet he has to tell Hazael what is to be. Hazael, a nobody as he himself recognizes (v. 13), will become one of the most formidable threats to Israel's national life during his 40-year reign in Damascus (2 Kings 10:32–33; Amos 1:3–5), yet the story sees this as the will of Israel's God. The reason is that Israel must be punished for its sins and Hazael is the foreign king ordained by God to do it (compare Hosea 13:16).

Elisha's word to Ben-hadad in verse 10 is no riddle. He does recover. And he does die. We await with trepidation the fulfilment of Elisha's word to Hazael.

FOR REFLECTION

We too have seen the sort of cruelty which makes Elisha weep.
It is impossible for us to believe that such things are ever
the will of God. We have come to see, thanks be to God,
that God weeps over them as we do.

TWO JUDEAN KINGS

We are nearing the end of the stories about Elisha, the second of two
major sets of stories about individual prophets in Kings. These stories
have contained many strange scenes and much detail as they have
taken us into the lives of ordinary people in Israel and Judah. Above
all, however, they have illustrated the key role of the prophets. They
have shown that it is through these heroes, and often at great cost to
them, that God makes his will and his ways known, in matters both
small and great, to his people. The question is always whether or not
the people in general and their leaders in particular will listen to what
they are being told. The answer is that usually they will not.

Here the scene changes to Judah to outline the reign of Jehoram,
mentioned already in 1 Kings 22:50 and 2 Kings 1:17, as he succeeds
his father, Jehoshaphat, as king. Care is needed here because now we
have two kings with the same name ruling at the same time; and to
add to the confusion, the name is sometimes shortened to 'Joram'.
The interlude is a sad one, for both Jehoram of Judah and the son
who succeeds him are tainted. Jehoram is married to Athaliah, a
daughter of King Ahab (v. 18) and the sister of Jehoram of Israel,
which makes their son Ahaziah a great-grandson of King Omri (v. 26).
The statement in verse 27 that Ahaziah was 'son-in-law to the house
of Ahab' tells only half the story: he was related to that fated house
also by blood! We shall hear more of Athaliah in due course. It is not
surprising that, with these connections and this pedigree, both these
Judeans receive the dismissive treatment usually reserved for the
northern kings, that they 'walked' in the wrong 'way' and 'did what
was evil in the sight of the Lord' (vv. 18, 27).

Jehoram of Judah (850–843)

The relationship between Israel and Judah was not an equal one.
Israel was both bigger and more prosperous than its southern neighbour and was the dominant state in the region, due in no small part
to the calibre of Omri (see Study 37). The marriage of Jehoram to
Athaliah is the only marriage between the ruling houses of the two
kingdoms of which we are aware. Judah was in reality little more than
a vassal of Israel and such a marriage must have been deeply offensive

to those in Judah who remembered how the rebel northern kingdom had come into being.

Jehoram's reign is tainted, and verses 20–24 show that his wrongdoing has serious and inevitable consequences, namely that Edom and Libnah (a city on the Philistine border) successfully revolt against Judean rule. The details in verse 21 are not clear, but it looks as if Jehoram was lucky to escape from the battle as his army was routed. The defeat is brought into even sharper relief by the comment that Edom has been in revolt 'to this day'. Verse 19, however, reminds us that there is a fundamental difference between Judah and Israel, no matter how similar the behaviour of their kings might be. It is that the Lord has a special relationship with Judah because of his promise to David. Judah might suffer setbacks and reversals but it will not be destroyed. The lamp of David will continue to shine (see 2 Samuel 21:17; 1 Kings 11:36; 15:4).

Ahaziah of Judah (843–842)

Ahaziah of Judah (not to be confused with his deceased uncle Ahaziah of Israel, whose reign was equally brief—see 1 Kings 22:51 to 2 Kings 1:17 and the comments in Study 50) reigns for only a year (vv. 25–29). Once more, the fighting ground between Israel and Aram is the border town of Ramoth-gilead (which is also called Ramah in verse 29), and Hazael of Aram's attacks on Israel have begun there. Ahaziah accompanies his uncle to fight the Arameans and visits him in Jezreel where he is recovering from his wounds. The mention of Jezreel should strike a chord. It is the place where Naboth had had his vineyard, and Elijah's words about what would happen to those who had stolen it from him are still not, as yet, completely fulfilled (see 1 Kings 21:21–24). Will this prove to be a fateful visit?

A PRAYER

Grant us, Lord, to understand the burdens and responsibilities of political life and the grace to pray for those carrying them.

A BLOODY COUP (I)

The deaths of two kings

Two of the three changes which Elijah was commissioned to bring about have now taken place: Elisha has succeeded Elijah as prophet and Hazael has become king of Aram in Damascus (1 Kings 19: 15–18). This chapter describes the third. It is a racy account of three brutal acts of violence. Jehu is the divinely appointed killer carrying out the first of the sanctioned killings and ordering the other two.

The role of Elisha

Elisha carries out the commission given to his master to anoint Jehu, one of the commanders of the Israelite army in Ramoth-gilead, as king of Israel (vv. 1–3). He does so by sending one of his junior prophets, who is fit enough to get away quickly should things go wrong. We are familiar with high-profile prophets playing leading roles as either supporters or opponents of kings (Nathan and both David and Solomon, Ahijah and Jeroboam, Elijah and Elisha with Ahab and Jehoram) but this is the first prophet to have been involved in a coup attempt since Samuel had anointed the young David while Saul was still the ruling king (1 Samuel 16:1–13).

The young prophet says more to Jehu than Elisha had said to him. Note the two expansions in the first sentence in verse 6. The young prophet adds the words 'the God of Israel' after he has named the Lord. Here the storyteller reminds us of what has been at stake. Ahab and Jezebel and their 'house' have not accepted that it is the Lord, the Lord alone, who is 'the God of Israel'. This point is made in the second addition too, which speaks of Israel as 'the people of the Lord'. 'One God, one people' was how it was intended to be. This dynasty must end because it has not been true to that ideal. The rest of the young prophet's speech spells this out and tells Jehu how to do what the Lord requires of him. This dynasty is to be wiped out as the previous two had been (see 1 Kings 15:27–30; 16:9–13).

Verse 11 is an interesting insight into how prophets were some-times perceived in ancient Israel. Compare Jeremiah 29:26 and Hosea 9:7 where similar opinions about the sanity of prophets are found. NRSV's 'babble' is translated equally strongly by NJPS as 'rant'. This may be a derogatory reference to the way prophets speak when they are caught up in their ecstasies, or, less dramatically, a sarcastic comment about what they say even when they are not. Either way, scepticism towards and ridicule of prophets was not unknown.

Jezreel

Once his companions are told what has happened, they acknowledge what the 'madman' has done and proclaim Jehu as king (v. 13). He loses no time in setting out for Jezreel where Jehoram is recovering from his wounds. The pace of the narrative is as fast as Jehu's driving. NJB's version of the exchange between Jehu and the horsemen sent out to meet him—'Is all well?' 'What has it to do with you whether all is well?'—is better than the translation in NRSV, though GNB probably captures the sense of Jehu's reply best with, 'That's none of your business!'

Jehoram's suspicions are aroused and both he and Ahaziah of Judah set out armed to meet Jehu. Their chariots meet at 'the property of Naboth the Jezreelite' (v. 21). Not only is the place itself significant, as the conversation between Jehu and Bidkar will make clear, but so is what it is called here. It has not been 'Naboth's place' for about fifteen years, since Ahab had appropriated it, but as far as the writer is concerned it was as it had always been—Naboth's inherited land.

Jehoram of Israel dies in his chariot (v. 27). Ahaziah of Judah is mortally wounded in his. Ahab, father of the one and grandfather of the other, had died in the same way (1 Kings 22:29–37). The cursed family is sharing a common fate, though the Judean king does receive a proper burial in the ancestral royal tombs in Jerusalem, as befits a descendent of David (v. 28).

The oracle mentioned in verses 25–26 is the one Elijah gave to Ahab in 1 Kings 21:19. The information that Jehu was nearby when that oracle was given is news to us. Though it may have been slow in coming, we see that the 'word of the Lord' is taking effect (v. 26).

A PRAYER

Grant us, Lord, to recognize the ambiguities of violence and the grace to pray for those who use it.

A BLOODY COUP (II)

Jezebel's misdeeds

Until the young prophet mentioned her name in 9:7, we had not heard anything of Jezebel since 1 Kings 21:25. His comment reminds us that she had murdered the Lord's prophets (see 1 Kings 18:4). Jehu's reply to Jehoram's question in verse 22 puts the blame even more pointedly where it belongs and does so in very strong language. There can be no 'peace' (that is, no prosperity and happiness) until Israel is rid of Jezebel's 'whoredoms and sorceries' (NRSV). Here Jezebel's malign influence is expressed in two complementary ways. The first is by the powerful metaphor of prostitution, a metaphor for apostasy especially prominent in Hosea (1:2; 2:2; 4:12–14; 5:4; 6:10; 9:1). The second is by describing the foreign religious practices she has introduced and promoted by the pejorative term 'sorcery' or 'witchcraft'. We are forcefully reminded here of the seriousness of the damage done by this foreign queen. She has seduced Israel away from her true love and true lover and introduced her, as it were, to the squalid ways of adultery and vice.

Jezebel's fate

Verses 30–37 describe Jezebel's gruesome death. She has seen and heard what has happened outside the city, but she does not panic or attempt to escape. She puts on her make-up and, properly dressed, stands by her upstairs window. She is defiant to the end.

In verse 31 we see more of our storyteller's skill. Jezebel greets Jehu exactly as the two horsemen and her own son had done. There, as elsewhere in 2 Kings (for example, 4:26; 5:21 and 9:11) the greeting is best translated by 'Is everything all right?' Here, of course, she and we know that everything is not all right. So when she calls Jehu by the name of the last one who had mounted a violent coup and who had only lived a week to enjoy his new power (see 1 Kings 16:9–20), her words are not only full of sarcasm but possibly full of foreboding too. Does Jehu think that he is going to fare any better than his usurping predecessor? Does Israel?

Jezebel is thrown from an upstairs window by two or three officials. These may or may not have been eunuchs: the word can mean that but it need not. The same word is translated as 'official' by NRSV at 2 Kings 8:6. If they were eunuchs, this would be another example of this foreign queen importing foreign practices into Israel which were forbidden in Israel's law (Deuteronomy 23:1; Leviticus 21:20; 22:24). Jezebel's death seems to be portrayed as death by 'stoning'. This form of capital punishment was not a matter of pelting someone to death with stones, which was how an enraged mob could kill its victim (as in 1 Kings 12:18), but one of throwing the victim off a cliff and, if necessary, finishing them off by dropping rocks onto them. Given that this form of punishment is prescribed for 'blasphemers', those who sacrifice children, 'mediums and wizards' and those who entice Israelites to worship other gods, it is the appropriate punishment for Jezebel (Leviticus 20:2, 27; 24:23; Deuteronomy 13:6–11; 17:2–7).

As the account of Jehoram's death had concluded with a statement that the 'word of the Lord' had been fulfilled (9:26), so this account of Jezebel's end concludes in the same way (vv. 36–37). It points out that the words of both Elijah and Elisha about the dogs and Jezebel's corpse have been proved true (see 1 Kings 21:23 and 2 Kings 9:10), though neither prophet had said anything about her remains being scattered like dung.

FOR REFLECTION

The words of the prophets have proved true. Jezebel has received due punishment for her evil ways. God's will has been done and his enemies destroyed. In this instance, evil has been seen to be punished and it is natural to rejoice that the murderess has got her just deserts. But in the light of Jesus' teaching about loving our enemies, is such a natural reaction the right one?

67

A BLOODY COUP (III)

The death of all the royals

The final verse of chapter 9 stated bluntly that nothing had been left of Jezebel. The opening verse of chapter 10 tells us that many more will have to die before there is nothing left of the house of Ahab and Jehu's mission is complete (1 Kings 9:8).

The numbers in this passage (70 in verse 1 and 42 in verse 14) are probably to be understood in general rather than precise terms. 'Seventy' is frequently used in the Old Testament to convey the sense of 'a large number' (for example, Exodus 1:5; Ezra 8:14; Isaiah 23:15; Jeremiah 25:11).

More deaths in Jezreel

Jehu's next strategy is to write to the civic leaders in Samaria telling them to appoint a new king (v. 1). According to the Hebrew, he writes also 'to Jezreel' but a small change in this word would enable us to translate it as 'of the city'—that is, of Samaria—which seems more likely. These leaders immediately see that letter for what it is and submit to Jehu's authority. He then puts their decision to the test in a second letter and they comply. The resulting piles of heads are one of the most gruesome sights in the whole of Kings. The next morning Jehu addresses the people, for this is Israel, with its long tradition of involving the people in the making of its kings. This time, however, the people are not there to make any choice about who will rule over them. They are there as witnesses to the fact that the nation's civic leaders have been part of Jehu's conspiracy. In this way Jehu protects his back very neatly indeed. In his conclusion he reminds everyone about who is really responsible for everything that has happened—it has all been part of the will and purpose of God as this was made known through the prophet Elijah. The killing has not ended yet. All known local supporters of the former royal house are liquidated (v. 11).

Deaths in Beth-eked

All that having been done, Jehu leaves Jezreel for Samaria. On the way he meets relatives of King Ahaziah of Judah 'coming down' to visit their royal cousins in the north (v. 13). They might be innocent people who happen to be in the wrong place at the wrong time, but what are people who are travelling from Jerusalem to Samaria doing on the road to Jezreel, which is miles out of their way to the north? Some commentators, less plausibly, suggest that they are going down from Samaria to see their relatives in Jezreel, unaware of what has happened in Samaria since they left. Anyway, they all die too, for they are also part of the house of Ahab.

Jehonadab, son of Rechab

Jehonadab, son of Rechab, comes to meet Jehu (v. 15). We are given no information about him at all in the narrative here, but it seems that whoever he was, he was important enough for Jehu to need to verify his loyalty. The 'hearts as one' dialogue is not about friendship or affection, but is concerned to establish if they are of a common mind. Once that is established, Jehonadab rides with Jehu into Samaria, where Jehu finishes the task given to him. More details of the man are supplied in Jeremiah 35:1–11 where Jonadab (as he is called there) appears as the original leader of the 'Rechabites'. These were a puritanical sect who insisted on living in the old, nomadic ways, who resisted such advantages of a settled life in Canaan as wine, and stood for the religious and cultural purity of Israel's earliest days. We can therefore see why Jehu should want to demonstrate his 'zeal for the Lord' to one whose own zeal was quite out of the ordinary (v. 16) and why he valued Jehonadab's support subsequently (see 10:23–27). Jehu's 'zeal for the Lord' is the same as Elijah's (1 Kings 19:10, 14).

When they arrive in Samaria, Jehu completes the task of wiping out the family and supporters of Ahab (v. 17). At the end of this third set of killings, as at the end of the preceding two in 2 Kings 9:26 and 36, the point is made that everything has been done that the 'word of the Lord' via Elijah had said should be done.

A PRAYER

Lord, as violence breeds violence, have mercy on both its perpetrators and its victims.

The ASSAULT on BAALISM

Jehu of Israel (842–815)

Jezebel herself has been removed from the scene, as have all members of the royal house and its supporters. Jehu next turns his attention to ridding the land of the worship of Baal which she had promoted. He intends to finish the war on Baal and Baalism which Elijah had started.

A massacre in the temple

Jehu pretends to be an ardent worshipper of Baal, calls all the worshippers of Baal to the temple of Baal in Samaria and massacres them when they are inside the building. His soldiers take the sacred pillars (plural in the Hebrew in v. 26) and/or pillar (singular in v. 27) out of the inner shrine and burn it or them, demolish the temple and desecrate the site. Baal is 'wiped out' from Israel just as the royal house which had served him has been (vv. 18–28).

The temple in question is the one Ahab had built in Samaria (1 Kings 16:32). It appears to have been built on the same standard pattern as the temple of the Lord in Jerusalem, with nave and inner sanctuary (the 'citadel', v. 25). Likewise, much of what went on in its worship—'solemn assemblies', priests, prophets, burnt offerings, sacrifices, the king acting as high priest—was common to the worship of other gods across the region, the worship of the Lord included. The reference to 'vestments' for all the worshippers in verse 22 is interesting and without parallel in the Old Testament. Ordinary worshippers in Israel would have worn their 'best clothes' or at least 'clean clothes' (Exodus 19:10), while priests wore vestments of linen. It looks as if worshippers of Baal did dress differently at least for some services, though why, and what their special dress was, are unknown.

The pillar (or pillars) which Jehoram had removed are back (2 Kings 3:2). If all the prophets, priests and worshippers of Baal were assembled inside the temple building itself, then either it was a huge building or there were nowhere near as many worshippers of Baal as Elijah had thought there were! The temple having been destroyed, the site is desecrated by being turned into a disposal tip for human excrement (v. 27).

Jehu and the 'law of the Lord'

Verses 29–31 teach that success in one area is not enough. Like all his predecessors, Jehu continues in the 'sins of Jeroboam': he supports the two royal chapels at Dan and Bethel with their golden bulls (1 Kings 12:25–33). He has done well enough, however, to be told (presumably through a prophet) that his sons will reign for four generations (v. 30). Though this is more than any northern king before him, it is far from the 'eternal dynasty' granted to David and his successors in the south. The overall conclusion in verse 31 is negative. The Deuteronomic Historian is working with the model of kingship in Deuteronomy 17:14–20 and one of its key requirements is that the king shall keep Torah, the Law of the Lord or 'the Teaching of the Lord' (NJPS). Another key feature of Deuteronomy is that the people of God shall love the Lord their God with all their heart, soul and might (as we have seen in the *Shema* in Deuteronomy 6:4). This Jehu fails to do.

Such failure is one of the themes of the whole narrative in Kings and so, by now, we expect verse 32 to follow verse 31. If Jehu is not keeping the Torah and so is continuing to walk in wrong ways, then there will be consequences brought about by Israel's own God. Thus, although Hazael's conquests of Israelite territory east of the River Jordan are listed in some detail in verses 32–33, verse 32 provides the heading for them—'the Lord began to trim off parts of Israel'. Hazael is little more than the tool that the Lord uses. It was the Lord's intention to make him king of Aram and now he sets about the work against Israel which the God of Israel has commissioned him to do (1 Kings 19:15–17; 2 Kings 8:12–13).

A PRAYER

*Lord, we would love you with all our heart and soul and might,
walk in all your ways and do all your good and perfect will;
yet we do not. Forgive us and help us.*

A WICKED QUEEN

Queen Athaliah of Judah (842–837)

Verse 1 picks up the story of the royal line of David in Judah. 2 Kings 9:27–28 told us of the death of King Ahaziah, killed by Jehu, and in 2 Kings 10:12–14 we read of the deaths of more of the Judean royal family at his hands. Athaliah, the queen mother in Judah and, remember this, the daughter of King Ahab and Queen Jezebel of Israel, now sets out to destroy all the Judean royal family including her own grandchildren. We are told nothing about her motives, though the note in verse 3 that she subsequently ruled over Judah for six years surely says enough. She wanted power. She took it. None of the usual formulae used to speak of a king's accession or his death are used about either the beginning or end of her reign. She is a usurper—out of place and out of order.

A baby is rescued

Verse 2 introduces us to another palace plot. Keeping tabs on who is who in all of this intrigue is not easy, but Jehosheba is Ahaziah's step-sister, one of King Jehoram of Judah's daughters by one of his other wives. In the parallel account in Chronicles, she is married to the priest, Jehoiada, which explains how she is able to keep her young nephew hidden for so long in the temple complex. One more child among the many priests' children in the temple living quarters, or among the young devotees like Samuel had been, would have been hard to notice.

Jehoiada, who appears in verse 4 and plays a leading role in what follows, is clearly a senior priest responsible for the temple and able to command the temple guards and the 'Carites' or 'Carians' (NJB). He is probably the 'high priest' mentioned in 2 Kings 12:10. This is the only mention of these particular guards in the Old Testament; and the word is probably an ancient spelling mistake for the Cherethites (see 2 Samuel 8:18 and 20:23; 1 Kings 1:38) who formed the royal bodyguard and who were possibly Cretan mercenaries. 'Carians' would have been mercenaries from Cilicia. When the time is right, Jehoiada makes a pact ('covenant'—*berith*) with them, sealed by an oath, to support the 'king's son'.

A boy is crowned

Everything goes to plan, even though the details are somewhat difficult to follow. The royal bodyguards and the temple guards, either armed with extra weapons from the royal treasury or carrying David's own spear and shields (or bows) which might have been used at coronations, surround the temple, and the seven-year-old Joash is proclaimed king by acclamation in the temple courtyard, as Solomon had been at the Gihon spring (see 1 Kings 1:38–40 and ch. 7). Joash, or Jehoash as he is sometimes called, is crowned and given the 'covenant' or 'testimony'. This word (*eduth*) is used in the plural in 1 Kings 2:3 and 2 Kings 17:15 and 23:3, where it is another word for all the commandments which the king himself is to keep and which he is to see that everyone else also keeps. Perhaps it was the summary statement of his responsibilities that the new king was given—'a copy of the laws governing kingship' as GNB puts it, or a certificate or warrant certifying his appointment as king, or the 'insignia' of his office. The word is not found in Deuteronomy 17:18–20, but that key passage about kings receiving a copy of the Torah and then living by it is not very far away here.

Athaliah, an Israelite who usurps the throne of Judah, is one more foreign queen to be added to the already long list of those whose marriages wreaked havoc among God's people (see 1 Kings 11:1–9; 16:31–33). The contrast with Joash is plain. Joash is given power; she had taken it. She does what she wants; Joash is given instruction about doing what God wants.

A PRAYER

Lord, thank you for the nurse whose name we don't know, for her care of the one remaining child of David's line and for what that care might have cost her. Thank you for all the other nameless, ordinary people without whose commitment your will cannot be done or your kingdom come.

The END of the WICKED QUEEN

The people choose

2 Kings 11:1–12 presents the accession of Joash as a conspiracy between a princess, her husband who was a leading priest, the royal bodyguard and the temple guard. The only ordinary person in the story is the nameless nurse. In verse 13 we see that the 'people' join the guards to acclaim Joash as king and in the following verses the 'people' are mentioned a further eight times. This reminds us of the ancient tradition that the king is chosen from and by the people, or at the very least approved by them, as Saul (see 1 Samuel 10:24), David (see 2 Samuel 1:4; 5:1–5) and even Solomon (see 1 Kings 1:38) had been. It also makes a powerful statement about what the monarchy is for. It exists for the benefit of the people and not vice versa. The monarchy in Judah might be a hereditary one, but the sons of David ruled with the consent of the people, and to be king in Judah was to take responsibility, under God, for the well-being of God's people. 'People of the land' later became a technical term for those Jews who didn't take their faith too seriously, but there is no trace of that later derogatory meaning here.

Athaliah's death

Athaliah is the only woman to have ruled in Israel or Judah but the account of the way she seized power made no comment on the fact that she was a woman. Neither does the account of her death. She hears the noise in the temple, just as Adonijah had heard the noise when Solomon was acclaimed king (1 Kings 1:41). Unlike him, she rushes to investigate. What she finds is a king who, among other things, is standing by the pillar 'according to custom'. She had taken the throne by force, without consent and contrary to custom. The contrast with Joash could not be plainer.

Jehoiada commands that she be taken out of the temple and killed. This is not because killing her is an evil deed, but because nothing blemished could be offered as a sacrifice in the temple—such an offering would desecrate the holy place. That is the very reason why Mattan, the priest of Baal, is not only killed in the temple of Baal down the street, but in the most holy part of that temple (v. 18). In so doing, the people desecrate even the ruins of the place.

New covenants

Jehoiada had taken the initiative to restore a descendant of David to the throne, and verse 17 tells of his initiative in going on to make two new 'covenants' (*berith*). The first is a new start with God in which the great covenant on Mount Sinai is renewed, as it had been in Joshua's day (Exodus 19:5; Deuteronomy 5:2; Joshua 24:25). God, king and people are committed to each other. He is their God; they are his people (Exodus 6:7). As a consequence of this and a sign of their commitment to it, the people descend on the temple of Baal—presumably built and staffed under Athaliah's patronage—and destroy it as Jehu had destroyed the one in Samaria (2 Kings 10:17–28). With the new covenant made, Athaliah dead and that temple destroyed, it looks as if the curse of Baalism, so fervently promoted by Queen Jezebel in Israel and by her daughter in Judah, is finally ended.

Jehoiada's second covenant is between the king and the people, possibly along the same lines as the one in 2 Samuel 5:1–3. After the episode with Athaliah, there needs to be a return to monarchy on the proper Judean model. The boy king is then led from the temple through the city to the palace, where he is enthroned (v. 19).

The people celebrate. The city is now quiet after all the unrest it has seen since that unfortunate marriage between Jehoram of the house of David and Athaliah of the house of Omri some dozen years before. The grandson of that marriage, the infant who was saved by his aunt and his nurse (a description which immediately makes us think of Moses, bulrushes and Miriam) is seven years old as he begins to reign.

A PRAYER

*For new hopes and new beginnings
and for those by whom they come,
thanks be to God.*

A KINGDOM *under* THREAT

Jehoash (or Joash) of Judah (836–797)

This is a long reign which receives the writers' stamp of approval (v. 2), albeit with the usual caveat (compare v. 3 with the similar note about his great-grandfather, Jehoshaphat, in 1 Kings 22:41–44). The 'high places' which Jehoash allowed to continue were not 'pagan' ones as GNB puts it, but shrines at which the Lord was worshipped. He dies, however, at the hands of his own people, the first king of Judah to fall victim to a coup, and this is reported without comment or explanation (vv. 20–21). In between we read a rather confusing account of his lukewarm attempt to repair the temple (vv. 4–16) and a brief note about how he was forced to pay tribute to King Hazael of Aram (vv. 17–18). His tardiness about the temple, the national disgrace of being forced to buy off Hazael and the manner of his death are not what we would expect after the introduction to his reign in verse 2.

'Jehoiada instructed him'

Verse 2 makes the point that Jehoash was able to 'do what was right in the eyes of the Lord all his days' because 'the priest Jehoiada instructed him'. No doubt Jehoiada acted as regent for the first years of the young king's reign, but more than that is meant here. The verb translated 'instruct' (NRSV) is cognate with the noun Torah ('law', instruction, teaching, guidance) and this verse is a clear allusion to the key text about how kings ought to behave in Deuteronomy 17:18–19. Jehoash, at least, came near to doing what kings should do—which was to live and rule as instructed by God's teaching.

Temple repairs

In verses 4–8 we see that Jehoash set up a scheme to pay for necessary repairs to the temple, funded by a combination of taxes and voluntary giving, but nothing got done (though it seems to have taken him a long time to realize that) and eventually it was decided that temple repairs were not the business of the priests (v. 8). I can think of many priests and ministers today who would be only too delighted with such a suggestion! Verses 9–12 describe the new system by which repairs were funded and carried out. Coins were not yet in use, so talk in some translations of money being counted and bagged might be misleading. REB and GNB are probably right when they say that the silver would be 'melted down' (v. 10), ready for being 'weighed out' to pay workmen and suppliers. Verses 13–16 read like auditors' notes. They explain that repairs were paid for out of the special donations collected in the 'Repairs Chest' and that the priests' salaries continued to be paid for in the usual way, which was from their fees for offering sacrifices. They also note that ongoing costs for temple expenses and worship resources were not met from the repairs fund.

Verse 15 could begin many discussions. Verses 15 and 7 don't reflect very well on the priests, for put together they suggest that repairs got done and money was properly accounted for only when the priests were kept away from both. Verse 15 would not, of course, be acceptable accounting practice today, but is honesty really such a rare commodity nowadays?

Temple treasures

Chapter 12 begins by dating the accession of Jehoash in terms of the reign of Jehu in Israel. Verse 17 is the first mention of Hazael since 1 Kings 10:32, where he is spoken of as the Lord's agent in 'trimming off' parts of Israel. Mention of these two should remind us that they, with Elisha, were the three people Elijah was commissioned to anoint as God's agents, and that their work was to punish (1 Kings 19: 15–17). Hazael has expansionist policies and, after success against the Philistine city of Gath, he moves inland to Judah. This is the second time that Jerusalem has been threatened (see 1 Kings 14:25) and the price which Jehoash is prepared to pay for peace is enormous. Is it for this that his servants assassinated him? He dies a flawed but true son of David.

FOR REFLECTION

Others might instruct us in the will and ways of God,
as Jehoiada instructed Jehoash, but in the end it is our decision
whether or not to do that will or walk in those ways, and it is a
decision we must make daily.

TWO KINGS *of* ISRAEL

Jehoahaz of Israel (815–799)

Verses 1–2 and 8–9 follow the usual format for statements on the reigns of the kings of Israel. The new king 'does what is evil in the sight of the Lord' for he has no option. It is politically unthinkable for him, or any king of Israel, to demolish the temples at Dan and Bethel and order Israelites to worship in Jerusalem. As that is the only course of action which would satisfy the writers of Kings, their judgment on Jehoahaz is the same as it was on all his predecessors and will be on all his successors. Verse 6 notes that the sacred pole, the symbol of the goddess Asherah, is back in the city after this king's father had removed it (2 Kings 10:26–27).

Verses 3–7 are reminiscent of the cycles of events which are such a feature in Judges: Israel 'does what is evil in the sight of the Lord'; God delivers them into the hands of an enemy; they cry for help; God sends them help; the enemy is defeated and the land 'has rest' for a period before the cycle begins again. The king intercedes and God sends a 'saviour' (v. 5), though we are told nothing of who or how.

God's anger

We have seen examples of God's 'anger' in the stories so far but verse 3 is the first explicit mention of the 'anger of the Lord' in Kings, a phrase which occurs steadily throughout the Deuteronomic History (for example, Joshua 7:1; Judges 2:14; 3:8; 10:7; 1 Samuel 11:6; 2 Samuel 6:7; 24:1). This language causes a problem for many. We can ascribe the best of human emotions to God and say, for example, that he 'loves' us, but when the Bible ascribes the harsher emotions, as it does here, we draw back.

Exodus 34:6–7 is an important mini-creed which crops up often in the Old Testament (for example, Numbers 14:18; Psalms 86:15; 103:8; 111:4; 145:8; Joel 2:13; Jonah 4:2; Nahum 1:3; Nehemiah 9:17; 2 Chronicles 30:9). It speaks of both God's love, which is 'steadfast', and his anger, which is 'slow', and it contrasts how long-lasting is the one and how brief the other. The Old Testament is fully aware of the shadow sides of human life and of how damaging 'iniquity', 'sin' or 'wickedness' can be. This is not something to be treated lightly or dismissed easily. The prophets, for example, insist that sin, in all of its chameleon colours, makes God 'angry' because it fouls up his creation and spoils life for its victims. The result is hatred where there should be love, plus despair, darkness, sadness, injury and doubt (as Francis of Assisi puts it in his famous prayer). In the face of all this, it would be a poor God who did not get angry, just as anyone who looks at the misery of so many people and so much of our planet and feels neither pain nor rage can hardly be human. A God who is not angry at the causes of these things would be less than human. Thus the God of the Bible gets angry because he sees what has happened to his creation and feels for the victims of the injustices of the powerful, for 'he has made nothing in vain and loves all that he has made' (as we say in the Burial Service). As good parents get angry when they see their children hurting themselves and hurting others, so God's anger is, in fact, a sign of his love. However, he is 'slow to anger', patient with sinful people (Psalm 103:8), and his anger is not his last or greatest word—that is the love which seeks to put all things right.

Jehoash (or Joash) of Israel (799–784)

Here is more possible confusion, because there had been a king of Judah with the same name which also occurred in both longer and shorter forms. Jehoash gets the usual beginning and ending formulae with nothing in the middle (vv. 11–13), though in the ending formula there is a note about his war with Judah which is covered in 14:8–16. The impression given is of the inexorable passing of time with no change for the better. We are now into the fourth dynasty in Israel, but everything goes on as before. Jehu's coup may have been instigated by the Lord, but neither his son nor his grandson walk in the Lord's ways.

FOR MEDITATION

Reflect on Exodus 34:6–7.

The DEATH of ELISHA

Verses 14–21 supply some details of Jehoash's reign and tell of the death of Elisha, who has been unmentioned since 2 Kings 9:1. The king visits the dying prophet and cries over him the same strange words Elisha himself had cried over his dying master (see 2 Kings 2:12 and the comments in Study 52). Elisha then performs a last symbolic act and, though dead, a final miracle. Now the two great defenders or champions of Israel—Elijah and Elisha—are both dead and we are left wondering about the future.

Working a miracle even in his grave

Elisha tells the king to shoot an arrow eastwards and then strike the ground with the arrows. This kind of symbolic action is designed not only to declare what God's intention is, but also to be part of the process of bringing it about. The prophet's bad temper persists even in his terminal illness and the king feels the force of it. He does, however, defeat the Arameans three times (v. 25).

Verse 20 is another one of those fascinating incidental verses in which we glimpse the social conditions of the time. The territories west of the Jordan river were regularly raided by Moabites from the east. Such is the panic these raids cause that a funeral procession is abruptly terminated by shoving the corpse into the nearest rock tomb. In those days, bodies of wealthy people were buried on slabs or ledges in natural or manmade cave tombs, and when they had completely decomposed the bones were collected and stored in jars or recesses in the same tomb. The bodies of the poor were interred in the ground. Ending the stories of Elisha with this miracle story is intended to impress upon readers just how important a prophet he had been.

Abraham, Isaac and Jacob

Verses 22–23 pick up on verses 3–5 and take us back before the death of Elisha into the reign of Jehoahaz. The covenant explains God's action in verse 4. God had made a number of covenants with his people. The covenant with Moses was the one whose terms were kept in or which was symbolized by the 'Ark of the Covenant', as we saw in 1 Kings 8:21 (see Study 19). Having built the temple and installed the Ark in it, Solomon had spoken of the Lord as a God who kept his covenant promises and who had been loyal to his covenant with David (1 Kings 8:23–26), though the story goes on to show that Solomon himself had not been loyal to that same set of promises and commitments (1 Kings 11:11). Verse 23 speaks of a more ancient covenant than either of these—a set of promises and commitments which bound God to Israel and Israel to God, going back beyond David (for example, 1 Kings 8:24) or Moses (see Deuteronomy 5:2) to the great ancestors Abraham, Isaac and Jacob (see Deuteronomy 29:13–14). This ancestral threesome is referred to often in Deuteronomy (1:8; 6:10; 9:5, 27; 30:20; 34:4). The only time it has been mentioned in Kings so far is when the prophet Elijah used it in calling on God in the contest on Mount Carmel (1 Kings 18:36).

In verse 23, two words in particular describe the Lord's attitude to Israel—'grace' and 'compassion'—which take us straight back to that central, credal statement about the covenant God in Exodus 34:5–7 (see Study 72).

The last sentence of verse 23 in NRSV captures the ambiguity of the Hebrew perfectly: does it mean that God eventually banished them or that he has never banished them yet? God's love for Judah has been repeatedly stated, but at the very least, this is the first hint in Kings of generosity and future possibility for Israel.

Events in Aram

Verse 24 picks up the story of the arrows in verses 15–19. The three victories of Jehoash over the new Ben-hadad (almost every king of Aram was called Ben-hadad) are exactly what the dying prophet had said would happen (v. 19). This note reinforces the theme in Kings that the prophets are God's special messengers whose words should be heeded.

FOR MEDITATION

Read Psalm 103:15–18, which speaks of both the transience of human life and the endurance of divine love.

PRIDE & *a* FALL *in* JUDAH

These verses deal with the war between Jehoash of Israel and Amaziah of Judah, a major incident in the reign of Jehoash which was so summarily covered in 13:10–13. Attention focuses on the incident from the side of Amaziah. Verses 15–16 are an editorial hiccup, a second end-of-reign statement about Jehoash repeating the one already made in 13:12–13.

Amaziah of Judah (797–769)

Amaziah receives the usual qualified approbation for the kings of Judah, though sadly he is more like his father Jehoash than his ancestor David (see 2 Kings 12:2–3). David's reign had been marked by success and victories; Jehoash's reign had seen Judah seriously defeated by the Arameans (2 Kings 12:17–18). Like the others, Amaziah fails to remove the 'high places', the local sanctuaries where the Lord was worshipped. Nothing less than the centralization of the worship of the Lord in the temple in Jerusalem would satisfy the writers of Kings, and no king of Judah has yet attempted anything like that.

Verses 5–6 give a point in his favour. He kills those who had murdered his father (see 2 Kings 12:20–21), an action the writers clearly regard as obvious and necessary. In Israel, successful coups had resulted in the wholesale killing of the families of the previous kings (for example, 1 Kings 15:29; 16:11). Amaziah does not follow that example, a point of which the writers clearly approve. The command referred to in verse 6 is from Deuteronomy 24:16 (compare Jeremiah 31:29–30 and Ezekiel 18:2–4, 20), and it represents a different approach to family solidarity from that seen in the sad story of Achan in Joshua 7:24–25.

David had annexed Edom, and Jehoram had lost it (2 Samuel 8:13–14; 2 Kings 8:20–22). Jehoash's victory—probably somewhere near the Dead Sea—followed by the capture of the Edomite capital Sela ('The Rock', which has sometimes, mistakenly, been identified with the modern tourist haunt of Petra), was significant enough to boost his morale, as we shall see, though 'ten thousand' should be understood to mean a large number rather than a precise one. So far, so good.

Judah and Israel at war

Fired up by this victory, Amaziah challenges Jehoash of Israel, who tries to shrug it off in language reminiscent of Judges 9:8–15. Amaziah challenges Jehoash to a 'trial of strength' (NJB). Jehoash warns him against pride, ambition and pretention. No clues are given as to why Amaziah is spoiling for such a fight. Is he possibly attempting to remove the three-generation-old dynasty of Jehu in Israel to replace it with himself, as the foremost living descendant of the previous dynasty?

Amaziah does not listen and the result is the inevitable defeat of Judah—inevitable because of the sheer difference in size between the two states. As with the 'ten thousand' dead Edomites in verse 7, we need to remember that it is very easy to get the wrong impression of size, distance and scale in all these stories. The nation of Israel, for example, was barely thirty miles wide by a hundred from top to bottom and, though firm estimates are impossible, its total population in this period is unlikely to have been more than a quarter of a million. In other words, it was about the size of modern Cornwall with only half its population. Judah was tiny, only a quarter of the size of Israel and with less than a tenth of its population.

The result of such an uneven contest was humiliation for Amaziah, destruction of 200 metres of the city wall in Jerusalem and the second stripping of the temple in a generation (see 12:17–18). Verse 14 (and the parallel in 2 Chronicles 25:24) is the only reference to hostage-taking in the Old Testament. This picture of Jerusalem with its king defeated, its wall partially destroyed, the temple ransacked and hostages taken adds up to a foretaste of the events of 597 and 586BC. And all because 'Amaziah would not listen' (v. 11). The Deuteronomic Historians have already blamed royal pride and its refusal to listen to advice for the division of the kingdom (see 1 Kings 12:1–19); now they hint at its potential to destroy it completely.

A PRAYER

May the God who scatters the proud in the imagination of their hearts grant to those to whom power is given for the good of all the humility to use it well.

A MURDER & *a* REPRIEVE

The murder of Amaziah

Amaziah is the second king of Judah in succession to be murdered
(v. 19). No reasons for the conspiracy are given, and as his murder
takes place at least fifteen years after the fiasco he had caused in
Jerusalem, that traumatic event cannot be the reason for it. This murder involves no change of dynasty because his son Azariah ('Uzziah'
in GNB and NJB) is made king by 'all the people', but the downward
slide of the dynasty of David is serious. David's reign had been prosperous and popular. Solomon's had been prosperous and increasingly
unpopular. Since then, the prosperity of the separate kingdom of
Judah had gone steadily downhill with only occasional moments of
upturn. One such occasion was Amaziah's defeat of the Edomite
army and the return of Edom to Judean control, which eventually
enabled his son to rebuild the port of Elath (vv. 7, 22). The overall
trend was downwards too in the popularity of the kings. Things have
gone badly wrong when Judeans can murder two of the 'Lord's
anointed' kings in succession.

Jeroboam II of Israel (784–753)

Jeroboam II's reign parallels that of Omri a century before (see 1 Kings
16:23–28 and Study 37). Both reigns are treated briefly and dismissed
with the predictable condemnation reserved for all the northern kings,
although, judged by other standards, both were exceptionally strong
and effective rulers. Jeroboam II extended Israel's borders to their
widest extent for years and was fully supported by the prophet Jonah
(vv. 23–29).

Quite a bit of information about the social conditions in Israel
during Jeroboam II's reign can be gleaned from the books of the
prophets Amos and Hosea, who operated at this time. Amos addresses
a nation at peace and enjoying considerable wealth and prosperity,
though he is forthright in his accusation that this is built on the
poverty and exploitation of a growing underclass (see Amos 2:6–8;
5:10–15; 6:1–7; 8:4–6), and although Hosea focuses on the religious
situation, the same picture emerges (see 4:1–19; 7:1–7; 10:13–15).

Their verdicts on Jeroboam II's reign are as negative as the writers of Kings', though for different reasons. The traditional condemnation of the wrong ways of worshipping the Lord which went on in Israel is repeated, but nothing is said about the injustices of which Amos so passionately speaks, nor about the religious apostasy which was such an issue for Hosea.

That state of prosperity and peace is reflected in verses 25 and 28. Lebo-hamath was the old northern border in Solomon's time (1 Kings 8:65) and the Sea of the Arabah is the Dead Sea. Under Jeroboam II of Israel, the borders of Israel extended as far north, and under Azaziah of Judah, they extended as far east (v. 22) and south (v. 25) as they had in the heyday of Solomon! This is how far and how much the Lord is able to 'save' his people when they cry to him in distress! So if verses 11–14 are a foretaste of the events of 597 and 586BC, as we said in the last study, verses 25–28 are a foretaste of return and restoration, because it is not the Lord's purpose to 'blot out the name of Israel from under heaven' (compare 2 Kings 13:23). That would be real reassurance for readers in the distress of the exile, for whom the whole story is being told.

Verse 25 contains the only reference to the prophet Jonah outside the book which bears his name.

FOR MEDITATION

The northern prophet Hosea was active at this time
and the poignancy of God's love for Israel is expressed powerfully
in Hosea 11:8–9:

How can I give you up, Ephraim?
How can I hand you over, O Israel?
How can I make you like Admah?
How can I treat you like Zeboiim?
My heart recoils within me;
my compassion grows warm and tender.
I will not execute my fierce anger;
I will not again destroy Ephraim;
for I am God and no mortal,
the Holy One in your midst,
and I will not come in wrath.

76   2 KINGS 15:1–12

Another NORTHERN DYNASTY ENDS

Uzziah (Azariah) of Judah (769–741)

Uzziah (or Azariah as he is called in these verses) succeeds his murdered father (see 14:19–21). His long reign is treated very briefly in verses 1–7 and its success is subject to the usual caveat in verse 4. A much fuller description of his reign is given in 2 Chronicles 26. Like Omri of Israel a century earlier, Uzziah of Judah was a powerful and successful king with an international reputation, though that fact is not obvious in the treatment each ruler receives in Kings. Isaiah the prophet experienced his vision in the temple in the year of Uzziah's death (Isaiah 6:1).

Verse 3 repeats the statement made in 14:3 that Uzziah's father 'did what was right in the eyes of the Lord'. Given that Amaziah had been murdered at the age of 54, doing right is not to be seen as a guaranteed recipe for a happy, successful and long life. The same point is made in Uzziah's case, for verse 5 notes that the Lord 'struck the king with leprosy', with the result that his son, Jotham, acted thereafter as regent. No reasons for this are given in Kings, but Chronicles puts it down to his pride and details the incident in which 'the leprous disease broke out on his forehead' (2 Chronicles 26:16–20).

Why?

'Why has this happened to me?' and 'What have I done to deserve this?' are two of the commonest questions ministers are asked in the course of their pastoral work, and 'Why do bad things happen to good people?' is a question asked by many believers. There is no agreed answer to this problem of suffering. Some people answer it using verse 5 here, that such things happen in people's lives because God makes them happen. They are the will of God, and he knows best. Some say that there are no reasons at all and use words like 'chance' and 'accident', or, 'It's just one of those things.' Between those two approaches lies the view that although the world is as it is and 'chance and change are busy ever', in and through it all runs the thread of God's loving purpose which, in the end, will work everything together for good.

Zechariah of Israel (753–752)

The long period of relative prosperity and peace in both Israel and Judah, from 780 to 740BC, comes to an end in Israel with the death of Jeroboam II. His son, Zechariah, reigns for six months before being ousted and killed by Shallum 'before the people' ('in public', NRSV) or, following the Greek, 'at Ibleam' (NJB, GNB, REB), which is where the dynasty had first come to power (2 Kings 9:27). What is said in verses 8–11 about his short reign is completely predictable.

It is very easy to lose the plot in these chapters of Kings as king succeeds to king, so verse 12 is one of those very useful markers which remind us of the longer story and of where we are in it. As far as Israel is concerned, God had made his will for it known through his word to Elijah at the door of the cave: he was to anoint Jehu as king (1 Kings 19:16). Subsequent to that, Jehu had been told that his dynasty would last for four generations (2 Kings 10:30). Verse 12 reminds us that everything has happened as God had said it would, for which NRSV uses the word 'promise'. As far as the dynasty of Jehu is concerned, the situation is as the prophets had said it would be. Ancient readers would be reassured that all the other promises which God had made—not least the promise to David—could be relied upon. Modern readers believe that God's kingdom will come and his will be done on earth as it is in heaven, and they pray for that to happen, which gives them the courage and perseverance to live in the meantime.

A PRAYER

Lord, grant us the faith to persevere
and the confidence to trust in your eternal purpose.

TERROR *in* ISRAEL

The picture which emerges in these verses is one of confusion and terror. Israel is racked by coups and menaced by a resurgent Assyria.

Shallum of Israel (one month in 752–751)

The assassin Shallum lasts for only a month before he is killed by Menahem from Tirzah, the former capital.

Menahem of Israel (751–742)

Previous coups have been marked by the slaughter of the deposed king's family and relatives. Verse 16, however, describes a new terror. Tiphsah, which had marked the northern extreme of Solomon's power (1 Kings 4:24), is sacked and barbaric war-crimes are committed by a new king with ambitions to rule an empire as big as Solomon's. The prophet Amos condemns the Ammonites for such things (Amos 1:13–15) but here they are committed by Israelites on those who used to be their own subjects.

Verse 19 introduces a terrifying prospect. Assyria is on the rampage. For most of their history, the fate of the small kingdoms of Canaan was determined by the superpowers of Egypt in the south and various Mesopotamian kingdoms in the north. The reason for the relative prosperity of Israel under Jeroboam II and Judah under Uzziah is usually explained by the fact that for those few years there was pressure in Canaan from neither quarter. Now Assyria emerges as the world power from the north and it will dominate the region for a hundred years with devastating effects.

Tiglath-pileser III came to power in 745BC, taking the throne name of 'Pul' when he seized the throne of Babylon in 729. He certainly engaged in campaigning in the region but whether the events of 738BC described in verses 19–20 should be regarded as a full-scale invasion of Israel is not clear. In any event, as others before him, he was either bought off by Menahem (as suggested in v. 20) or bribed to support him against his rivals (as suggested in v. 19). The sums are enormous. A thousand talents of silver weighs over thirty tons and the sum required from 'all the wealthy' was twenty ounces of silver each. Israel becomes, in effect, a vassal state of Assyria.

Pekahiah of Israel (742–741)

Menahem's son, Pekahiah, succeeds his father and lasts for two years before losing his life to another rebel. Nothing is said about events in his short reign (vv. 23–26).

Pekah of Israel (741–730)

There are two uncertainties in the account of this new king. The meaning of 'Argob' and 'Arieh' in verse 25 is unclear: they might be the names of places or of people. The 20-year length of Pekah's reign in verse 27 is certainly a mistake (vv. 30 and 33 cannot both be right).

More important is the note in verse 29 about the return of the Assyrians and their policy of exile. The population of these territories in the north of Israel is transported to Assyria, being replaced by exiles from other territories conquered by the Assyrians. By such mass deportations Assyria was able to control its growing world empire and minimize the danger of local rebellion.

Pekah too falls victim to a coup (vv. 27–31).

Jotham of Judah (741–734)

By contrast, Jotham's reign in Judah is relatively uneventful. It is described in the usual way, with an added note about a building project in the temple. Verse 37 introduces a coalition which will seriously trouble Jotham's successor. Our curiosity is aroused when it is said that it is the Lord who is sending this unholy alliance against Judah. He would have good reason for sending it against Jotham's son, Ahaz, as we shall see in chapter 16, but Jotham has received a verdict of approval (v. 34). It may be that as time goes on, our storytellers are suggesting, successive kings of Judah have less and less excuse for not abolishing the worship of the Lord at the high places and centralizing it in the temple in Jerusalem.

FOR PRAYER

In these verses we have seen a glimpse of the suffering of the innocent when the powerful compete for power. Pray for today's victims of the violence of terror, oppression and war.

AHAZ *of* JUDAH (734–715)

The names of these kings can easily blur into each other, but if you confuse Ahaz of Judah with Ahab of Israel, that hardly matters because they were two of a kind. Ahaz of Judah 'walks in the ways of the kings of Israel'.

Verses 2–4 state the basic indictment. The least important of his failures was that he continued, as his predecessors had done, to allow the worship of the Lord at the 'high places'. Verse 3 accuses him, without going into detail, of the 'abominable practice' of child sacrifice (see 2 Kings 3:27 and the note in Study 55).

The coalition

The coalition mentioned in 15:37 reappears in verse 5, besieging Jerusalem and giving the Edomites the opportunity to liberate Elath which had only recently been recaptured (2 Kings 14:22). The ancient scribes recognized that the Hebrew is wrong in verse 6, for it says that Rezin liberated it for the Arameans who live there 'to this day'. A geographer couldn't make such a blunder, but a copyist easily could. The correction to Edom by NRSV is the correct one. These verses do not repeat the idea that the Lord was behind this attack, but the fact that verse 5 follows verse 4 is a broad enough hint. This Syro-Ephraimite war is usually seen as an attempt by Aram ('Syria') and Israel ('Ephraim') to compel Judah to join them in a defensive pact against Assyria, though none of the three quite different accounts of Ahaz and his reign (Isaiah 7; 2 Chronicles 28; and here) describes it in that way. Ahaz responds by buying the support of the Assyrians. Damascus fell, its king was killed and its people were exiled in 732BC.

No reference is made here to the prophet Isaiah who, according to Isaiah 7, warned Ahaz against taking this line. Given that 1 and 2 Kings have frequently and readily featured prophets, this silence is strange.

One like that, please

Verses 10–17 are a thinly disguised account of a vassal appearing before his overlord to declare allegiance and pay financial tribute (see v. 18). The story focuses, however, on the fact that the altar in

Damascus takes his fancy. He must have one like it. His command is obeyed. His new altar is placed in front of the temple, the old bronze altar is moved to the side and things continue as before. Is this another sign of Judah's vassal state, that things must be done in the temple in Jerusalem as Assyria dictates?

For an explanation of the various sacrifices in verse 15, see Study 21.

The old altar is set apart so that Ahaz can use it, though what for is not clear. Seeking God's guidance from a priest or prophet is not unusual in the Old Testament, and that is almost certainly what is meant here. 'Inquire' is, however, an unusual word, and given that an altar is involved, the reference is probably to the practice of seeking omens by examining the entrails of sacrificed animals. GNB expresses this well, saying that Ahaz wants it 'to use for divination'. This common religious practice is roundly condemned in Deuteronomy 18:10–12.

Paying the price

Verses 17–18 probably indicate the cost of the tribute mentioned in verse 8. The twelve bronze oxen which supported the 'sea' and the ten bronze 'stands' (see 1 Kings 7:23–26 and 27–39 respectively, plus the comments in Study 17) were melted down to pay the Assyrian king. There were, according to 1 Kings 7, ten bowls rather than the one suggested here in NRSV. We do not know what the 'covered portal' or the 'outer entrance for the king' were.

Put simply, Ahaz was a disaster. He encouraged the old religion of Canaan to resurface, he welcomed new foreign religious fashions and he revamped the temple to pay for foreign protection. Judah lost territory to Edom and became subject to Assyria. The signs are not good.

FOR PRAYER

The Deuteronomists judge Ahaz to be a failure. He was, however, trapped in an impossible position. Pray for those world leaders today whose options are severely limited.

The FALL of SAMARIA

Hoshea of Israel (730–722)

Verse 1 picks up events in Israel from the mention of Hoshea's successful coup against Pekah in 15:30. Verse 2 begins in the way that readers of the story of the kings of Israel have by now come to expect, but then takes a new turn. Hoshea's way of doing evil is different. He brings the wrath of the Assyrians, now ruled by Tiglath-Pileser's son, Shalmaneser, on to Israel by breaking his vassal obligations. He withholds tribute and joins in a coalition of states in alliance with Egypt. Hoshea is arrested and the Israelite capital besieged. In 722BC, the city falls, and its inhabitants are exiled. In his annals, Sargon, who has deposed Shalmaneser, claims the conquest and reports, 'I besieged and conquered Samaria and led away as booty 27,290 of its inhabitants', a number which probably refers to adult males. The place names cannot be located. All of this is treated in the most matter-of-fact way: we do not smell the siege, see the blood or hear the cries of grief and loss.

Why?

Verses 6–18 explain how such a thing could happen. The Israelites are the Lord's people, rescued from Egypt and bound to him in a covenant which made them his people and him their God. They had, however, worshipped other gods, followed the customs of other nations and, note, 'followed the customs which the kings of Israel had introduced'. The meaning of this Hebrew phrase is uncertain, but as it is in NRSV it makes explicit something that has been implicit in the history so far. The sufferings of Israel and Judah are to be laid at the feet of the kings: their failure to live by the rule of Deuteronomy 17:14–20 has had disastrous consequences.

Verses 9–12 point out that the people themselves are not blameless either. The Hebrew in the first part of verse 9 is obscure, but 'secretly' doesn't make much sense, for the sins listed are highly visible. The Israelites have combined the worship of the local gods with unofficial worship of the Lord in 'high places' which they multiplied. This list of apostasy and syncretism adds up to much religion but little commitment to the God who had given them their new life in their new land. Strangely there is no direct reference to the 'sin of Jeroboam' which has usually featured in the condemnations of the northern kings, only the passing reference to the two 'calves'. Two modern translations of the middle sentence in verse 15 (which is also found at Jeremiah 2:5) are particularly noteworthy—'Pursuing futility, they themselves became futile' (NJB) and 'They went after delusion and were deluded' (NJPS). The key word is the famous 'vanity' of Ecclesiastes 1:2, a word used elsewhere as a synonym for idols and false gods (for example, Deuteronomy 32:31; 1 Kings 16:13, 26).

Verses 13–17 insist that this has been done in the face of repeated warnings from 'prophets and seers' (who are the same thing—see 1 Samuel 9:9). They have deliberately and repeatedly turned aside from God's guidance and gone their own ways. They have sinned, not through ignorance or weakness, but through their own deliberate fault. This makes the 'therefore' of verse 18 inevitable.

Learning the lesson

Anyone looking for a summary of the teaching of 1 and 2 Kings can find it in verses 7–18. As the footnote in the New Oxford Annotated version of the NRSV puts it, 'These verses are the most important in the entire book for the understanding of the theological and ethical viewpoint of the Deuteronomists.'

But will Judah learn from this lesson? Judah has already been accused of several of the sins listed here, both from the early days under Rehoboam (1 Kings 14:21–24) and very recently under Ahaz (2 Kings 16:3–4). Also listed are two sins which Israel has not been accused of committing, but which Judah will commit in time—the worship of 'the host of heaven' (v. 16), which was a particular feature of worship in Mesopotamia rather than Canaan; and the practice of divination (v. 17), although that might be implied in 16:15 (see the comment in the previous study). The implications of Israel's fate for Judah's future are plain to see, but will Judah see it?

A PRAYER

Lord, as we watch scenes of war and terror on our television news,
help us to remember that real people are involved
and to pray for them.

AFTERMATH

Judah

Verses 19–20 leave us in no doubt of the answer to the question posed at the end of the last study. Judah does not learn the lesson. These two verses stand as a heading to the rest of the book. We are about to read of how Judah came to share the same fate as Israel. The smaller southern kingdom has followed its larger northern sister in failing to keep the Lord their God's commandments. It has followed the novel customs Israel had invented. It will also follow Israel into banishment. 'All the descendants of Israel' will eventually share the same fate.

Israel

Verses 21–24 summarize the reasons for Israel's banishment given in 17:7–18 and make good their omission of any reference to Jeroboam, son of Nebat. He is fairly and squarely blamed for 'driving' Israel away from obedience to the Lord and 'making' them commit great sin. Israel has 'continued' in all his sins and failed to 'depart' from them. Here, as so often in the story, much is laid at his door (see 1 Kings 15:34; 16:19, 26, 31; 22:52; 2 Kings 10:29; 13:2, 11; 14:24; 15:9, 18, 24, 28).

Verse 23 notes that the prophets had given them repeated warning, but NRSV's use of 'foretold' for the Hebrew 'said' or 'spoken' gives a misleading impression of their work, which was more often to exhort and plead, or warn and threaten, rather than to predict.

Exiles from elsewhere

In verses 24–28 we see the outworking of the Assyrian deportation policy. Having removed the Israelites—probably the whole population rather than only the leadership, though opinions differ here—they are replaced with exiles from elsewhere. Sargon's own records say, 'I restored the city and made it more habitable than before. I brought into it people of the countries conquered by my own hands. I set my own official over them as District Governor and imposed on them tribute as on an Assyrian city. I made them mix with each other.' The area is renamed 'Samaria'. Note the end of verse 24: the land had been Israel's promised land, given to them by God to 'possess' (Deuteronomy 1:8, 21, 39; Joshua 1:11 and so on), but that process is now completely undone as other nations 'take possession' of it instead.

The lions of verses 25–26 appear as God's agents to punish disobedience, but that raises two major questions. First, it is one thing for God to punish Israel for failing to keep the commandments which he had clearly told them about and which they had agreed to observe as their part of a covenant. It is quite another for him to set lions on to strangers who have never heard of the Lord and certainly not entered into any kind of agreement with him, just because they do not 'worship the Lord' (which is NRSV's better translation here of 'fear the Lord').

Second, the idea of a god or gods of the land was a common one. Many of the Israelites themselves had taken it for granted that, as they now lived in Canaan, they should pay proper attention to Baal, the god of Canaan. If you wanted local crops to grow, for example, then you needed to follow local custom in planting and harvesting, and that included the proper sacrifices to the local god. The king of Assyria knows all about such things and is quite happy to make the necessary arrangements to enable the newcomers to worship the Lord, whom he sees as the local god of Samaria. The Deuteronomists, however, have so far taken a very different line. For them, the Lord was not the God of a place but of a people—one particular, called and chosen people; not a local god but the God of gods (Deuteronomy 6:4, 10:17).

Verse 25, however, seems to call that into question. It is a frightening thought, and one that all believers should bear in mind, that the Israelites could not only be dispossessed of their promised land but also cease to be God's people and disappear into oblivion, as has happened to the ten 'lost' tribes. Verse 25 suggests that the Lord now has a 'new' people to replace them.

FOR PRAYER

The twentieth century has produced more refugees and displaced persons than ever before.

Lord, help us to remember that and to remember them.

MANY GODS

At first, the newcomers do not worship the Lord (17:24). Then, instructed by an Israelite priest sent by the king of Assyria, they worship the Lord alongside the gods they have brought with them. This is not good enough, according to the writers of Kings, who condemn them for trying to add the Lord to their existing pantheons as if he was just another god, just as they had condemned the old Israelites for doing the same thing. What is surprising and almost unprecedented in the Old Testament is that verse 25 appears to expect the incomers to replace the Israelites as the Lord's new people. The only precedent for this, and it is not a very strong one, is that a 'mixed multitude' accompanied Moses and the descendants of Abraham in the exodus out of Egypt (Exodus 12:38). Now, it seems, this multi-ethnic and multi-faith mixture, deported and transported from many places, are to be seen as the Lord's new people in Samaria. If they are to be so, however, they must follow the old guidelines (vv. 34–39). Sadly, however, and persistently, these new Israelites do what the old Israelites did (v. 40).

Many gods

In verses 29–31 we see each ethnic or national group worshipping its own god or gods, many of them otherwise unknown to us. We can almost feel the writer's scorn—what gods are these if each nation 'makes' its own? Here we see two attitudes to 'other faiths', one pluralist' and the other 'exclusivist', fundamentally at odds. Both of these positions have their descendants today, when the differences between the great world faiths are clear for all to see as these faiths and their followers live shoulder to shoulder on our small planet. For the 'pluralist', all religions point to ultimate spiritual realities, as in each one faith takes shape within a particular time and place and culture. All religions, therefore, lead to God, though some might do it better than others. They are to be respected because they are true for those who belong to them. The 'exclusivist' sees such ideas as completely wrong. As there is only one God, so there is only one true religion, and only one true way of thinking about him and worshipping him. All other religions are pagan, idolatry and superstition and so on.

They are to be opposed and their members converted to the true faith. The question of the 'other faiths' is one of the major ones facing all religions in the 21st century.

A message for Judah

The stress on 'to this day' in verses 34 and 41 lead some to see this situation as the beginning of that division and opposition between 'Jews' and 'Samaritans' which certainly existed in New Testament times (John 4:9 and so on) and still exists today.

Whatever we make of this chapter, the lesson for Judah is plain enough. Samaria has fallen and Israel is no more. The nation of Israel has become the Assyrian province of Samaria. Those Israelites who have managed to remain in their homeland have now added yet more gods to their list. Verse 40 sums up their situation. They continue as before. They have not listened.

From this point on, the story will be the story of Judah alone. As it proceeds, we will see if Judah will listen or continue as before. For those for whom the story was finally written, who know how it ends, the big question is whether the judgment passed on Israel in verse 40 will also be true of them. Whether they are in exile or struggling to survive in their homeland, will they listen so that they do not continue in their former ways?

A PRAYER

Lord, you call for the undivided allegiance of those who worship you. Help us to see what are the other gods we put alongside you, that we may worship you alone.

The GREATEST *since* DAVID

Hezekiah of Judah (715–697)

After so many chapters reporting the worst, the opening of this one is a refreshing change. The new king in Judah is the opposite of his father. He is the greatest king since David (v. 5). Verses 4–8 show the different facets of his greatness.

- He closed the traditional places of worship and broke down the sacred stones or pillars which were such a feature of them. The Deuteronomists disapproved of both of these and saw this move as long overdue (see Deuteronomy 12:2–7 and 16:22). He then turned his attention to the temple. No mention is made of the bronze snake, 'Nehushtan', in any of the descriptions of the temple furnishings in Kings (for its origin, see Numbers 21:6–9). The reference to 'the sacred pole' (the *asherah*) suggests that a single one of these ancient, dubious symbols is intended, though there has been no mention of one of these in the temple either. For the explanation of 'high places' see Study 9 on 1 Kings 3:2–4; for 'pillars' see Study 33 on 1 Kings 14:23, and for 'sacred poles' see Study 32 on 1 Kings 14:15.

- He 'trusted in the Lord'. This is the key debating point in the confrontation with the Assyrian spokesman in verses 19–24.

- His life was a model of faithful living in God's ways—verse 6 emphasizes that by saying the same thing in three different ways.

- The 'Lord was with him' as he had been with David (2 Samuel 5:10).

- He rebelled against Assyria and 'would not serve him' (v. 7). For him, the Lord alone could be served (Deuteronomy 6:13), unlike his father, who had lacked real trust in God and had relied on Assyria instead (2 Kings 16:1–8).

- He successfully tackled the 'old enemy', the Philistines (v. 8).

A problem with dates

Verses 9–12 are another summary of the fall of Samaria, reminding us that this event forms the backcloth to Hezekiah's reign. Verse 9 conflicts with Sargon's annals, as we saw in Study 79, where he claims the final victory for himself. Note again the classic explanation of the tragedy in verse 12.

In the Introduction, we looked at some of the general difficulties in producing a time-chart of the reigns of the kings of Israel and Judah. Hezekiah's reign presents us with one of the biggest single problems. There are two fixed points in this period—that Samaria fell in 722BC and that Sennacherib began to campaign in Canaan in 701.

Confrontation

After the glowing introduction, verse 13 comes as a nasty surprise. Sennacherib, Sargon's son and successor, invades Judah. Having just been told that Israel was exiled and Samaria fell because they didn't keep God's covenant, Hezekiah's faithfulness is to be put to the test.

Hezekiah responds to the invasion by surrendering and accepting the same vassal status that his father had had. The tribute is huge, ten tons of silver and one of gold, and it is paid from the treasuries of the palace and the temple, supplemented by melting down some of the temple furnishings (1 Kings 15:18 and 2 Kings 16:8). That, however, is not the end of the matter. Sennacherib sends 'a great army' which surrounds Jerusalem.

The three officials who accompany the army are given their Assyrian titles in NRSV: the Tartan, the Rab-saris and the Rabshakeh.

2 Kings 18:13—20:19 is repeated almost word for word in Isaiah 36—39, showing how the words of the prophet Isaiah were proved true. That Kings has so far failed to mention Isaiah is baffling.

FOR PRAYER

Hezekiah is pictured as a hero—a combination of religious reformer and patriot. Give thanks to God for those like him in every age and place.

The RABSHAKEH'S CHALLENGE

The Assyrian trio stand in a significant place (18:17), at least to readers familiar with Isaiah 7. It is the place where Isaiah the prophet had confronted Hezekiah's father. At the time, Jerusalem was besieged by the coalition of Arameans and Israelites, and the prophet's message was that the king should do nothing except trust in God. Exasperated by Ahaz's attitude, Isaiah told him straight that though he would survive this puny siege, his land would soon have to face the Assyrians, brought there by God (Isaiah 7:17). Now the Assyrian spokesman is challenging his son on that very spot. Hezekiah sends out a trio of his own.

Verse 20 gives the reason the Rabshakeh and the army are there. Hezekiah had rebelled against Assyria, possibly with Egyptian encouragement, and the tribute he had sent when the rebellion failed is obviously not going to persuade Sennacherib to forget it.

The Rabshakeh's first challenge is for the king, and it is about 'trust', a word which features seven times in verses 19–24 and again in verse 30. He answers his own question:

- You surely can't be trusting in Egypt, for Egypt is a 'broken reed'.

- You surely can't be trusting in the Lord, for you've just closed down most of his places of worship.

- You surely can't be trusting in your own resources because you haven't got enough.

His clinching challenge is the hardest of all: 'How did I and this army get here at all if it wasn't by the Lord's will and power?'

The trio recognize the strength of his arguments and ask him to speak in Aramaic, which the listening crowds don't understand. (It was only after the exile that Aramaic, the language of the Assyrian empire and then of international diplomacy, would become the everyday language of Palestine. When that happened, it was Hebrew which became the language that the ordinary population could not follow.) The Rabshakeh neatly turns that one and addresses the people, loudly and in Hebrew, first with a warning, then an offer and finally a question. Eating from your own vine and fig tree is not quite the idiom which expresses the Hebrew idyll of peace and freedom (that is to *sit under* one's own vine and fig tree as in 1 Kings 4:25; Micah 4:4; Zechariah 3:10), but it is temptingly close to it. The offer in verses 31–32 is so close to the Deuteronomic 'choice' theme (see Deuteronomy 30:15–20) that NIV actually closes the invitation with the phrase, 'Choose life and not death'. He is offering them freedom instead of siege, food instead of their own excrement and clean water instead of their own urine. The Rabshakeh is preaching to them in almost classic Deuteronomic language, style and theology! The Lord is acting via the king of Assyria, he says, which is, of course, exactly how the fall of Samaria is explained in 2 Kings 17:5–6 and 18:11–12. Do not let Hezekiah deceive you now, he preaches. Surrender and all will be well!

It is traditional to regard the final torrent of questions as an arrogant boast in which the king of Assyria claims that he is so powerful that none of these local gods can withstand him, but these questions need not be read like that. Read in the light of verse 25, they can be read as suggesting that the king of Assyria has not been stopped by these gods because his conquest has their support! None of them have 'delivered their nations out of his hand'; rather they have delivered them into it. Why, then, should Jerusalem expect deliverence from the Lord?

The people do not answer. The given explanation is that thay have been commanded to be silent. The appearance of the trio reporting to Hezekiah tells a different story. Torn clothing was the traditional sign of distress and mourning. These three are terrified by what they have heard. Their appearance says it all.

A PRAYER

Lord, at times when doubts and fears are strong, our trust in you is fragile and our hold on you is trembling, strengthen us by the knowledge that your grasp of us is mighty.

A PROPHET & *a* PRAYER

Blasphemy

The king's reaction to the report of his delegation is to tear his clothes as they had done. They react like this because they take the Rab-shakeh's words to be mockery of 'the living God' and they are appalled at this blasphemy (vv. 3–5). So, to the terror of their situation is added the fear of being caught up in the Lord's punishment of the blasphemy. The description of the Lord as the 'living God' in verses 4 and 16 are the only occurrences of this description in Kings. It occurs in this form over a dozen times in the Old Testament (for example, Deuteronomy 5:26; 1 Samuel 17:26, 36; Psalms 42:2; 84:2; Daniel 6:20, 26). This is closely related to the common form of swearing an oath or making a powerful statement by saying, 'As the Lord lives' (for example, Judges 8:19; 1 Samuel 14:39, 45), or in direct speech from God as reported by prophets, 'As I live, says the Lord' (for example, Numbers 14:21, 28; Isaiah 49:18; Ezekiel 5:11). The implication in this way of speaking of God is that the Lord is the only true and living God, which is spelled out unambiguously in Hezekiah's prayer in verses 15–19.

Isaiah the prophet

Verse 2 is the first mention in Kings of Isaiah the prophet. According to the book of Isaiah, his ministry took an important new turn on the death of Uzziah, Hezekiah's grandfather (Isaiah 6:1). The event in Isaiah 6 is often called Isaiah's 'call', but as that experience is actually recounted in chapter 6 and not chapter 1, it is perhaps best described as beginning a new stage in his work as a prophet. He had much to say to Hezekiah's father, Ahaz, as we noted in Study 78.

Hezekiah sends two of the original delegation with the 'senior priests' to ask for Isaiah's prayers for the 'remnant that is left' (v. 4), an important theme and word in Isaiah (Isaiah 10:20–23; 11:11–16). One important role of prophets was as intercessors (see 1 Kings 17: 17–24; 2 Kings 4:34–37; Jeremiah 14:7–9; Amos 7:1–6).

Isaiah assures the king that the Lord will deal with Sennacherib (vv. 6–7).

Events in the south

The Rabshakeh returns to the Assyrian base in the captured Judean city of Lachish, 25 miles south-west of Jerusalem, leaving the army to maintain the siege. When he finds that Sennacherib is besieging the nearby town of Libnah, and also finding himself under threat from Egypt, he sends a letter to Hezekiah telling him not to get the wrong impression from any rumours he might hear. Sennacherib might be otherwise engaged at the moment, but given his track record he will be successful and he will be back.

'King Tirhakah of Ethiopia' is the name of Sennacherib's opponent in NRSV. He did not become ruler of Ethiopia until 690BC, so this is another small dating problem. Some of the places listed in verses 12–13 have been mentioned already in 18:34. Most of them cannot be located with any certainty but the list effectively illustrates the principal feature of the political map of the ancient Near East at this period, namely, the multiplicity of small city states and local kingdoms. Israel and Judah were, in terms of their place on the world scene, little different than scores of other such minor kingdoms.

Hezekiah's prayer

When Hezekiah received the report from the delegation, he went into the temple (v. 1). When he receives the Rabshakeh's letter, he does the same and 'spreads it before the Lord' (v. 14). Hezekiah's prayer in verses 15–19 has affinities with the view of God expressed in Solomon's prayer in 1 Kings 8:23 and 27 and with the picture of God painted in the work of Isaiah of Babylon in Isaiah 40—55. It acknowledges the transcendence of God (compare Isaiah 6:1–4) as creator of all that is, and it contains an aside mocking the status of the other gods (compare Isaiah 44:9–17). It appeals to God to 'save' them. That had been Ahaz's appeal to the Assyrians (2 Kings 16:7) and also what he had done for Israel in the time of Jeroboam (2 Kings 14:27).

A PRAYER

O Lord, save thy people,
And bless thine inheritance.

Psalm 28:9 and the *Book of Common Prayer*

CURSE & BLESSING

An oracle of Isaiah

Verses 20–28 are the first example in Kings of the sort of prophetic oracles that make up most of the books of the prophets. This 'word of the Lord' that Isaiah has been given to pass on to Hezekiah uses the typical poetic style of parallelism, in which things are said twice with the repetition being used to make contrasts, emphasize or advance the message.

The opening stanza speaks the response of 'virgin daughter Zion' and 'daughter Jerusalem' to the arrogant shoutings of Sennacherib. The city is as vulnerable as a young girl, but it despises the bullying tyrant and is not afraid of him in the least (v. 21).

The second stanza exposes the arrogance of the Assyrian king against the Holy One of Israel, picturing it in the most exaggerated terms (vv. 22–24). Sennacherib never invaded Egypt, let alone conquered it. The message is plain: his claims are nonsense. For another condemnation of Assyrian boasting, see Isaiah 10:12–19. The 'Holy One of Israel' is the book of Isaiah's distinctive way of speaking about God, a title used only four times outside the book but 31 times within it. To call God 'holy' is to acknowledge both his power and majesty and his love and purity. To call him the 'Holy One of Israel' is to focus on his special relationship with Israel and to see both the joys and the demands which that brings to both parties.

The final stanza takes up the Rabshakeh's claim in 2 Kings 18:25, but gives it a twist. Yes, Sennacherib has done everything so far in the power of the Lord as he claimed, but the Lord knows all about him and sees his arrogance. As he has controlled his past, he will control his future too, and Sennacherib will find himself dragged back whence he came, as his hooks (or nose-rings, by which prisoners were chained together) have dragged away so many others (Amos 4:2).

A sign for Jerusalem

As Isaiah had given Ahaz a sign of the timescale in which he would destroy the enemy coalition (Isaiah 7:11, 14), so he gives Hezekiah a sign that the siege will be over within three years and that the 'surviving remnant' currently besieged in Jerusalem will again plant and prosper (vv. 29–31). He gives Hezekiah the same explanation too, that this will be done through the 'zeal of the Lord of hosts' (see Isaiah 9:7). The power behind the deliverance of Jerusalem is God's jealousy ('jealous love', NJB) or 'zeal' (see Isaiah 37:32; 63:15)— a word which is translated as 'fury' in Isaiah 42:13 and 59:17. The 'Lord of hosts' (for this title, see the comment in Study 39) is the 'jealous God' of the second commandment (Exodus 20:5) whose fierce passion we have seen in 1 Kings 14:22. The same zeal had empowered Elijah (1 Kings 19:10, 14) and Jehu (2 Kings 10:16).

In the meantime, the besieged remnant are assured that the Lord will defend his city for the same reason that he has not removed bad Judean kings, for the sake of his and David's reputations (see 1 Kings 15:4; 2 Kings 8:19).

The fate of Sennacherib

The siege of Jerusalem was lifted in 701BC and Sennacherib returned to Nineveh, where he was assassinated in 681 by two of his sons who then fled to Armenia (Ararat). The cause of the lifting of the siege has caused much speculation. The commonest suggestion is that it was the result of plague. This comes either from 2 Samuel 24:15–16, which makes a link between God's angel and plague, or from the story recounted by the Greek historian, Herodotus, that Sennacherib was forced to withdraw from his assault on Egypt because mice had gnawed through the army's bowstrings (see the link between mice and plague in 1 Samuel 6:4–5). Mention of the 'angel of the Lord' in verse 35, however, ought to be enough to deter readers from such guesswork. As in Exodus 3:2; 14:19 and 1 Kings 19:5, the appearance of angels is intended to make the point that this event was another of the Lord's mighty works.

A PRAYER

Give peace in our time, O Lord.
Because there is none other that fighteth for us,
but only thou, O God.

The Book of Common Prayer

86 2 KINGS 20:1–11

SENNACHERIB & HEZEKIAH

Before we read on about Hezekiah, let us see the events of 2 Kings 18—20 from another angle.

From the Assyrian archives

One of Sennacherib's own accounts of his encounter with Hezekiah can be seen in the British Museum. Reading it, we see the human realities of invasion, defeat and exile:

> *As for Hezekiah, the Jew, who did not bow in submission to my yoke, 46 of his strong walled towns and innumerable smaller villages I besieged and conquered... I took out from them 200,150 people, young and old, male and female, innumerable horses, mules, donkeys, camels, large and small cattle as spoils of war. He himself I shut up like a caged bird in Jerusalem, his royal city... I fixed upon him an increase in the amount to be given as presents for my lordship, in addition to the former annual tribute... 30 talents of gold, 300 talents of silver, precious stones, large blocks of red stone, inlaid ivory couches and chairs, elephant hide and tusks, ebony wood, box wood and all kinds of treasures, as well as his daughters, concubines and musicians he sent me later to Nineveh, my lordly city. He sent a personal messenger to deliver the tribute and make a slavish obeisance.*

Memorials like this one and the Moabite Stone (see Study 54) are interesting for many reasons, not least because they confirm that there were such events as the Bible stories portray and give the 'other side's' point of view of them. By his own account, Sennacherib did not take Jerusalem, an escape for the city which gave rise to the idea that it was inviolable. This mistaken idea would later cause problems for the prophet Jeremiah, whose message would be that it was the will of God for the city to be destroyed.

Hezekiah's illness

Verses 1–7 refer to a serious illness suffered by Hezekiah at some unspecified time during the invasion or invasions by the Assyrians.

Isaiah's announcement of his imminent death naturally devastates the king. Verse 7 recognizes that Hezekiah's illness is caused by a boil. Deuteronomic orthodoxy, on the other hand, had another explanation for such a deadly illness. In its way of looking at things, virtue was rewarded and vice was punished, and so Hezekiah must have sinned. Verse 3 illustrates Hezekiah's problem with this verdict on his life. He pleads with God to think again because his life has been good rather than bad. Prompted by God, Isaiah returns and gives him God's revised verdict plus a fig-poultice remedy.

Another sign

Isaiah had had trouble with Hezekiah's father not believing what he told him (Isaiah 7) and, in the process, refusing the prophet's offer of a sign. Hezekiah, on the other hand, asks for such proof to confirm Isaiah's words. There follows another of those miracles which remind modern readers that we are reading a theologically motivated story, intended to show that God has to be taken seriously if human life and society are to function properly. The sign Hezekiah is given is a mini-version of Joshua and the day the sun stood still (see Joshua 10:12–13), either with the sun's shadow on a sundial (NRSV) or, as in most translations, on the palace steps.

Hezekiah was introduced as the best king of Judah yet—even the best there would ever be (1 Kings 18:5). His estimate of himself in verse 3 is fully in keeping with what we have read so far of his life and character. Yet this sickness does, given the conventions of the book, raise a doubt in our minds. It raises a doubt about Hezekiah, but it raises a greater doubt about the future. If this greatest of all kings came this close to premature death, what is the ultimate future of the kingdom of Judah if it does anything less than 'walk before God in faithfulness and with a whole heart and do good in his sight'?

A PRAYER

O Lord, make clean our hearts within us.
And take not thy Holy Spirit from us.

The Book of Common Prayer

87

The FINAL VERDICT *on* HEZEKIAH

The first mention of 'Babylon'

Verses 12–19 depict Hezekiah receiving a visit from the envoys of the king of Babylon. Merodach-baladan ruled in Babylon from 721 to 710BC when he was expelled by Sargon. On Sargon's death in 705, he attempted to take power again and to initiate a wider rebellion against Assyria, though without success. It may be that a memory of his seeking for supporters is reflected here. What is certain is that in meeting him we encounter the fateful name of 'Babylon' for the first time. The apparently innocent mention of that name in verse 12 is soon followed by the first prediction of the exile to Babylon in verse 17.

Folly or pride or both

Hezekiah welcomes the envoys and boasts to them by showing them everything he has. This is seen by later Jewish commentators as another sign of the pride of which he is accused in 2 Chronicles 32:25. Another Assyrian inscription also depicts him as arrogant. In it, Sennacherib says, 'I laid waste the wide district of Judah and made the overbearing and proud Hezekiah, its king, bow submissively at my feet.'

The visit of the envoys brings Isaiah back on to the scene, predicting terrifying exile to Babylon and the plundering of palace and temple, including the mutilation and enslavement of some of Hezekiah's own sons. Verse 19 reveals another flaw in Hezekiah's character.

The words 'prophet' and 'prophecy' have been used with a variety of meanings in many different religions and contexts over at least three millennia, but in many modern minds they have only one meaning. A prophet is someone who predicts the future. Prophecy is prediction. That understanding of prophets and prophecy has not been dominant in the prophets and prophecies we have met so far in Kings. There we have seen that a prophet was God's spokesperson, declaring God's will in a particular time and place and pointing out the consequences for those involved if his will was not done. Here, therefore, we see Isaiah the 'foreteller' as well as the 'forthteller', pointing out the future outworkings and consequences of their present actions. Nothing like this has been said to Judah and Jerusalem before, and Isaiah gives no reason for what will happen. That becomes clear in what follows.

The tunnel

The concluding statement about Hezekiah's reign in verses 20–21 gives a new piece of information about his reign, that in it he had carried through a major project to improve the water supply to Jerusalem. Hezekiah's Tunnel was a magnificent piece of engineering and it still carries water from the Gihon spring in the Kidron valley to the Pool of Siloam inside the city. It runs for nearly 600 metres and to construct it 'he tunnelled the rock with iron tools' (Ecclesiasticus 48:17) with two sets of tunnellers starting from either end. The story of how they nearly passed each other in the middle is told in the Siloam Inscription which was discovered carved in the tunnel wall about twenty feet in from the Pool of Siloam in 1880.

Obituary

Hezekiah's obituary in verses 20–21 does not quite do him justice. It mentions his water tunnel but little else. Two more things need to be said to his credit if we are to be true to the story told about him in Kings. First, at the end of his reign there was still a nation to hand on to his son—and that, in the circumstances, was no mean achievement. He had rebelled against Assyria and then submitted again and survived. His country had been invaded and submission impoverished it. But Judah still existed. Credit must be given to Hezekiah for that.

Second, he had attempted to reform the nation's religious life— not radically, and nowhere near as rigorously as he might, but he had made the attempt and his grandson, Josiah, would try again (2 Kings 22). Hezekiah was one of the better kings of Judah, despite his flaws.

FOR REFLECTION

In prophet's word he spake of old,
He speaketh still.

From the hymn 'Praise to the Living God'
translated from a medieval Jewish doxology

88

NO SON *of* HIS FATHER

Manasseh of Judah (697–642)

In 2 Kings 18:5, Hezekiah, despite his flaws, is called the greatest king of Judah since David, who also, of course, was deeply flawed both as a man and as a king. In Manasseh, in complete contrast to the father, we have a son who was Judah's worst king by far. Manasseh reigns longer than any king in Judah's history, but in his reign he follows in his grandfather Ahaz's footsteps and repeats all that was worst in his ancestor Ahab of Israel.

Verses 2–9 list his misdeeds. We have seen most of these 'abominations' before (see the references given in Study 82), including the child sacrifice, 'soothsaying and augury' from his grandfather's time (see 2 Kings 17:17). The 'mediums and wizards' of verse 6 are new. These practices are condemned in Deuteronomy 18:10–14. There is no ambiguity about the 'sacred pole' in verse 3. It is an image of the goddess Asherah (v. 7). Note the two quotations citing what God had 'said' (vv. 4 and 7), which point back to Deuteronomy 12:5 (see Study 13)—plus the fact that they have not 'listened' (v. 9). The king is accused of 'misleading' his people through his failure to observe Torah (see Deuteronomy 17:18–19). The quotations serve to emphasize that Manasseh's actions were not committed in ignorance. The mention in verse 16 that he 'shed much innocent blood' should be added to the two mentions of the name of Ahab in the catalogue of apostasy. In both Manasseh and Ahab, the sin of apostasy and the crime of terror go hand in hand (see Study 45).

The message of Isaiah to Hezekiah in 2 Kings 20:16–18 is repeated by unnamed prophets in 21:11–15. These prophets, like Moses in verse 8, are called God's 'servants', a traditional title of the Davidic king of which Manasseh is no longer worthy. He has made the chosen people worse than the Amorites, one of the local peoples who had lived in Canaan before the Israelites took over. Because of him, Jerusalem will share the fate of Samaria, and Judah's monarchy will go the way of Israel's. Even the remnant promised by Isaiah (2 Kings 19:31) will be prey and spoil for their enemies. They have gone wrong since they left Egypt, so they can reap what they have sown for the last 700 years!

Kings makes no mention of any change of heart on Manasseh's part, whereas in 2 Chronicles 33:1–20 we read of his repentance and changed ways. The Prayer of Manasseh, from the Apocrypha of the Eastern Orthodox churches (now available in any NRSV with Apocrypha), is a classic penitential prayer written later and attributed to Manasseh to express his penitence. For Kings, however, he is the worst of the worst.

Freedom and responsibility

Modern readers of the Bible often forget that ancient Israelites had little or no belief in any individual life beyond death, and that even in the time of Jesus, Jewish conservatives like the Sadducees dismissed the whole idea as a modern heresy. According to the writers of Kings, therefore, goodness must be rewarded and badness punished in this life because there is no other. How come, then, that the worst of the kings of Judah can reign longer than the best of them?

Note, first, that while there is some dispute about the precise length of his reign (55 years in verse 1 but 45 in the dates above), the writers make no attempt to conceal its great length. Nor do they hesitate to expose his wickedness. These two facts might sit uncomfortably side by side, but our writers have the courage to admit both of them.

Note, second, that their theology is not as crude as some accuse it of being. They recognize, for instance, that their principle does not necessarily operate on a simple individual basis—that someone's suffering might not be the result of their own sin, nor their prosperity the reward for their virtue! They also recognize that things do not always happen immediately. They know that there is a space between cause and effect. It is this space which, for example, gives human beings the freedom to choose between good and evil, to err and sin and then recognize their mistakes and choose differently. It is this space which enables them to see a God who teaches, advises, warns and encourages but who does not plan the minutiae of people's lives or compel their responses. This is the space where human freedom and responsibility are exercised and choices made.

A PRAYER

Pray for those trapped by the choices they have made
and those trapped with them.

In FATHER'S FOOTSTEPS

Amon of Judah (641–640)

Amon walks in his father's evil ways and not in the 'way of the Lord' (v. 22).

Instead of the worship of the Lord, the Lord alone, in the temple in Jerusalem, Amon promotes the worship of the Lord together with his goddess consort, Asherah, plus the worship of Baal and the stars (the heavenly host), at many altars in the temple. Jeremiah 44:15–23 gives us a fascinating glimpse of the worship of the 'queen of heaven' in Jerusalem at this time, as do the inscriptions discovered at Kuntillet Ajrud, in the far south of Judah, which refer to 'Yahweh and his Asherah'. Amon also patronizes the high places where the Lord used to be worshipped, as well as supporting the worship of Baal across the country. Images and idols abound. He permits and encourages religious practices which prophets have condemned for centuries, including the sort of occult magic that had brought down the house of Saul when he consulted the medium at Endor (compare 2 Kings 21:6 and 1 Samuel 28:3–25). What this amounts to is that he has 'abandoned' the Lord, the 'God of his ancestors' (v. 22). It makes the powerful point that in doing these things Amon is betraying not only the Lord but also his family honour and his national heritage.

Verses 20–22 give us a particularly crisp example of the common biblical metaphor of religious faith and life as a journey or a walk along a particular road or path. This is a favourite metaphor in the Wisdom literature (for example, Proverbs 1—3) and throughout the Psalms, and it is frequently used by Jesus in his teaching, most clearly of all in Matthew 7:13–14. It reminds us that religion is not simply a question of right belief or stimulating worship, but of lifestyle and ethics too. The importance of 'discipleship' and 'pilgrimage' in modern spirituality captures the elements of commitment and movement in this ancient but still helpful metaphor.

Amon is the third king of Judah to fall victim to a palace coup (the others are Jehoash, and his son Amaziah—see 2 Kings 12:21–22; 14:19) and the fifth to die a violent death (Ahaziah had died from wounds received in battle, and Athaliah the usurper queen had been assassinated—see 2 Kings 9:27; 11:16). The 'people of the land', that is, ordinary Judeans as distinct from those at court or in the military, killed his killers and put his son, Josiah, on the throne to succeed him. Amon and his father are both buried in the 'garden of Uzza'. This is probably best taken to refer to a garden Manasseh had built beside the palace in Jerusalem for his Arabian wife, Meshullemeth, which contained a shrine to the Arabian astral god, Uzza. Solomon's failings are being repeated here, though on a much smaller scale in keeping with Jerusalem's and Judah's greatly reduced circumstances (see 1 Kings 11:1–13). The apostasy of father and son continues with them to their tombs (or even to the same tomb if NJB is right).

A recap

If we pause in 640BC to take stock, the picture is bleak. For eighty years Judah has stood alone. The northern kingdom has been resettled with exiles from other parts of the Assyrian empire and Samaria is now an alien place. It is sixty years since Jerusalem was besieged by the Assyrians and then, somehow, saved from destruction. In that time, however, the religious reforms instituted by Hezekiah have been more than undone by his son and grandson. Judah and Jerusalem are now indistinguishable from any of the other small cities and minor kingdoms of the region. That had always been the case in terms of politics and economics, but now it is also true in terms of religion. There is nothing different in the temple in Jerusalem from what you would find in the temples of Gaza, Damascus or Tyre. Manasseh and Amon have seen to that. What chance, then, has an eight-year-old, put on the throne by the mob? What chance has Judah?

A PRAYER

Eternal God, you have set forth the way of life for us in the teaching of your servant Moses, in the words of your prophets of old and above all in the life and work of Jesus Christ. Help us to turn from old and deathly ways and to walk in your ways of life and peace.

FINDING *the* BOOK *of the* LAW

Josiah of Judah (639–609)

The contrast is startling. This eight-year-old does not follow in his father's or grandfather's footsteps but walks in the ways of his ancestor David (vv. 1–3). He does so in every detail ('all the ways'), without any deviation (a clear allusion to verse 20 in the key background passage of Deuteronomy 17:14–20). We should not, however, be surprised, for an anonymous prophet had spoken of his coming 300 years before (1 Kings 13:2).

His faithfulness to David's ways led him to repair and restore the fabric of the temple, which by this time was 300 years old. As yet, however, he sees nothing wrong with the various symbols and images which his grandfather had introduced into the temple's worship. The refurbishing project is well under way (v. 5), with honest and reliable builders (v. 7, as in 2 Kings 12:9–15), when in 621BC the 26-year-old king is brought up with a jolt.

The book of the Torah

In the course of the repairs, a book is found which the high priest describes as 'the book of the Torah (Law)'. He shares the discovery of this scroll with the secretary who, being an accountant, first gives his financial report before reading the 'book' to the king. The effect is electric. The king is badly shaken by what he hears, calls a meeting of his leading officials and then instructs them to 'go and inquire of the Lord'—that is, to find a prophet and ask what this all means (vv. 11–13).

Everyone agrees that this 'book of the Torah' is very closely related to the book of Deuteronomy, which calls itself 'the book of the Torah' in Deuteronomy 29:21; 30:10 and 31:26. Most agree that the 'book' which Shaphan read to Josiah probably consisted of chapters 12—26 and 28 of our present book. Beyond this broad agreement there is much speculation, much of it futile because the origins of the book of Deuteronomy itself are shrouded in mystery. It may well have originated in Israel and been brought down to Jerusalem after the destruction of Samaria in 722, but that is not certain. Some suggest that the 'discovery' of the book was a ploy, that the Deuteronomists planted it so that it might be found. Others say that Hilkiah brought out the old book which Josiah's grandfather had thrown out of its appointed place (see Deuteronomy 31:26 and 2 Kings 14:6), but did so tentatively because he was unsure of what the grandson's reaction might be. Others recognize that we cannot know the details.

If this link with Deuteronomy is correct, it is clear why Josiah was appalled by what he heard. Most of what he had grown up with in the temple was completely at odds with the teachings of Deuteronomy about the single-minded loyalty which the Lord required from his chosen, covenant people. His grandfather's legacy (seen in 2 Kings 21:2–9) could not have been further from what Deuteronomy says that the Lord had commanded his people through Moses. Brought face to face with that, Josiah tears his clothes in the classic gesture of despair, sorrow and remorse. We must wait until 2 Kings 23 to see if this is anything more than a dramatic gesture.

The people of the book

The finding of this scroll must be one of the most significant events not only in Kings but in the whole of the Old Testament. Jews, Christians and Moslems all are, in one way or another, 'people of the book', and this passage is the one where the idea of a 'holy book' first appears. Up to this point, the religion of ancient Israel had holy places and holy people but no 'holy scripture'. It had no sacred texts from which guidance for faith and life could be sought, no authorized collection of stories or teaching, no readings for worship or study. It is hard for us to imagine that, and it would take about another 200 years before their first 'sacred book' was authorized and agreed. This discovery marks the start of the process which would lead to Ezra publishing and authorizing 'the Torah' (see Nehemiah 8) and continue, for Christians, until our Bibles as we know them first appeared.

A PRAYER

Thanks be to God for his gift of the Scriptures.

HULDAH *the* PROPHETESS

An anonymous prophet had spoken of the coming of Josiah (1 Kings 13:2), and Josiah's initial response on hearing the words Shaphan reads to him confirms the impression of him given in 2 Kings 22:2. He sends to God's current spokesperson in Jerusalem for advice and guidance. Unlike many of his predecessors, he is a king who is prepared to listen to prophets and heed God's teaching.

Josiah's delegation go to the Lord's current spokesperson, Huldah. She might be a prophetess, with all the status attaching to that crucial role in Kings, but the writers still define and describe her first and foremost in terms of her husband, her husband's family and her husband's job (v. 14). Women in positions of authority are few and far between in the Old Testament, and the two we have encountered so far in Kings—the foreign Queen Jezebel of Israel in 1 Kings 16 to 21, and her daughter Athaliah who usurped the throne of Judah in 2 Kings 11—hardly commend themselves as role models. In addition to Huldah, four female Israelite prophets are mentioned in the Old Testament and three of them are named. They are Miriam, sister of Moses and Aaron in Exodus 15:20; Deborah, the prophetess and 'judge' in Judges 4:4; the dubious Noadiah in Nehemiah 6:14; and Isaiah's wife in Isaiah 8:3. The fact that Deborah is referred to as 'a' prophetess rather than 'the' prophetess in Judges 4:4 may indicate that the phenomenon of a woman in this role was not as unusual as the scarcity of their names and appearances in the Old Testament might suggest. We see something of Huldah's importance in that her role is obviously familiar to the national leaders and they go to her rather than summoning her to come to them.

Plain speaking

Like her male predecessors, Huldah is not awed by the king's messengers or particularly respectful of the king himself, calling him 'the man who sent you to me' (v. 15). Her message is blunt. Josiah will die in peace (though in fact he won't) but disaster will hit 'this place'. Note those four references to 'this place' in verses 16, 17, 19 and 20. Two of them also speak of the 'inhabitants' of the city but the focus in Huldah's speech is on the destruction of the city of

Jerusalem. This is a new and surprising development. In the reign of Josiah's great-grandfather, Hezekiah, the city had been saved from the Assyrians (2 Kings 19:32–36), though Isaiah the prophet had warned Hezekiah that his 'sons' would be deported to Babylon. In his turn, Josiah's grandfather, Manasseh, had been told by the prophets that the whole population would be handed over to their enemies and the city 'wiped clean' like a dish (2 Kings 21:10–15). Now, however, Josiah is told that disaster will come on the city itself as well as on its inhabitants. Huldah is explicit. She promises Josiah that he himself will not see the disaster which is coming on the city. The repentance which she ascribes to him in verse 19 is reminiscent of that ascribed to Hezekiah in 2 Kings 20:5, though there is no suggestion that Josiah reacted to this in the all-too-human way that Hezekiah did (2 Kings 20:19). She insists that the Lord's anger against the city is unquenchable.

By this point it is clear that God's patience is over. He saved the city from the Assyrians 'for David's sake' (2 Kings 20:6) but, despite the fact that Josiah walks in all of David's ways (2 Kings 22:2), that is no longer enough to guarantee the City of David's survival. The slide downwards has gone so far that not even Josiah's dedication, nor the thoroughgoing reforms we shall read about in 2 Kings 23, can prevent the disaster which is coming on 'this place'.

Huldah places the blame for the coming destruction of Jerusalem clearly on its inhabitants. Here, in a nutshell, we read the message of the whole Deuteronomic History. The catastrophe of the fall of Jerusalem has a simple explanation: 'It's your own fault. You have brought all this upon yourselves.' There are, needless to say, many explanations for the traumatic events of 597 and 586, not least in terms of ancient Near Eastern power politics and economics. These might explain how those events came about; but they do not, for the Deuteronomic Historians at least, explain why. For the why, we must listen to Huldah.

A PRAYER

Lord, help us to see, individually and corporately, that our attitudes and actions have consequences.

JOSIAH'S REFORMS

Josiah's reaction to the message of Huldah is to institute a sweeping religious reform. She had confirmed that the scroll found in the temple was indeed a word from God and Josiah acts immediately to put its teaching into effect.

A new covenant

Josiah calls leaders and people together and reads the scroll 'standing by the pillar'—or on the dais—in the king's customary place (2 Kings 11:14). Verses 2 and 21 (and the parallel in 2 Chronicles 34:30) refer to the scroll as the 'book of the covenant'. Exodus 24:7 is the only other place where this phrase is used, so the choice of this different title for the scroll would seem to be a deliberate attempt to portray Josiah as a second Moses. We see the two different senses of the word 'covenant' in verses 2–3. 'The covenant' which is the subject of the scroll is that set of promises and commitments (for which words like 'contract' and 'agreement' are useful translations) which bound God to the nation and the nation to God. The 'covenant' which Josiah makes before God is to keep that agreement, and for this the word 'promise' is a good translation.

Cleansing the temple

Josiah orders the cleansing of the temple (vv. 4–7). In the light of 2 Kings 25:18 and Jeremiah 52:24, 'the priests of the second order' is translated in the singular as the deputy high priest in REB and 'the priest next in rank' in NJB. Everything associated with the worship of any god other than the Lord is removed from the temple, including the two altars which Manasseh had erected to the 'hosts of heaven' (2 Kings 21:5) and the image of Asherah which he had installed (2 Kings 21:7). They destroy that statue and desecrate even its ashes by scattering them in the local cemetery. Josiah burns everything else that can be burned and, killing two birds with one stone, scatters the ashes at Bethel when he destroys that altar which the Deuteronomic Historians had always considered to be at the heart of the northern kingdom's failings (see v. 15; 1 Kings 12:25–33; 15:26, 34). He deposes all the priests of these other gods and destroys the rooms which the temple prostitutes (probably male but possibly of both sexes) used for their fertility rites and where the women 'wove for Asherah'. This is usually taken to mean weaving vestments for use in the worship of this goddess, but something much more lively is probably meant here.

Centralizing everything

Josiah attempts to centralize the worship of the Lord in Jerusalem by destroying the local 'high places' where he had been worshipped previously and by bringing all the priests to Jerusalem. This is the policy advocated in Deuteronomy 18:6–8, though Jerusalem itself is not named there. The local priests either did not co-operate or were not allowed to, though the reference to their eating unleavened bread indicates that they retained their priestly status (v. 9; see comments on 2 Kings 23:21–22 in the next study).

Cleansing the city

Josiah next purges the city of its various sacred places (vv. 8b–14). The 'high places of the gate' may be either shrines at this particular city gate or, following a tiny change in the Hebrew, the 'altars dedicated to the goat-demons' (GNB). For the cult of these satyrs or desert-spirits, see 2 Chronicles 11:15. Topheth was the shrine of Molech in the valley of Hinnom where human sacrifice had been practised (see Jeremiah 32:35 and the comment on 2 Kings 3:27 in Study 55). The horses and chariots of the sun (which have not been mentioned before), the roof altars in the palace of Ahaz and Solomon's old shrines for Astarte, Chemosh and Milcom (see 1 Kings 11:6–8) are all destroyed and desecrated. These were so evil that our authors call the Mount of Olives on which they were built the 'Mount of Destruction' (NRSV) or 'Corruption' (NIV) (v. 13).

Some of these details are obscure but the picture is clear. Josiah carries out a thorough reform, designed to rid Jerusalem and Judah of all traces of the worship of any other god than the Lord.

A PRAYER ✓

Lord, teach us to know what this text means, that 'You shall worship the Lord your God, him only shall you serve'.

The REFORMS SPREAD

The altar at Bethel

The reforms spread. From Jerusalem, through Judah, and into the old heartlands of Israel, Josiah's reforming zeal moves to effect change.

Verse 15 returns to a key theme of 1 Kings 12 to 2 Kings 17, that the life of the northern kingdom was fundamentally and fatally flawed from the start because of King Jeroboam's 'sin'. That sin had been to build the sanctuaries at Dan and Bethel (see 1 Kings 12:25–33 and comments in Study 29). In his reforming and centralizing zeal, Josiah desecrates and destroys the altar and sanctuary at Bethel just as he had all the other sacred places of the Lord in Judah as well as those of the other gods. At Bethel, as in other places, the Lord was worshipped either alongside other gods or in the same ways, depending on whether you translate 'asherah' in verse 15 as 'sacred pole' or as the name of the goddess (see comments on 1 Kings 14:15, Study 32).

Verses 16–17 point back to the story in 1 Kings 13. The bones of that dead prophet are left undisturbed. What he had spoken about has now taken place. This is another little reminder in the ongoing story that prophets are to be taken seriously.

Other altars in Samaria

In verses 19–20 we see an even more rigorous policy than Josiah has been pursuing in Judah. Instead of simply desecrating the altars to other gods and deposing their priests (as in v. 5), he destroys and desecrates the high places of Samaria and kills their priests on site before returning to Jerusalem.

Here we need to pause. Josiah is king of Judah but Bethel and the 'towns of Samaria' are in the old kingdom of Israel, which had long since been resettled by the Assyrians as part of their empire. So what is Josiah doing there? It may be that this story reflects something that actually happened and about which the writers of Kings are not particularly interested, namely that as well as being a religious reformer Josiah was an ambitious king with an eye to expanding his kingdom northwards as the power of Assyria waned. It may also be that these two are linked. Perhaps Josiah was free to rid Judah of all 'foreign' gods because Assyrian power was in serious decline? That decline ended with the fall of Nineveh to the Medes and Babylonians in 612BC, which is celebrated in the book of Nahum.

The Passover

Back in Jerusalem, Josiah orders the celebration of the greatest Passover since Moses. It is to be done as the discovered scroll says it should be done. If we are right in saying that that scroll is essentially Deuteronomy 12—26, then the Passover instructions mentioned in verse 21 can be found in Deuteronomy 16:1–8.

After the exile, Tabernacles at the beginning of the new year in September, Passover in March or April and Weeks or Pentecost forty days later became the three great pilgrim festivals in Judaism, and they remain important to this day for the Jewish community. At Passover, each family gathers for a meal of lamb and bitter herbs and retells the exodus story. The classic account of the origin of the festival is found in Exodus 12:21–27 where it is celebrated on the eve of the escape from Egypt. It may have begun earlier than that, but it came to be linked with the events of the exodus as the great celebration of the liberation of Israel. In the longer story, the last mention of Passover was in the time of Joshua in Joshua 5:10–11.

Verse 22 insists that the like of Josiah's Passover celebration had not been seen even in the great days of David and Solomon, a statement which prepares us for the point made in verse 25 that there had never been a king like Josiah. Josiah's way of celebrating Passover, centralized in Jerusalem, was a new departure and it was a magnificent experience! What had been a local celebration, in which the paschal lamb was killed at the nearby holy place before being eaten in the family home, was now one which necessitated a trip to Jerusalem to kill the lamb in the temple.

A PRAYER ✓

Liberating God, hasten the day when all humanity can celebrate in the freedom and peace which is your will for all.

A SAD END

The odd corners of religion in Judah

Verse 24 opens a window on to some of the other religious practices in Judah which Josiah brings to an end. Most of what has been mentioned previously in 2 Kings 23 can be classed as public or official forms of religious activity, sanctioned by tradition and royal patronage. In addition to such 'public' religion there was then, as there is now and always has been, a wide range of 'private' religious practices. 'Mediums' and 'wizards' were mentioned in 2 Kings 21:6 as examples of the more dangerous forms of private religion encouraged by Manasseh, and this verse adds two more plus the general catch-all, 'abominations'. 'Teraphim' were 'household gods', as in the story of Jacob and Rachel in Genesis 31:17–35. Those mentioned in 1 Samuel 19:13–15 are near to human size and shape but many examples of small figurines, both male and female, have emerged in archaeological excavations in the region in recent years which are probably much the same sort of thing.

No king like Josiah

Verse 24 concludes that Josiah 'established' the words of the law or teaching written in the scroll which Hilkiah had found, and that leads into the statement that there had never been any king like him. Nor would there be. He fulfils supremely the requirements of a king found in Deuteronomy 17:14–20 and of an Israelite in Deuteronomy 6:4–5. This verdict on Josiah supersedes that on Hezekiah in 2 Kings 18:5.

'The fierceness of his great wrath'

Verse 26 brings us back down to earth. Things had been going so well with Josiah that it was beginning to look as if 2 Kings 22:17 and 20 might be overstatements. Perhaps Josiah had stopped the rot? Perhaps the great virtue of this king might be able to turn the fortune of his people? No, say verses 26–27, emphatically not! Not even Josiah's great achievements can undo the consequences of Manasseh's wrongdoing and the cumulative effects of years of wrongdoing before him. Verse 26, however, does not use this sort of cause-and-effect language. Instead it speaks of 'the fierceness of the Lord's great wrath' and the ways in which Manasseh had 'provoked' the Lord to this excess of fury. For this very passionate and human way of talking about God's anger, see my comments in Study 72. Despite Josiah, Judah will go the way of Israel, Jerusalem will go the way of Samaria, and the temple in Jerusalem will go the way of the one in Bethel. Having chosen the city and singled out the temple, the Lord can be forced to abandon his choice! The words of the prophetess stand.

Josiah's death

Nineveh had fallen in 612BC but the Assyrians were still fighting to hold on to the remains of their empire. Why tiny Judah should want to get involved in the international power struggles of a dying empire is impossible to say, but in 608 Josiah led his army against the Egyptians who were marching north. Historically, we know that they were going to the aid of the Assyrians, and most translations say that, but AV and NJPS read the text correctly when they say that they were going north to attack the Assyrians. The original writer just got it wrong. Josiah is killed. His dead body is returned to Jerusalem from Megiddo by chariot just as his unfaithful ancestor Ahaziah's had been (2 Kings 9:27–28). He was 31 and had reigned for 23 years.

Verse 28 contains the standard formula for marking the end of a reign, but the two verses which follow are difficult. Had not the prophetess also said that Josiah would be gathered to his ancestors and his grave in peace (2 Kings 22:20)? How, then, can he be killed in battle? Can the words of a prophet no longer be trusted? The alternative version in 2 Chronicles 35:20–24 tells us more. There Pharaoh Neco tries to dissuade Josiah from attacking him by telling him that he is going north at God's command, but Josiah refuses to listen. His death is the result of his disobedience to God. The account in Kings makes no mention of that. Verse 26 explains why: Josiah reaps what his father has sown.

The fate of Judah is sealed. Josiah is dead and the prophetess has told us what will follow his death.

FOR PRAYER

Pray for those whose faithfulness goes without reward and whose lives are blighted by the sins of others.

TWO EVIL SONS

The defeat and death of Josiah in battle at Megiddo in 609 effectively brought the nation of Judah's freedom and independence to an end. Judah was now subject to Egyptian rule and in these verses we see how Pharaoh Neco exercised it. The short reign of the next king and the way that he was replaced are a clear reminder that the nation is under sentence of destruction.

Jehoahaz of Judah (609)

On the death of his father, the people took Jehoahaz, a younger son of Josiah, and made him king (23:30). Some commentators speculate that the 'people of the Land' bypassed the elder son and appointed a younger brother as part of an anti-Egyptian conspiracy, and that these same 'people of the land' paid, literally, for this political error of judgment later (see v. 35). Verse 32 gives the Deuteronomic Historians' judgment on Jehoahaz, and the way that it is phrased needs to be noted. The decline of Judah has been such that this bad king can be described for the first time as doing evil 'just as his ancestors had done'. It has become normal for the kings of Judah to do wrong! Verse 33 shows what the Pharaoh thought of the people's choice: he imprisoned him and then took him to Egypt 'where he died'.

Jehoiakim of Judah (609–598)

The Pharaoh demonstrated his authority as overlord by appointing Eliakim, an older son of Josiah, as king and by renaming him Jehoiakim (vv. 34–37). The name itself has no particular significance, but the fact that Pharaoh gives it to him clearly does. Though a king of David's line continues on the throne in Judah, the normal process of election and anointing has not taken place. Judah is now clearly a vassal state of Egypt with a puppet-king who is forced to pay nearly four tons of silver and one talent of gold (35 kilos) in tribute, which he raises through taxation. This is not a very large sum when compared to that paid by Hezekiah to Sennacherib (2 Kings 18:14–15) but it is the first time that tribute has been collected from all the people in this way (Menahem had only taxed the rich—see 2 Kings 15:20); and the sense of the Hebrew verb (captured in the NRSV by 'he exacted') is that the taxation policy was pursued energetically. In the early days of the nation, Solomon had treated Israelites like slaves and been resented for it (1 Kings 5:13; 12:4); now in its latest days his descendant is doing the same. The writers think no better of him than they did of his brother and describe his reign in the same way. NRSV is wrong in including the word 'all' where it does in verse 37. The verse does not say that 'all his ancestors' have done wrong but that he does 'all the wrongs' that his ancestors have done. The nation might be heading for disaster, but not all its kings have 'done evil in the sight of the Lord' as Jehoahaz and Jehoiakim have done.

Jeremiah the prophet

As we pointed out in the Introduction, the whole story in Kings is paralleled in 1 Chronicles 23 to 2 Chronicles 36 and from time to time, though not very often, we have noted what the account in Chronicles has to say. We noted too that 2 Kings 18:13—20:19 is repeated almost verbatim in Isaiah 36—39, and drew attention to certain points there. No mention is made in Kings, however, of any of the prophets whose books we have in the Old Testament and who operated in the period covered by Kings, except for Isaiah. That silence is very strange, given the importance of prophets in Kings, and strangest of all in the case of Jeremiah. He is only mentioned briefly in 2 Chronicles at 35:25 and 36:12, 21–22, but according to the book of Jeremiah he played a very significant public role at this time. His word to Jehoahaz (or Shallum, as he calls him) is found in Jeremiah 22:11–12, and his first word to Jehoiakim is found in Jeremiah 22:18–23. Most famous of all is his confrontation with Jehoiakim via Baruch and the scroll in Jeremiah 36.

FOR REFLECTION

As events in Kings move steadily to their terrible climax,
Psalm 130 provides both a prayer and a perspective
with which to read on.

The BABYLONIANS ARRIVE

King Josiah had been killed at Megiddo in 609BC attempting to stop Pharaoh Neco 'going up to the King of Assyria to the river Euphrates' (2 Kings 23:29). The newly rising power of Babylon, in alliance with the Medes, destroyed the Assyrian capital of Nineveh in 612BC, much to the delight of the prophet Nahum. The Egyptians were defeated by the Babylonians at the battle of Carchemish in 605BC.

Nebuchadnezzar

In 604, Nebuchadnezzar, the victorious general at Carchemish now crowned king of Babylon, sent his army west and south into Palestine and almost everything crumbled before him. Jeremiah, it seems, advocated complete surrender to the Babylonians (Jeremiah 21:8–10; 25:1–14) but Jehoiakim refused to do this, at least until he saw the size of the army lined up against him. He capitulated and for three years Judah was a vassal state of Babylon.

Nabu-kudurri-usur reigned as king of Babylon from 605 to 562BC so 'Nebuchadnezzar' is more correctly written as Nebuchadrezzar, the form found in Ezekiel and often, though not always, in Jeremiah. Having difficulty in spelling foreign names is obviously nothing new!

Rebellion

Just as his father had died meddling where he needn't have done, so Jehoiakim decides to rebel against Babylon (v. 1). Egypt had remained strong enough to give Nebuchadnezzar a very bloody nose when he attempted to invade Egypt in the winter of 601, and that defeat may have prompted Jehoiakim to take this action. In retrospect it looks like bad judgment on his part to withhold tribute from Nebuchadnezzar just at the moment when he was smarting from that setback. For the moment, however, he got away with it. Nebuchadnezzar's army was in some disarray and all that he could do about Judah was to let marauding bands of Babylonians and more local adventurers from Syria, Ammon and Moab—all of whom had been vassal states of Israel and Judah in the old days—raid and pillage. Babylonians are called 'Chaldeans' here and occasionally elsewhere in the Old Testament. Chaldea was an important province in south-east Babylonia.

Egypt stayed put behind its natural boundary, so there was plenty of room in Palestine for some settling of local scores and opportunistic plundering. That may have been the historical reality, but the Deuteronomic Historians believe that there were other forces at work. To them, these raiders were doing the Lord's will, punishing Judah and contributing to its destruction 'as the prophets had said it would be'. The end of Judah and Jerusalem is inevitable.

The reference to Manasseh in verse 3 and the judgments on both of Josiah's sons in 2 Kings 23:32 and 37 (and his grandson in v. 9) seem to indicate that although Josiah had been a truly great reforming king, the legacy of his father was simply too strong and deep to be overcome. Commentators frequently point out that Jeremiah says little about Josiah and certainly does not hold him in the high regard in which he is held by the writers of Kings. They suggest that a possible reason for this is that although his reforms may have been radical, they were in reality of little effect.

In the middle of all this, Jehoiakim dies. Nothing is said about his burial: perhaps it was as Jeremiah had said it would be (Jeremiah 22:18–19), especially if, as some commentators suggest, he actually died during the siege.

Jehoiachin of Judah (598)

Jehoiachin (also called Jeconiah in 1 Chronicles 3:16 and Jeremiah 24:1, and Coniah in Jeremiah 22:24) does as badly as his father and reigns as briefly as his uncle (vv. 8–12).

The Babylonian army, reorganized and re-equipped, returns to the area and besieges Jerusalem. In next to no time, Jehoiachin surrenders to Nebuchadnezzar himself. The last sentence of verse 12 dates his surrender, and the first fall of Jerusalem which follows it, to the eighth year of Nebuchadnezzar's reign—though Jeremiah 52:28 calls it the seventh. Babylonian records date the event precisely to the second day in the month of Adar in the seventh year of Nebuchadnezzar's reign, which would have been 16 March 598.

The end has now begun in earnest and the account of how it progresses will make harrowing reading.

FOR PRAYER

Pray for the victims of terror, war and violence in today's news.

The FALL of JERUSALEM

Deportation

The king, the royal family and the palace officials are taken prisoner by Nebuchadnezzar. They, together with anybody who is anybody, are 'carried away to Babylon' (vv. 13–16). This includes not only the royal family and the governing class, but all the civil service, the army and the skilled tradesmen, or possibly only those who work in the 'defence industry'. There is, you will spot, a bit of repetition here and a discrepancy in the numbers—10,000 in verse 14, but 8000 in verse 16. Jeremiah 52:28 gives the very specific figure of 3023, to add to the confusion. Among these exiles is Ezekiel, who will begin his ministry in Babylon, and left behind is the prophet Jeremiah, though Kings mentions neither.

Hezekiah had boasted to his Babylonian visitors of the treasures his kingdom possessed, and Isaiah had castigated him for it (2 Kings 20:13–19). Now the Babylonians begin to carry away those treasures, including Solomon's gold vessals, just as Isaiah had said would happen.

A remnant remains

Only the 'poorest people of the land' remain in Jerusalem. In later Judaism, 'the people of the land' and the 'poor' become almost technical terms. The 'people of the land' were those who didn't take the Torah as seriously as they should, at least as far as the religious leaders were concerned. Quite opposite, the 'poor' were those who were specially noted for their piety. This leads, among other things, to the debate about who and what Jesus means when he says, 'Blessed are the poor'—which Luke takes to mean the economically poor (Luke 6:20) and Matthew understands to be the 'poor in spirit' (Matthew 5:3)—but that is another question. Here the reference almost certainly is to the bottom-of-the-pile, lowest social group, working-class poor, with the kind of overtones that these terms often carry today.

'As the Lord had foretold'

This last phrase in verse 13 is a key one. All the way through Kings, the prophets have been pointing out to the kings of Israel and Judah that actions have consequences. History is not inevitable. It is not decreed by God's plan and design, nor does it just happen. It is created by the decisions and actions of human beings. The Lord has been able to foretell what will happen by his spokespeople, the prophets, because, to put it at its crudest, 'you reap what you sow'. The Deuteronomists are, needless to say, wise enough to recognize that this is not necessarily a simple and direct one-to-one relationship of cause and effect. According to their reading of the history of their nation, Jerusalem and Judah are now reaping what their kings have sown over centuries.

Zedekiah of Judah (598–587)

Nebuchadnezzar appoints Mattaniah, a full brother to Jehoahaz (he of the brief reign in 2 Kings 23:31–34), as king in place of his deported nephew (v. 17). To demonstrate that he is in total control of the situation, Nebuchadnezzar changes this king's name to Zedekiah, as Pharaoh Neco had changed his half-brother Eliakim's name to Jehoiakim (2 Kings 23:34). The Babylonian Chronicle indicates that Nebuchadnezzar 'appointed a king to his liking'. This may have been because Mattaniah and his dead brother were part of an anti-Egyptian faction, for it is clear from the much fuller information given in the book of Jeremiah that Jerusalem was faction-ridden at this time. There were obviously other, more risky, royal uncles whom Nebuchadnezzar needed to avoid when choosing his puppet-king, and these accompanied their deposed nephew to Babylon.

His choice, however, makes no difference in the long run. Verses 19–20 note that Zedekiah too 'does what was evil in the sight of the Lord', as Jehoiakim—the one who had rebelled against Nebuchadnezzar in the first place—had done. It is because of what he does that the long-expected and long-threatened event now takes place. The Lord 'expels' Jerusalem and Judah from his presence. His occasion for doing this is that, as his half-brother had done, Zedekiah rebels against Nebuchadnezzar.

FOR REFLECTION

Zedekiah's despair and hopelessness lead to an act of sheer folly, and Jerusalem is destroyed as a result.

The DESTRUCTION of JERUSALEM

The end of the line?

Even though the situation he inherited was hopeless, Zedekiah managed to make it worse. With Egyptian encouragement, according to Jeremiah 27:3–7 and Ezekiel 17:15, he 'rebelled against the king of Babylon'. Unwise. Very unwise. His rebellion brings the Babylonian army back to the city, and in 588 the third and final siege of old Jerusalem begins. The dates of all this are given three times (in verses 1, 3 and 8) to emphazise the significance of this terrible end. The siege lasted for nineteen months until the food situation became impossible, and then the king and the army tried to break out of their prison and escape. The beginning of verse 4 is obscure. Most translations suggest that the city wall was breached—though whether from outside or inside is not entirely clear—and then the king and his men slipped out through the breach, but REB thinks that the phrase means that the city capitulated. Either way, the picture of the king and his armed escort deserting the city and leaving its people to face the Babylonians is hardly edifying. It is therefore no surprise that the army deserts him in the same way in verse 5. It is hardly possible to imagine the terror behind the words so matter-of-factly put in verse 3, but the less squeamish reader can see how Deuteronomy 28:52–57 describes such a situation in general or read about this particular siege in Lamentations 4:10, which is one of the psalms of anguish produced out of it.

The bulk of the Babylonian (Chaldean) army had left the scene long since, but enough troops remained to maintain the siege and they had no difficulty in pursuing and capturing the escapees. The king and his troops had tried to get away eastwards down into the Arabah, the great rift valley of the Jordan River between the Sea of Galilee and the Dead Sea, where David had taken shelter when he was outlawed by Saul (1 Samuel 23:24). They didn't get far. Less than twenty miles away, near Jericho, Zedekiah was captured. To those who know the old story, verse 5 is full of irony. Zedekiah is trying to get out of the promised land by the same route that Joshua had come in, and he is defeated at Jericho, the place of Joshua's greatest victory (Joshua 6).

Even though verse 7 describes what the Babylonians did to Zedekiah in equally matter-of-fact tones, it is impossible to disguise its horror. This is the son of David, blinded, exiled and bereft of heirs. Given that because there was no belief in any real life after death among the Israelites at this time, a man's hope for the future lay in his family (and a woman's didn't count much at all), this is the end for Zedekiah. It looks like the end of David's line, too.

The end of the city?

A month later, one of Nebuchadnezzar's generals arrives in Jerusalem on a mission of total destruction (v. 8). The temple, the palace complex and 'every important building' (NIV) are burned down. The walls are pulled down. The rest of the people, except the very poorest, are exiled to Babylon (832 of them, according to Jeremiah 52:29). Exile is the fate both of those who had opposed the Babylonians and of those who had supported them. The reference to the 'deserters who had defected to the king of Babylon' in verse 11 gives another insight into the factions and the politics of the siege. All are deported to Babylon.

Jerusalem is no more. All that remains of the City of David and the magnificence of Solomon is a ruin. The people of Israel are now no threat to anyone, a leaderless bunch of 'vinedressers and tillers of the soil'—labourers and peasants—whose state is a long way from the destiny which God had intended for them when they had come into the land under Joshua seven or eight hundred years previously. Instead of 'each living under his own vine and fig tree'—the ideal picture of life, liberty and happiness painted in the Old Testament—the remaining Israelites are to be slaves in other people's vineyards and tillers of other people's soil.

FOR REFLECTION

'O God, why do you cast us off for ever? Why does your anger smoke against the sheep of your pasture?'

Read the rest of Psalm 74 and feel the pain and trauma of this event.

99

2 KINGS 25:13–26

To BABYLON & *to* EGYPT

After giving us a stark overview of the fall of Jerusalem and the destruction of the temple in verses 8–12, the story now gives two details of these terrible events before moving on.

Destruction

Verses 13–17 contain the last mention of the temple in Kings and describe the way in which it was finally stripped and emptied before it was burned down. The passage, however, goes way beyond simple description. For the bronze pillars, 'stands', 'sea', pomegranates and lattice work, see 1 Kings 7:13–39 and the comments about them in Study 17. Verse 15 makes the point that the Babylonians placed no religious value whatsoever on anything they took from the temple. The only value they saw was the cash value of the gold, silver and bronze, and the cash value of the bronze alone was considerable (v. 16). On the other hand, the writer refers to the temple as the 'house of the Lord' three times in these short verses, as well as reminding us of its builder, the great and magnificent Solomon. He intends us to see the contrast and feel the difference between what might have been and what is. David's own 'How are the mighty fallen!' (2 Samuel 1:19) and the words of Luther's hymn that 'tower and temple fall to dust' just about sum it up. The greatness of Israel is no more, its faith and religious heritage are ashes and rubble, and its glories are reduced to a set of figures in the profit columns of Babylon plc.

Death

Apart from Zedekiah's sons and the soldiers killed in the fighting, there has been no mention in the descriptions of the events of 598, or these of 587, of any other bloodshed—until now. Verses 18–21 describe the killing of five priests, two army officers, five government officials and sixty men rounded up off the streets. This was not random violence but a state execution, ordered by Nebuchadnezzar and carried out at his base in Riblah. The charge, no doubt, was treason, as both leaders and people are found guilty of sharing in Zedekiah's broken oath of allegiance to Babylon. At the very least, Nebuchadnezzar makes an example of what happens to rebels. We might complain at the injustice of the fact that the innocent and powerless sixty die alongside the responsible and powerful twelve, but we have seen enough of this sort of thing in our own times to know that, sadly, this is the way the world is. For the Deuteronomists and their first readers, on the other hand, whose presuppositions and preoccupations were very different from the individualism of the modern West, it would be impossible to differentiate between the 'innocent' and the 'guilty' in this way at all.

'So Judah went into exile out of its land'

This final sentence in verse 21 does not, however, end the story of exile. Anybody who is anybody is exiled to Babylon, though, unlike Jeremiah 52:28–30, Kings gives no final statistics. Nebuchadnezzar appoints Gedaliah, a Judean not of the royal house, as governor. His father had been a trusted adviser of Josiah and friend of Jeremiah (2 Kings 22:12; Jeremiah 26:24), and Gedaliah himself had had much to do with the prophet (Jeremiah 39:14; 40:6). Archaeologists have discovered records of this period in the ancient town of Lachish, in which a Gedaliah, 'comptroller of the household' of Zedekiah, is mentioned—probably the same person. However, he is killed and his supporters murdered within months by a very minor royal who obviously disapproves of his eminently sensible policy (v. 24).

Gedaliah had made a promising start to restoring the land to some semblance of order, by gaining the co-operation of the soldiers who had escaped capture and were possibly still fighting a guerilla war, but it comes to nothing. Fearful of the Babylonian reaction to this, the remnant flee to self-imposed exile in, of all places, Egypt. According to Jeremiah 42—44 they take the prophet Jeremiah with them, but here, as everywhere else, Kings makes no mention of him at all. Back to Egypt. The wheel has gone full circle.

FOR REFLECTION

Although it is very painful reading, you can dip almost anywhere into the book of Lamentations and read what this experience felt like to those involved. Its final paragraph (5:19–22) takes us to the heart of the questions raised in this unimaginable trauma.

The STRANGEST of STRANGE ENDINGS

A king's pension

Between verses 26 and 27 there is a jump of 25 years and 800 miles; from Jerusalem to Babylon and from 587 to 562BC. We find ourselves catapulted into the exile, to meet up again with King Jehoiachin of Judah, last heard of in 2 Kings 24:8–14, where his three-month reign ended abruptly when he was carried off to Babylon. That 18-year-old is now 55 years of age when, in an amnesty at the beginning of his reign, a new king of Babylon orders Jehoiachin's release from prison, gives him a pension and accords him dining priviledges at the royal table. Babylonian cuneiform tablets actually record a ration for him and his five sons. Very nice for Jehoiachin, but a very odd way indeed to end both Kings and the whole Deuteronomic History which begins with Joshua. Evil-merodach recognizes and to some extent reinstates the royal line of David, last mentioned in the mutilated King Zedekiah in verse 7 and the murderer Ishmael in verse 25.

Historical realities

In the last few chapters, I have tried to help you feel what the events of the fall of Jerusalem might have felt like to those who lived through them. Once the terror and trauma were over, what remained was a huge sense of loss. They had lost their 'promised land', their king of David's line who was God's anointed son, their holy city and, in it, God's holy temple, the one place where he had 'caused his name to dwell'. They had every reason to believe that the chosen people had become unchosen, or that their God had been shown up to be a second-rater in the divine league tables. Everything that had given their nation its identity had been lost. Small wonder that Psalm 137 says they sat weeping by the rivers of Babylon, their despair only alleviated by desires for vengeance.

The exile is still regarded by most Old Testament scholars as the most crucial event in the history of ancient Israel. It could have been the end of everything; instead it was the beginning of much. The small nations contemporary with ancient Israel and Judah—Ammon, Edom, Moab, Syria, together with the Philistine city states—all disappeared from history, as, of course, did Israel when it was exiled by the Assyrians in 722. Judah did not. Against all the odds, both the land and the people—usually known from here on as 'Judeans', which soon became shortened to 'Jews'—survived.

The exile was not the end. The credit for that lies with three prophets (Jeremiah, Ezekiel and the anonymous one whose message we find in Isaiah 40—55) and the Deuteronomists. These prophets explained the exile and pointed to a future. The Deuteronomists wrote the long explanation we have been reading, edited the words of Jeremiah and some of the other prophets and began the publishing process which resulted first in the Torah (the books of Genesis to Deuteronomy) and eventually in the whole set of religious literature cherished by Jews and Christians alike. The explanation they all gave—'It's your own fault, especially your king's'—might sound simplistic but it worked.

A sign of hope?

Old films used to end with 'The End' appearing on a blank screen. No such words appear at the end of 2 Kings. Some old serials used to end each episode with 'To be continued'. Those words don't appear here either, but that is what the curious ending of verses 25–30 adds up to. It is an inkling of hope. The long story which began with Joshua 1 (or should it be Deuteronomy 1, or even Genesis 1?) is not over yet.

But how will that long story end, and what will happen next? That is up to you and me—and God. Because the story is still being written. The question is, will we learn the lessons of the past which the Deuteronomists have been trying to teach?

A PRAYER

Lord our God, we thank you for your gifts of life and faith, for our calling as your people, and for the story we have just read. We confess that the sins and mistakes and sad, sorry failures of which we have read are features of our lives too, and so our world continues to be marred and spoiled. Help us to learn the lessons of Kings, that life and peace and hope are found when we walk in your ways and pay heed to your teaching. So may we move into your future, upheld by your grace, that your kingdom may come and your will be done in your world, in your Church and in our lives. Amen.

NOTES

NOTES

NOTES

NOTES

NOTES

NOTES

NOTES

NOTES

NOTES

NOTES

NOTES

NOTES

NOTES

NOTES

NOTES

NOTES

NOTES

NOTES

NOTES

NOTES

NOTES

THE PEOPLE'S BIBLE COMMENTARY

VOUCHER SCHEME

The People's Bible Commentary (PBC) provides a range of readable, accessible commentaries that will grow into a library covering the whole Bible.

To help you build your PBC library, we have a voucher scheme that works as follows: a voucher is printed on the last page of each People's Bible Commentary volume (as above). These vouchers count towards free copies of other books in the series.

For every four purchases of PBC volumes you are entitled to a further volume FREE.

Please find the coupon for the PBC voucher scheme overleaf.

All you need do:

- Cut out the vouchers from the last page of the PBCs you have purchased and attach them to the coupon.

- Complete your name and address details, and indicate your choice of free book from the list on the coupon.

- Take the coupon to your local Christian bookshop who will exchange it for your free PBC book; or send the coupon straight to BRF who will send you your free book direct. Please allow 28 days for delivery.

Please note that PBC volumes provided under the voucher scheme are subject to availability. If your first choice is not available, you may be sent your second choice of book.

THE PEOPLE'S BIBLE COMMENTARY
VOUCHER SCHEME COUPON

TO BE COMPLETED BY THE CUSTOMER

My choice of free PBC volume is (please indicate your first and second choice, as all volumes are supplied subject to availability):

☐ 1 and 2 Samuel

☐ 1 and 2 Kings

☐ Chronicles to Nehemiah

☐ Psalms 1—72

☐ Psalms 73—150

☐ Proverbs

☐ Nahum to Malachi

☐ Mark

☐ Luke

☐ John

☐ Romans

☐ 1 Corinthians

☐ 2 Corinthians

☐ Galatians and Thessalonians

☐ Timothy, Titus and Hebrews

☐ James to Jude

☐ Revelation

Name: . . . .

Address: . . . .

. . . .

Postcode: . . . .

TO BE COMPLETED BY THE BOOKSELLER

(Please complete the following. Coupons redeemed will be credited to your account for the value of the book(s) supplied as indicated above. Please note that only coupons correctly completed with original vouchers will be accepted for credit.):

Name: . . . .

Address: . . . .

. . . .

Postcode: . . . .

Account Number: . . . .

Completed coupons should be sent to: BRF, PBC Voucher Scheme, First Floor, Elsfield Hall, 15–17 Elsfield Way, OXFORD OX2 8EP

Tel 01865 319700
Fax 01865 319701
Registered Charity No. 233280

THIS OFFER IS AVAILABLE IN THE UK ONLY
PLEASE NOTE: ALL VOUCHERS ATTACHED TO THIS COUPON MUST BE ORIGINAL COPIES.